Handbook of American Indian Religious Freedom

Handbook of
American Indian Religious
Freedom

Edited by Christopher Vecsey

CROSSROAD • NEW YORK

1991

The Crossroad Publishing Company
370 Lexington Avenue, New York, NY 10017

Printed in the United States of America
Typesetting output: TEXSource, Houston

Library of Congress Cataloging-in-Publication Data

Handbook of American Indian religious freedom / edited by Christopher
Vecsey.
    p. cm.
    ISBN 0-8245-1067-4
    1. Indians of North America–Religion and mythology. 2. Indians
of North America–Legal status, laws, etc. 3. United States.
American Indian Religious Freedom Act. 4. Peyotism–United States.
5. Sacred space–United States. I. Vecsey, Christopher.
E98.R3H18   1991
299'.793–dc20   90-49393
                                                          CIP

Contents

◇

Prologue

CHRISTOPHER VECSEY

Under the sponsorship of Senator James Abourezk (Dem., S.D.) and Representative Morris Udall (Dem., Ariz.), both houses of Congress passed a resolution in 1978 regarding American Indian Religious Freedom.[1] This public law of the 95th Congress recognized the "inherent right" of American citizens to religious freedom; admitted that in the past the United States government had not protected the religious freedom of American Indians, due either to insensitivity or misunderstanding; proclaimed the "indispensable and irreplaceable" role of American Indian religion "as an integral part of Indian life"; and called upon governmental agencies to "protect and preserve for American Indians their inherent right of freedom to believe, express, and exercise the traditional religions." The resolution referred specifically to Indians' access to unspoiled sacred sites, the use of natural resources normally protected by conservation and other laws, and participation in traditional Indian ceremonies as areas of Indian religious practice to be protected. This American Indian Religious Freedom Act (AIRFA) was an attempt to direct policy comprehensively toward promoting the free exercise of Indian religions.

Circumstances Past and Present

More than a decade later it is argued that American Indian religious liberties have not been safeguarded by AIRFA. It is our hope in this volume to examine AIRFA's impact (or lack thereof) on Indian religious freedom and to suggest ways in which Indians can gain greater protection of their religious rights. This book derives from the American Indian Religious Freedom Act Conference held at the Newberry Library in Chicago, April 7–9, 1988, co-sponsored by the National Conference of Christians and Jews, Inc., and the D'Arcy McNickle Center for the History of the American Indian. Elliott Wright and Rose Marie Ohm (from NCCJ), and

Frederick E. Hoxie and Jay Miller (from the McNickle Center) were the principal organizers, and Alfonso Ortiz of the University of New Mexico served admirably as the convener. To these persons, and to the many participants at the conference, we owe and acknowledge many thanks. We also appreciate the generosity of the Native American Rights Fund (NARF) for sharing its expertise and resources in the preparation of this volume.

Although the 1988 conference focussed upon AIRFA, the legal, historical, and religious issues that are embedded in the complex tangle of relationships between Native American peoples and the United States transcend the words and perspective of the resolution. AIRFA symbolizes this complex and is perhaps a foundation upon which future progress rests rather than a mere comment upon past failures. Nevertheless, the chapters that follow attempt to unravel and hold up for scrutiny the salient strands of the tangle that must be understood if one is to understand and promote American Indian religious freedom in our day.

Our tasks are threefold. First, there is the need to identify the specific areas in which Indian religious practices are undermined by federal, state, and local policies and by private enterprises. Second, there is a need to help non-Indians understand the conceptual bases for American Indian religious practices, to make those beliefs and practices more comprehensible. The third need is to suggest practical considerations, for instance, to protect the free exercise of Indian religions in the face of other conflicting claims and values.

There are three primary situations in which American Indian religious practice becomes entangled with American jurisprudence:

1. When Indians are accused of criminal activity: transporting or ingesting peyote (*Lophophora williamsii*); hunting animals out of season or killing endangered species; or when Indians are prohibited from expressing features of their Indian way of life (e.g., braided hair), or participating in Indian rituals such as sweats or pipe ceremonies especially in the confines of institutions such as prisons or schools.

2. When revered artifacts are kept from the communities that use them religiously and are displayed against their will; or, when Indian bodily remains are taken from burial grounds and treated in a manner perceived by Indians as sacrilegious.

3. When Indians encounter governmental policies or private enterprises, the results of which may endanger Indian religious traditions: when a dam will make inaccessible a pilgrimage site or burial ground; when a road, power line, or resort will create inappropriate activities in a sacred site, etc.

Indians find their religious practices endangered in the following situations:

- the degradation of geographical areas deemed sacred sites;
- the maltreatment of Indian burials, particularly bodily remains;
- the prohibition against capture, kill, and use of endangered or protected species;
- the regulations regarding the collection, transport, and use of peyote;
- the alienation and display of religious artifacts;
- the prevention of Indian rituals and behavior, particularly in authoritarian institutions.

As Sharon O'Brien — professor of government at Notre Dame University and scholar of American Indian law in the United States — explains in her chapter, AIRFA was designed to address these situations in order to ameliorate Indian predicaments. O'Brien places AIRFA in the context of an extended history of U.S. persecution of Indian religions, as well as the countervailing liberalism that swelled in the 1930s and again in the 1970s in America.

She argues, however — as do all our authors — that AIRFA has contributed little to promoting Indian religious freedom. Whereas some have argued and hoped that the resolution might provide Indians with substantial aid in their claims and others have noted that the act constitutes statutory recognition of the federal government's trust responsibility regarding Indians, a survey of court cases of the 1980s reveals a judicial disregard for the act. "No teeth" is the most common depiction of the resolution, and O'Brien observes that recently there have been attempts to create new federal laws that can serve as watchdogs guarding Indian religious rights — watchdogs that can bite. In the meantime, O'Brien finds, the courts have applied more stringent tests to Indians in their religious cases than to other peoples' religious claims; Indians have been required to prove that the infringement of certain religious practices will necessarily lead to the demise of their religion, whereas in other cases the claimants must prove only that their religious rights are being infringed upon. O'Brien concludes that a decade after AIRFA Indian religions are still endangered within the United States.

It is instructive that in the present day Indian religions are not regularly threatened in ways that were common earlier in this century. We do not see persistent prohibitions against Indian medicine people; indeed, in some areas the Indian Health Service accommodates traditional medical specialists. We do not see blanket prohibitions against Indian rituals on reservations. Sun dances, ritual clowns, kiva services, peyote ceremonies are usually allowed to flourish, and at certain religious events multitudes of non-Indian tourists witness the proceedings with approval. In certain respects Indians are allowed to practice their religions in peace, without harassment (beyond that of the tourists).

On the other hand, it should be noted that Indian cultures have already altered many beliefs and practices to make their religions more palatable to non-Indians. Over the centuries Indians have ceased certain practices — ritual cannibalism, human sacrifice, widespread scatology, explicit sexuality — under pressure from non-Indians, in a process often referred to as "acculturation." Some aboriginal culture traits that could be religiously grounded — polygamy, revenge warfare, self-mutilation as part of mourning, etc. — have been erased or subdued. As a result, contemporary Indian religions are hardly scandalous, or even titillating, to non-Indians. It is remarkable, considering how "domesticated" and "safe" these religions are, that Indians need AIRFA to protect their religious freedom.

A Native American practice with a long history of non-Indian interference is the ritual ingestion of the peyote cactus. Omer C. Stewart, professor emeritus of anthropology at the University of Colorado, author of monumental histories of the peyote religion, and longtime courtroom witness on behalf of Indian Peyotists, reviews the legal history of Peyotism from the seventeenth-century Spanish Inquisition in America to the time of AIRFA's passage in 1978, with a note on the 1990 Supreme Court ruling against Indian peyote use in *Employment Division v. Smith*.[2] From the late nineteenth century, U.S. laws have prohibited peyote use; and despite the creation of the Native American Church as an agency for securing First Amendment protection for Peyotism, despite the reforms of the Indian New Deal of the 1930s, and despite successes in many state and federal courts, Indian ingestion of sacramental peyote is still subject to United States scrutiny, legislation, interference, and even prohibition.

Walter and Roger Echo-Hawk demonstrate in their chapter that the treatment of Indian skeletons constitutes a vital religious concern for contemporary Indian Americans. The two authors — Walter Echo-Hawk is a senior staff attorney of the Native American Rights Fund, and Roger Echo-Hawk is a student of Pawnee tribal history — document the efforts of their Pawnee Tribe of Oklahoma to repatriate and rebury their tribal ancestors whose bodies had been taken from their graves by non-Indians and kept by museum officials who believed their scientific curiosity to be more important than Indian religious scruples regarding the treatment of the dead.

The two authors review the justifications made by museums for holding these bodily remains as property, but they argue that such policies undermine Indian religious practice. The Pawnees, e.g., have always held these remains to be sacred objects, buried amid religious ritual, to which periodic offerings were to be made by the living. For the Pawnees — as for other Indians — the tribal treatment of the dead continues to be a matter of moral and prudential concern.

Steven C. Moore is a NARF staff attorney who has represented American Indians seeking to protect sacred sites. In his chapter Moore argues that the U.S. government agencies have resisted the intent of AIRFA to protect the sacred sites of Native peoples in the U.S.; indeed, the Forest Service and the Bureau of Land Management have regarded AIRFA as an impediment to their bureaucratic interests and have attempted to subvert it.

Even more devastating to AIRFA and to American Indian sacred sites has been the Supreme Court ruling in *Lyng v. Northwest Indian Cemetery Protective Association* in 1988. In this case (which Moore argued before the Supreme Court), Yurok, Karok, and Tolowa Indians attempted to protect the "high country" within the Six Rivers National Forest in northern California — where for centuries their ancestors have gone for vision questing, purification, and other ceremonial activity integral to their religious life. The U.S. Forest Service proposed to construct a road through this sacred site, and although a federal district court in California and the Ninth Circuit Court of Appeals issued injunctions against the construction, the Supreme Court denied the importance of the site to the Indians' religion and removed the injunction. Moore surveys the arguments of the court — including the dissenting opinion — and writes that there is now a need to amend and strengthen AIRFA with new legislation if Indians' sacred sites are to be protected in the near future.

Deward E. Walker, Jr.'s, chapter provides the underpinnings to an understanding of American Indian sacred sites and their importance to American Indian religiousness. His essay depicts the phenomenology of Indian ecological spirituality, not only in general terms — differing from Christian religious traditions regarding the land — but in copious detail, especially regarding the Northern Plains Indians. His bibliography is a vast resource regarding Indian environmental religiousness. What he makes clear is that since land is the crux of historical and contemporary Indian-White conflicts, it also constitutes the central knot of the legal-religious tangle. Sacred sites are the major areas where Indian spirituality rubs against American legality.

Besides outlining the ways in which Indian religious phenomena are oriented to environmental access points or portals where the sacred is revealed, Walker details some thirty sites in Northwestern United States — out of hundreds with which he is familiar — which give order and orientation to Indian communities and their ways of life, their religions. He then criticizes the requirement of U.S. courts that Indians prove the centrality of specific sites to their religious practice before the courts will protect those sites from non-Indian devastation. At this time, only if a site's loss will lead necessarily to the extinction of the people's religion do the courts propose to protect Indian sacred sites. Walker states that sacred sites are fundamental to Indian religious integrity — the ability of a people to maintain their religious traditions complete and undivided —

and he encourages the courts to make integrity, rather than centrality, the criterion for protecting sacred sites. Unless a new court standard is established, he says, Indian religions will remain in jeopardy.

Understanding American Indian Religiousness

If Indian religions are threatened today, perhaps it is because non-Indians do not understand the beliefs and practices that make up the Native religions. Walker's essay and his sources attempt to overcome the obstacles to such an understanding.

Indian beliefs are encased in, and manifested through, linguistic structures that are completely foreign to English-speakers. Indian religions always exist for non-Indians *in translation*, through filters. This fact does not make them impossible to comprehend, although the problems increase in light of the hundreds of Native languages, representing hundreds of different local religious complexes, each with its own traditions (of course, today many Indian religionists speak English as a first language).

Moreover, traditional Indian complexes allow for diversity of belief, and even of practice, within a single community. In many cases Indian religions lack institutions of codification — credos, constitutions, canons, and the like — and thus in any one community one can find a variety of religious orientations. Monotheists, henotheists, and polytheists exist side by side, sharing a religious heritage. A village might possess different medicine or kiva societies, each with its own specialized knowledge and cultus; hence, an outsider might be hard-pressed to identify the "essence" of a particular tribal faith.

Indians belong to cultures that traditionally have been exclusively oral, or what we call "nonliterate." Without canonized, authoritative texts, one finds numerous versions of central narratives; one finds varying testimonies regarding the meaning of theistic utterances. Lacking the disputative tendency of some other religio-philosophical systems, indeed lacking the compulsion to systematize all beliefs into a theology, and thus lacking concepts such as heresy, Indian religious beliefs are daunting in their diversity.

Like all religions, those of Indians are historically permutable. They have changed over time and continue to change. Creative Indian thinkers have responded to the events of their days by adapting religious ideas and practices. Pan-Indian religious developments have occurred, complementing and augmenting local complexes. New religions — like the Iroquois Longhouse religion or the Indian Shakers — have combined ancient and new features, all adding to the difficulty of assessing and understanding traditional Indian religions.

There might even be the question of what constitutes "traditional"

Indian religions when one-third to one-half of contemporary Indians identify themselves (at least nominally or partially) as Christians. To hundreds of thousands of Indians, Christianity is a portion of their traditional religious configuration, however syncretized or compartmentalized with aboriginal features. In short, the array of religious phenomena might thwart non-Indian observers trying to understand contemporary Indian religions.

In addition to these difficulties is the Indian tendency to equate sacrality with secrecy. Given the long history of non-Indian hostility toward Indian religions, it is no wonder that Indians are reticent to discuss their religions freely. In some cases Indians are willing to let non-Indians gain misleading notions about Indian beliefs (e.g., Masau'u becomes the Great Spirit), and in other cases use analogies (Blue Lake becomes the Taos "church"), allowing non-Indians an easy but inexact glimpse into Indian conceptions. Many of the world's religions are presently engaged in searching dialogue; such is rarely the case between Indians and non-Indians.

Perhaps Indian religions are threatened partially because they are significantly different from non-Indian modes of religiousness, and thus are not understood or appreciated. As long as non-Indians (including legislators, executives, and judges) can write off Indian religious concerns as incomprehensible (hence, superstitious), Indian religions will continue to be threatened. But if Indian beliefs and practices can be elucidated, then Indian religions may gain protection. In American jurisprudence, religious freedoms have been gained only when religious claims have been clearly explained; therefore, education may be a step toward legitimizing Indian religions in the eyes of non-Indians.

It may be helpful to establish a frame of reference for discussing Indian religious ideas and practices by suggesting a number of definitions of "religion" that might hold true for Indians. We suggest a "number of definitions," because we often have in mind several distinct but related phenomena when we utter the word "religion." Each phenomenon could serve as a definition, but none describes the fullness of what "religion" encompasses.

Religion, then, consists of a people's conceptions of, and relations with, the sources of life. Such a definition presumes that religion is a shared complex, a tradition that is passed down by a people. It includes beliefs about that which is considered necessary for life to continue, that upon which human and other forms of life depend for persistence. It also includes the means by which people attempt to make contact with and understand the sources of their life, including ritualized means. These sources of life may be spiritual (souls, gods), or they may be material (the world of nature, the human community, including the dead).

Religion also consists of a people's way of life that is thought to be in harmony with the cosmic order. This way of life can include ethical norms, modes of production, social organization, ritual activity, as well as sartorial, tonsorial, and other styles or behavior patterns. This way of life is based in an attitude of piety, reverence, acceptance, and affirmation concerning the cosmic order; the way of life is an attempt to live in harmony with cosmic principles or patterns.

Both of these definitions attempt to include phenomena to which people often refer when they speak of religion: relations with the powerful spiritual world; socially embedded moral codes; ultimate concerns; reverential behavior; rituals. Both definitions combine beliefs and practices.

Indian religious beliefs seem always to posit the existence of a spiritual realm upon which life depends. This realm (perhaps personal, perhaps impersonal), indicated by terms like *manito, wakan, orenda,* and the like, is a numinous, normally unseen, qualitatively superior realm that reveals itself. It is a great mystery that manifests itself, makes itself felt, supports human existence, and toward which ritual is directed. It could be said that Indian religious beliefs consist partially of ideas regarding this spiritual realm that permeates the world.

The long debate in scholarly literature regarding the use of the term "supernatural" to describe this realm points out that the spiritual is so grounded in the physical world, so related to the human community, that it is often indistinguishable from the mundane. In short, the spiritual realm is not necessarily "wholly other" from the physical world. We can say that Indian religions refer at foundation to a spiritual realm, the existence of which orients people and gives them meaning; however, that realm is not removed from nature and humanity.

Furthermore, Indian religious beliefs also include views regarding human existence: how humans are grounded in matter, related to other life forms, kept alive by community, but supported ultimately by spiritual entities: souls, spirits, etc. Indian religious beliefs concern more than the spiritual world; theistic beliefs do not exhaust the range of religious speculation. Through their beliefs Indians express their values, their ethics, their anthropology, their science, as well as their metaphysics.

We cannot say *what* all Indians believe, except to say that their beliefs find expression in all the areas where Indian religions are threatened. If we look at the issues of sacred geography, of ancestors, of relations to animals and medicinal plants, of symbolic artifacts, of tribal identity, of ritual celebration, we shall find Indian religious beliefs, deeply embedded and profoundly felt.

If we cannot say *what* Indians believe, we can say something of *how* they believe. Beliefs can never be observed directly; they can only be perceived through their expressions. Indians express their religious beliefs (it is how they believe) in "myths" (the most important stories a people has to tell), in prayers, in songs and other verbal forms, but also in dance, gesture, style, demeanor, in their modes of production, in their social systems, in their ways of life. That is, Indians believe through their practices, in ways that often transcend verbal formulation. Indian beliefs are performed and embodied by living communities.

Indian religious practices include ritual activities: the stylized, repeated performances that mark the seasons and their patterns, the passages from one stage of life to another, the commemorations of formative events, and the crises of human existence. Indian rituals include thanksgivings, healings, purifications, initiations, blessings. They imitate animals; they mourn the dead; they conjoin the spiritual and human realms; they praise the cosmic order; and they seek answers. Some include whole communities; others are solitary. Some take years to plan; others are spontaneous.

But just as Indian religious beliefs include more than theistic conceptions, their practices include more than ceremonials. Indian religious practices include what foods can be eaten, what names can be addressed. Since languages are usually gifts from the spiritual realm, the speaking of the native tongue can be a religious act. Hunting, farming, the gathering of herbs can all take on religious significance, as can the deference paid to an elder, the care paid in tending a fire, or the averting of one's eyes before strangers. In short, a whole way of life has religious potential. The confrontation between Indian and non-Indian cultures, therefore, can often be interpreted religiously; in the areas where Indian religions are threatened, one can discern conflicting ways of life, conflicting religious configurations.

The issue is whether the U.S. through its federal agencies, its courts, its state and local governments, can acknowledge and respect (even protect) Indian religious traditions that are different from the religious traditions of non-Indians but that pre-date them by centuries upon centuries. A question exists whether the U.S. can make the intentions of the First Amendment and AIRFA palpable. The answer depends upon the will of non-Indians who hold political power: legislators, officials of the executive, judges, etc.

We hope that we can avoid the sanguine view that the U.S. government always has the best interests of Indians at heart. Such is not the case. There is a long history of intolerance, hostility, and persecution regarding Indian religions, a history that is not entirely over.

One can point to a long history of New World jurisprudence — including the foundational concepts of United States land title — in which Indian nations have been denied their sovereignty and rights to territory on the basis of their religions. Virtually from first contact Europeans reserved for themselves the privilege of "discovery" — a theological-legal construct — based upon their self-supposed legitimacy as Christian sovereigns. In the sixteenth century, Europeans termed themselves "discoverers," claiming that only a Christian sovereign could "discover" a land and its people. The rights of non-Christian people — the Indians being "discovered" — were supposed to dissolve in the face of the "discoverers." The "discoverers" were Christians; the occupants of the New World were heathens. The latter possessed no rights worthy of respect by their Christian conquerors (whose right to conquest was grounded in their Christian identity). By the nineteenth century, the United States was proclaiming its right to Indian lands precisely upon these justifications. The "civilized" (i.e., Christian) U.S. possessed its sovereignty over land because of the rights of "discovery"; the "savage" (i.e., non-Christian, or heathen) Indians lost the lands they occupied because of their traditional religious orientation. These distinctions — Christian/heathen, discoverer/occupant, civilized/savage — are inherent to the American heritage and live with us to this day.

One can point to the period between the 1880s and the 1930s, as O'Brien does, when it was government policy to curtail, prohibit, and stamp out salient Indian religious rituals — sun dances, give-aways, and other ceremonies — and Indian cultural practices grounded in religious orientations, such as polygamy and communal land ownership. Only with John Collier's administration of the Bureau of Indian Affairs did the most blatant persecution cease, and only then under loud protest from missionaries, B.I.A. officials, and others. Today there are still non-Indians who would rather see the disappearance of Indian religious forms, who still regard them as the "devil's work," even though the 1968 Indian Civil Rights Act applies the First Amendment's Free Exercise Clause to Native Americans.

On the other hand, we hope to avoid the sanguinary view that Indians are still completely under siege from an aggressive, heartless legal system that is incapable of understanding an Indian's religious viewpoint. The attitudes of many non-Indians are significantly different from what they were before Collier's time. There may not be an active and large-scale commitment on the part of non-Indian officials to preserve Indian religions, but there is at least a generalized predisposition to tolerate Indian religiousness. In the "New Age" of American religious pluralism, when Americans commonly syncretize astrological, Hindu, theosophical, and Christian patches into a piecework "lifestyle," we can assume some familiarity with Indian religious ways, and even acceptance of those ways, on the part of non-Indians. Hence we should not despair at convincing the American people and their legal system of the validity of Indian religious beliefs and practices.

There have even been successes in the past decades that indicate a willingness of that legal system to hear Indian religious claims. The return of Blue Lake to Taos Pueblo was based on the argument that continuing alienation from the lake meant continuing degradation of Taos religious integrity. The Pueblo convinced Richard M. Nixon and Congress that control and access to Blue Lake were essential to the free exercise of Taos religion.

In 1978 the Bald and Golden Eagle Protection Act of 1940 was amended to allow the secretary of the interior to allow Indians to take eagles "for the religious purposes of Indian tribes," such as could be consistent with conservation policies.

In 1984 the Santo Domingo Pueblo won a case against the *New Mexican* for the newspaper's publication of unauthorized photographs of religious ceremonials — photos taken from an airplane. The court understood the Indians' notion that dances are prayers, that secrecy can be essential in promoting the efficacy of prayers, that intrusions can desecrate and destroy a religious complex.

Certain museums — from the Smithsonian Institution to Stanford University — have agreed to return to Indian communities either skeletal remains or artifacts of their forebears, including, e.g., the 1989 repatriation of twelve contested wampum belts to the Onondaga Nation by the New York State Museum.

There have also been gains for Peyotists and some protections for Indian "lifestyle" and ritual in prisons. Despite these and other signs that Indian religious claims can gain serious hearings, most attempts to evoke AIRFA to promote Indian religious freedom have failed, most recently and significantly the "high country" road case, *Lyng* discussed by Moore, and the peyote case, *Smith* surveyed by Stewart.

It is not that U.S. justice regards Indian religious practices as reprehensible or repugnant, as it did a century ago. Neither is it that judges are incapable of understanding Indian religious motivation. Rather, other considerations get in the way of granting Indians free exercise of their religions. Some of these considerations are practical; some are based on legal principle. In other cases, however, Indians and their religions are simply not valued highly enough to change the minds of those in power who have other considerations in mind.

Take, e.g., the question of Peyotism, where there has been abundant scholarship and testimony bearing witness to its multidimensional religiousness. It is no longer possible for courts to reject Peyotism as a bona fide religion; therefore, its participants deserve free exercise of religious belief and practice.

Peyotism is grounded in a theistic worldview that posits a spiritual realm that has pity and compassion for Indians and that communicates spiritual power through the peyote cactus. Although this worldview is nondogmatic, variable, and syncretistic, there are common Peyotist beliefs regarding humans as beings dependent upon the Creator's will and benevolence for their continued existence. God created peyote to help Indians live, and to live correctly. Peyotism expresses a belief in a spiritual realm that possesses power, and a human world that needs it; a spiritual realm that possesses answers, and a human world that seeks them. Peyote is a means by which the spiritual realm shares power and answers; it is the means through which God and humans can communicate; it mediates between God and humans. Peyotists emphasize that peyote produces a direct experience of the divine, a heightened awareness of human incompletion and spiritual benevolence.

Peyotism also consists of a social code that promotes the mutual well-being of the individual and the group, the chartering of a moral, civil way of life. Peyotism is a means of expressing an ethic of community responsibility, of sobriety, of God-oriented morality, of obligations to family, nation, and humanity. Peyotist literature is full of examples of moral transformation, conversion, repentance, and the desire for a way of life based in brotherly love. Peyotist leaders conduct weddings and funerals; its members lend each other money, work together, and intermarry, like members of other religious traditions. They are drawn together as a community of believers and worshippers through a common ritual, as well as a common worldview.

Given Peyotism's beliefs in, and relations with, the source of life, and given the Peyotists' way of life, in harmony with the cosmic order, it has not been impossible to make the courts understand the validity of Peyotism as an American Indian religious complex, bearing some similarity to Christianity and crossing tribal boundaries. Nevertheless, there is still the suspicion that the cactus is a type of narcotic and that traffic in this substance across national or state borders is a possible criminal offense, apart from its use in the religion. Practical considerations intervene when an individual imports or distributes peyote. Is this person — who may be a Native American — providing Native American Church adherents with their "eucharistic" substance, or is the clientele a non-Indian student population looking to get high? When individual Indians are challenged in their possession of peyote, it is often individual motivation, not Peyotism, that is under question. But more important, when courts have weighed the rights of Peyotists against the interests of employers or the state, the religious freedoms of these marginal, powerless people have been disregarded and curtailed, as Stewart demonstrates in his summary of the *Smith* case.

Indians have made some substantial progress in regaining artifacts and human remains — both claimed to be religiously charged objects — that are alienated from Indians, held by museums and other institutions not controlled by Indian communities. Some Indians have claimed that repatriation of these items is crucial to the present practice and future viability of Native religions. The claimants charge that the artifacts are symbols of their religious faith, concrete expressions of their beliefs, and means by which relations are maintained with the sources of life. They are a focus of Native religious concerns, and the future of Indian religions is jeopardized by continued alienation. They further charge that the display of these religious objects constitutes a sacrilege, as well as an infringement upon religious practice.

We know of no case in which a court has forced return of religious artifacts to Indian representatives; however, over the last decade a number of museums (Heard, Wheelwright, Denver Art, etc.) have returned items voluntarily, because their directors were convinced that Native religions needed these objects to maintain their integrity. It is not inconceivable that a court could come to the same conclusion and force the return of museum-held objects, although there are many practical considerations concerning ownership of these commodities that would have to be settled. A century ago, when many of these artifacts were obtained from Indian communities (through various means), Indian religions were thought to be moribund. Today representatives of these faiths are proclaiming their traditions to be viable and are pursuing their continuation actively.

As the Echo-Hawks describe in their chapter, Indians are seeking the return not only of artifacts, but also the bodily remains of Indian ancestors taken from graves and held in museums. Tens of thousands of Indian bodies people the shelves and display cases of museums around the country. Indians note that in their religious traditions the ancestors are considered continuing members of the cosmos of relations, and their remains deserve proper treatment. Although in certain areas the dead are to be avoided as carefully as possible, in many cases the dead serve as intermediaries to the spiritual realm; or they are transformed into life-giving rain clouds; or they appear in dreams to provide advice and share powers. Indian beliefs posit that a human soul persists after death, and there are numerous Indian narratives regarding the land of the dead and its importance to living humans. Even where there is fear of the dead, there exists a sense of propriety toward their remains — either out of fear for ghostly reprisals, or out of a desire to maintain harmony with natural processes. The proper treatment of the dead is not unconnected to the ritual treatment of animal bones (one of the deepest strata of Indian religiousness), in which the bones symbolize the eternal, spiritual elements of being.

It does not take much to make a coherent case regarding the perceived sacrilege of exhuming, examining, and storing of Indian bodily remains, and one can see why the repatriation of ancestors' bodies is a religious issue to Indians. Why, then, is there such difficult headway, when refusal to repatriate would seem to be an infringement on Indian freedom of religion?

The museums argue that these skeletons are valuable for educational and scientific purposes. They also state that Indian remains will be repatriated only if the remains can be traced to living descendants, with the burden of proof on the Indian claimants. In short, they often refuse to return their human treasures. Why?

Non-Indians should have no trouble recognizing the religious attachment to ancestral bones. There are laws, after all, against grave-robbing from Christian or Jewish cemeteries. Perhaps there are considerations that outweigh whatever value non-Indian museum directors place on Indian skeletons as religious objects. Educational and scientific claims are not to be disregarded. Perhaps museum directors, who maintain their careers by possessing and displaying Indian artifacts and skeletons, cannot overcome their professional interests in order to respect Indian religious claims. Perhaps they value these objects too much as items of control to value them as objects of Indian religious attachment. Perhaps they do not value Indians, their religious scruples, or their ancestors enough in order to change their museum policies drastically. In the meantime Indians have made comprehensible claims that their free exercise of religion is being denied, with only the beginnings of positive effect thus far.

Finally, we observe the issues concerning sacred sites, issues that address the environmental dimension of Indian religions. Is it really so difficult to explain to the courts the substance of Indian beliefs regarding the environment? It should not be.

First, we have a huge literature upon which to draw for examples of Indian environmental religiousness: thick anthropological analyses of tribal ecoconsciousness, images from the popular media of ecological Indians. It can be proven that Indians have made empirical, effective use of the environments in which they live, and continue to do so. Indian knowledge of medicinal herbs, astronomical phenomena, domesticated plants, and animal behavior all show a way of life depending directly on nature and recognizing that dependence.

Indians have been more than efficient users of their environments. Their recognition of dependence on nature has taken the quality of devotion, a recognition of the earth as source of life, as nourisher, approaching the concept of Providence itself. And since the physical world has been the source of Indian life, it is no wonder that Indians have conceived their deities as aspects of nature, embedded in natural processes and sites. Spirits of animals, water, light, wind, crops, and land have filled (and continue to fill) Indian people's religious lives.

Indians have combined a practical use of the environment (as source of life) with a mythopoeic association with the earth (as source of life), a sense of consubstantiality expressed through totemic identification, through concepts of animal "owners," through myths of corn grandmothers, bears who adopt boys, girls who marry stars, and more. Indians have associated themselves with the world, identified themselves as equivalent (i.e., equal in value) members of a community in nature, while at the same time using nature for human ends.

Indians have viewed the world of matter as a primal substance, pre-existing the gods themselves, and it is the human role to fit into the patterns of this primordial substance. In addition, Indians have viewed the world as a place made of living beings, an animated universe of persons — human, nonhuman, spiritual — with souls. Animals, plants, streams, mountains have the potential for life and can be treated as persons who can express will and can suffer. In short, Indians have regarded the beings of nature as worthy of respect and ethical consideration. Indians have placed limits on their human freedom out of consideration for the welfare of nonhuman persons. Their religions are replete with questions regarding the proper relationship with the environment, questions concerning, e.g., the human justification for killing animals — who are humans' kin but who are necessary as food to support human life. Indians have apologized to their killed animals and treated their bones with ritual respect; they have thanked animals, plants, the earth itself, for being sources of human life.

If governmental agencies can be educated regarding the religious connections of Indians to specific areas of land, then a religious dimension becomes clear regarding all questions of land use, past and present. We understand that when Indians were removed from their lands in the nineteenth century, they were removed from places with a profound set of religious associations (one thinks of Choctaw women weeping their farewells to trees during the Removal). No less is true today when ski resorts, missile ranges, and logging roads come between Indians and their natural sources of life.

There is a vast contrast between Indian and non-Indian attitudes toward the environment in America. The non-Indian view sees nature as commodity, as virgin to be conquered, as empire to be controlled, as wilderness to be tamed, as playground, as a nonliving collection of natural resources to be exploited, as a matter to be measured quantitatively, as scenery, and as source of suffering and alienation. From its Judeo-Christian roots, from its capitalist orientation, from its technological prowess, non-Indian America has possessed values regarding the environment at variance with those of Indians.

Nevertheless, it is not impossible to make non-Indian officials understand the validity of Indian religious environmentalism. In court testimony, for example, Indians have made cogent presentations regarding not some vague concept of nature, but rather specific sites and natural entities. Indians have said:

- our ancestors arose from the earth here;
- our clan received its identity here;
- our parents are buried here;
- we receive revelation here;
- our culture-hero left ritual objects here;
- we make pilgrimages and vision quests here;
- our gods dwell here;
- our religion requires that we have privacy here;
- the animals, plants, minerals, or waters here possess power that is necessary to our medicines;
- hence, this sacred site must remain undisturbed, or we must have unlimited access to this place.

These are arguments that should carry weight. But when a judge hears of environmental spirituality within the context of a case concerning a public works project or some other enterprise valued by non-Indians, Indian religiousness is weighed against other considerations. We can explain Indian geopiety in terms that a non-Indian can understand and appreciate; however, Indian religious rights will not automatically be granted. And they often have not been granted. The Tellico Dam has buried Indian graves. Ski industry development has occurred where Hopi and Navajo spirits live on San Francisco Peaks. Tourists gawk at Rainbow Bridge. The "high country" seems doomed. Why have Indians not won these cases?

Perhaps it is because judges do not understand Indian religious environmentalism. Perhaps judges fear that the granting of these rights constitutes the "establishment" of Indian religions at the expense of other traditions, including the all-important American traditions of commerce and patriotism. After all, Christians have been forced by business and the state to give up their privileged time (formerly enforced by the old Sunday blue laws); perhaps Indians will continue to be forced by commercial and national interests to give up their privileged places (their sacred sites). Perhaps judges think that tourism, dams, or physical exercise are more weighty than Indian religions, or Indians themselves. The Yakimas can make it clear that they need unlimited access to Hanford nuclear reservation in Washington State. The U.S. does not deny that this is a sacred site to the Yakimas; however, the U.S. has used this area since 1943 for plutonium production, and "national security" interests may outweigh the hundreds of years in which the Yakimas have travelled to this land for vision quests and other religious services. The War Powers Act of 1943 may be more important in the minds of non-Indian officials than the rights of access reserved to Indians in an 1855 treaty. In sum, Indians seem not to win their rights even when they make cogent arguments because in the American legal system religious freedom is just one value, and rarely is it the highest value. Considerations born of competing values intervene.

Toward Greater Sensitivity

Robert S. Michaelsen — professor emeritus of religious studies at the University of California at Santa Barbara — draws upon his distinguished career of observing civil religion in America in order to assay the relationship between law and Indian religious liberty. He notes that the law presently acts as a bulwark between divisive interests in society, and thus acts as adversary to all special interests apart from the state itself. He asks why the law cannot be conceived differently, as a medium or gift between interests, perhaps imposing limits on the U.S. rather than on the Indians.

Like the other authors, Michaelsen recommends a number of strategies to enhance Indian religious freedoms: new federal laws, new standards to be employed as criteria in the courts. He realizes, however, that a sharply altered legal worldview is necessary in the United States in order to compel the law to defend Indian religiousness. He recognizes that American values have been formed partially *against* Indian culture, sovereignty, and religious lifeways. America gained its land, its sovereignty, its Christian autonomy, by denying Indians their freedoms. In the present day the religious hegemony is that of the state, which is the American church, and non-Indians impose it on the Indians against the Native Americans' will and against the higher ethic of America's own jurisprudence. The present agents of American government regard America as their land, under their control, and in this cosmology Indian religions figure small upon the horizon. Michaelsen provides the reader with a description of the salient court cases mentioned by our other authors, in order to document the values expressed by various United States judges. In the face of this set of values, Michaelsen proposes an American legal consciousness that prefers no religion — not even the American civil religion — but disparages none either. This proposition requires an openness to Native American religions as exponents of the human spirit.

In the past years American Indians have made some gains in promoting their free exercise of religion; however, more progress is sorely needed, as all our authors assert. What can be done to aid such progress? Perhaps Congress can draw explicit attention to the areas of Indian religious freedom that are under jeopardy, following, for example, some directions suggested in this volume. Perhaps government-related and government-funded projects could be subjected to "impact studies," similar to those mandated by the National Environmental Protection Act, the National Historic Preservation Act, and the Archaeological Resources Protection Act in the U.S., or the Protection of Holy Places Act in Israel. A consistent series of such impact statements might add up over time in public consciousness, creating an awareness of Indian religious concerns.

The difficulty with such legislation is that it appears as a specter to some Americans, seeming to give Indian religions a status superior in law to all other religious traditions in America. Americans can possibly understand special Indian land claims, because they arise from fundamental U.S. concepts of land title and aboriginal rights of occupancy. Indian claims to special health and educational facilities and to special hunting and fishing rights can be explained by reference to treaty stipulations and U.S. trust responsibilities. But Americans would need to be convinced of the legal bases for special legislation to protect Indian religious practices (as AIRFA tried to do), unless it can be shown dramatically that Indian religious integrity is presently in danger, under special attack, and in need of special protection. Legislation must make clear that it seeks protection for Indian free exercise — not Indian establishment — because Indian religions are the oldest traditions in America and their integrity is in danger.

To further the cause of public consciousness-raising, legal advocates must continue to press claims and cases that can educate Americans, in order to establish a series of precedents that will have a cumulative effect. Advocates should choose causes carefully, picking those cases that can clearly be presented as free exercise defenses. Moreover, the Indian religious freedom issue should not be enjoined in a case as a subsidiary issue, or as an afterthought, e.g., after environmental arguments have been exhausted. Indian advocates should not allow themselves to be used by other interest groups; this throws doubt on the validity of the religious freedom issues. Advocates should choose cases in which the religious practice to be protected can be shown to be crucial to the integrity of the Native religion of which it is a part. Demonstrating the integrity of a practice will probably require explicit discussion of the practice and its religious significance; hence, cases where secrecy cannot be compromised may have to wait for other precedents to accrue. The strongest claims will be those that concern Indian religious complexes as a whole, testified to by tribal authorities, rather than idiosyncratic practices of an individual Indian whose sincerity might be called into doubt.

Advocates of Indian religious freedom must be aware, however, of the ironies surrounding the legal pursuit of religious protections. By focussing on a specific site, artifact, or practice, Indians may draw too much public attention, stimulating the curiosity of pot-hunters, curiosity-seekers, and tourists. By overcoming strictures of secrecy, Indians may weaken the religions they are trying to protect. By explaining the beliefs that underlie their religious practices, Indians may create the effect of canonizing, dogmatizing, mummifying the religions that have thrived for millennia by virtue of their fluidity and diversity. The result might be a "fundamentalism" that insists on univocal explanations for religious phenomena that have long been polysemous. Indians must be careful in pressing their claims for religious freedom not to undermine the spirit of their traditional religiousness.

At the close of the American Indian Religious Freedom Act Conference in 1988, the vice-chairman of the Hopi Indian Tribe, Vernon Masayesva, addressed the participants with a speech that the conferees endorsed unanimously as a concise expression of the conference's sense. Masayesva's statement serves as the epilogue to the *Handbook of American Indian Religious Freedom* — depicting the present difficulties facing Indians seeking to practice their traditional religions and illuminating the path to ameliorate those difficulties. He reminds us that the Europeans who emigrated to America sought their own religious freedoms; the First Amendment has served as the voice for those longings. "The time has come," he says, "when protection of Indian religious rights must also become a reality." As a distillation of the chapters of this book, one can imagine no finer conclusion.

1

A Legal Analysis of the American Indian Religious Freedom Act

SHARON O'BRIEN

In the summer of 1978, Congress enacted the American Indian Religious Freedom Act (AIRFA), a legislative measure that reaffirmed Native American identity and culture. The act's preamble stressed that religious practices of Indian people were an "indispensable and irreplaceable" part of Indian cultures and acknowledged that the government's past actions had abridged traditional Indian religious practices.

Emphasizing freedom of religion as a fundamental right guaranteed by the First Amendment of the Constitution, the act proclaimed in section 1, "It shall be the policy of the United States to protect and preserve for American Indians their inherent right of freedom to believe, express, and exercise [their] traditional religions." Specific attention was given but not limited to: the right of access to sites, use and possession of sacred objects, and the freedom to worship through ceremonies.

Pursuant to this policy objective, section 2 mandated the president to direct federal agencies "to evaluate their policies and procedures in consultation with native traditional religious leaders in order to determine appropriate changes necessary to protect and preserve Native American religious cultural rights and practices." The act required that one year from the date of its enactment, the president inform Congress of changes necessary to bring administrative policies and legislation in line with the government's policy to preserve Indian religions.

The purpose of this chapter is to present an overview of the act's history, to review the courts' inconsistent interpretation of the act, and to assess the act's judicial effectiveness in preserving Indian religious rights.

Historical Background and Legislative History

Theoretically the First Amendment of the U.S. Constitution, "Congress shall make no laws respecting an establishment of religion, or prohibiting the free exercise thereof," should have precluded the need for AIRFA. Indians, however, have suffered religious persecution during the last two hundred years, an experience that has mirrored their initial three hundred years of their contact with the non-Indian. Early Spanish and Portuguese officials justified the taking of Indian lands on the basis of the Natives' heathen nature; land in return for knowing the "word" of God was considered an equitable exchange — an idea followed in varying degrees by the French, English, and Americans. In tandem with their lands, tribes increasingly lost their cultures as successive officials and missionaries sought to assimilate and Christianize them.

In the late 1800s, government officials, believing that traditional religious beliefs impeded Indian progress, established policies to destroy Indian religions. In 1882 Interior Secretary Henry M. Teller ordered an end to all "heathenish dances" and ceremonies due to their "great hindrance to civilization." Two years later, the Bureau of Indian Affairs implemented regulations to imprison for thirty days Indians found participating in their traditional rituals. Further orders required Indian males to cut their braids and outlawed the sun dance. The government's determination to stifle the Ghost Dance religion, which swept across the Plains in the late 1800s, culminated in the massacre of 390 men, women, and children at Wounded Knee in 1890. For this tragedy Congress awarded thirty Congressional Medals of Honor to soldiers of the Seventh Cavalry — the former unit of General Armstrong Custer.

Restrictions against Indian religions continued until President Franklin D. Roosevelt appointed John Collier as Commissioner of Indian Affairs in 1932. During his tenure, Collier, a former social worker and a student of Pueblo life and spirituality, ceased official prohibitions against Indian religious practices. The end to discriminatory policies did little to overcome the nation's general ignorance of and prejudices against Indian religions and the determination of Christian communities to proselytize Indian people.

Throughout the next three decades of war, termination, and social upheaval, Indian people struggled to maintain and protect their religious existence. In the mid-1970s, encouraged by a new era of self-determination for Indian people, traditional religious leaders gathered in New Mexico to testify against the government's unabated infringements of Indian religious rights. Federal authorities had arrested Cheyennes and Arapahoes for the possession and use of sacred eagle feathers under the 1976 Bald Eagle Protection Act. Customs officials had exposed and destroyed purified medicine bundles and refused to allow tribal members to transport sacred plants and animals across state and national borders. Police in a number of states had arrested Native American Church members for using peyote in their religious services. Archeologists and museum personnel had denied proper burial rights to Indian remains and had refused to return sacred objects necessary for ceremonies. And throughout the country, federal and state officials and private individuals had prevented tribal members access to sacred lands and had dispossessed them of sacred objects.

The awareness raised in New Mexico and at other meetings ultimately led to concrete proposals from the Indian community for changes in federal legislation. Indian leaders negotiated an agreement with federal conservation officials concerning the possession of eagle feathers for ceremonial purposes. And Indian groups across the nation initiated lobbying efforts for a bill to protect Native religious rights. On December 15, 1977, Senator James Abourezk introduced the American Indian Religious Freedom Act into the Senate.

Testimonies from Indians and Hawaiians detailing religious suppression generated widespread Senate support for the bill. The sole cautionary note expressed in the Senate hearings came from Justice Department spokesman Larry Simms. He relayed two points of concern from the administration — that the bill would require federal agencies to protect Native religions at the expense of society's larger interest and that the act could conflict with existing federal law, thereby violating the Equal Protection and Establishment Clauses. To avoid this dilemma, Simms proposed the inclusion of the statement, "[n]othing in this resolution shall be construed as affecting any provision of State or Federal Law" (Abourezk 1978, 11). The response by Abourezk that the act *intended* to modify existing federal regulations and laws dissuaded acceptance of the proposed change. Without further discussion, the Senate unanimously approved passage.

Approval in the House proved more difficult. Echoing the administration's views, various congressional representatives argued that the act conflicted with the Equal Protection and Establishment Clauses. Other representatives contended that the act would permit entry onto private lands for religious worship, allow the use of dangerous drugs, and endanger protected wildlife. In the Senate hearings, Senator Abourezk had stated that the bill would supplement the First Amendment by providing tribes with a statutory cause of action. Representative Morris Udall, in an apparent effort to secure the bill's passage, but using language that would return to haunt him (see *Lyng*), characterized the act as "the sense of Congress...merely a statement of policy" with "no teeth in it" (Udall 1978). The bill passed the House, without major revisions, 337 to 81.

On August 12, 1978, President Jimmy Carter signed the bill into law. In the accompanying statement, Carter acknowledged the bill's necessity. "In the past Government agencies and departments have . . . denied Native Americans access to particular sites and interfered with religious practices and customs." It would now be "the policy of the United States to protect and preserve the inherent right of American Indian, Eskimo, Aleut and Native Hawaiian people to believe, express, and exercise their traditional religion." The act, Carter continued, was "in no way intended to . . . override existing law, but is designed to prevent Government action that could violate . . . constitutional protections" (Carter 1979).

As mandated by section 2, President Carter appointed a task force composed of nine federal agencies, including the Bureau of Indian Affairs and supported by representatives from the American Indian Rights Fund and the American Indian Law Center, to identify necessary administrative and legislative changes in federal agencies and regulations. The task force requested all federal agencies to evaluate their policies and procedures in light of the act and conducted ten on-site hearings around the country. The task force submitted its report to Congress in August 1979. Contained in the document were some thirty-seven pages of recommendations for administrative and legislative changes regarding land, cemeteries, sacred objects, and ceremonies. To date only a small number of federal agencies, such as the Customs Service, the Fish and Wildlife Service, and the Department of the Navy, have altered a few isolated procedures to accommodate tribal religious practices.

This lack of administrative change coupled with few judicial successes led the House Subcommittee on Civil and Constitutional Rights in June 1982 to address the continuing problems of American Indians to practice their religions despite the passage of AIRFA. Testimony by American Indian witnesses and governmental officials clearly attested to the lack of federal administrative compliance with the law and congressional failure to rectify religious infringements through legislative reform. The committee hearings, while important for refocusing attention on the issue, failed to produce concrete results.

Six years later Congress again unsuccessfully attempted to rectify the inadequacies of AIRFA. In March 1988, Senators Cranston, Inouye, and DeConcini introduced legislation "to ensure that Federal lands are managed in a manner that does not impair the exercise of traditional American Indian religion" (S. 2250, 100th Cong., 2d Sess. 1988). Specifically, the bill sought to amend AIRFA by adding a new section that stated, "Except in cases involving compelling governmental interests of the highest order, Federal lands that have been historically indispensable to a traditional American Indian religion shall not be managed in a manner that would seriously impair or interfere with the exercise or practice of such traditional American Indian religion." The following year, as discussed later, Congress initiated another attempt to amend AIRFA.

Interpretations of the Act

AIRFA's vagueness and conflicting congressional statements concerning AIRFA's scope have produced three possible explanations of the act's intention. The most restrictive interpretation, and the one ultimately adopted by the Supreme Court in the 1988 *Lyng* decision, is that AIRFA merely represents a policy statement directing the executive branch to review its procedures and regulations. This view holds that the act does not mandate substantive changes, but is only procedural in nature, i.e., directing federal agencies to consider, in conjunction with other societal needs, the impact of their actions on Indian religious rights.

The second interpretation is that the act provides Indian individuals with substantive claims. Whether such claims are constitutional or statutory in nature is debatable. Several lower courts have held that AIRFA only lends support to those guarantees already provided to Indian plaintiffs by the First Amendment, that the act provides no additional statutory rights. Other courts have ruled that AIRFA provides tribes with a statutory claim to religious freedom that is in addition to their constitutionally guaranteed First Amendment rights.

The third and most expansive interpretation perceives AIRFA as a statutory recognition of the federal government's trust responsibility to protect and to preserve Indian culture and religion. This interpretation would require the federal government to provide a different degree of federal accommodation (as in the case of peyote usage) to Indian religious rights.

Case by Case Analysis of Decisions under AIRFA

The courts have heard approximately two dozen cases involving AIRFA. The most important of these have dealt with Indian efforts to obtain access to and protection of sacred lands from development or exploitation. The remainder have involved official regulation of individual activity, such as penal prohibitions against the wearing of headbands, long hair, and the use of peyote; penalties for killing or selling protected eagles; and the government's assignment of Social Security numbers. The following section provides a brief case by case analysis of the more important decisions with particular attention given to the courts' interpretation of AIRFA's function, scope, and objectives.

Headbands, Hair, Eagles, Sacred Objects, Funeral Arrangements,
Social Security Numbers, and Peyote

In the earliest non-land case to invoke AIRFA, *Oneida Indian Nation of New York v. Clark*, the Oneida Nation filed suit against the secretary of interior charging tribal election irregularities. At issue was the failure of the Bureau of Indian Affairs to extend a deadline to accommodate an individual's attention to religious responsibilities. The court found that the denial of an extension did not constitute a violation of the First Amendment, nor of AIRFA. Furthermore, the court ruled that AIRFA protected only those traditional Native religious rights secured by the First Amendment and did not create a separate cause of action.

Other courts, when faced with the necessity to balance Indian religious rights with land development, have reiterated the view that AIRFA provides no statutory protection. Most of the remaining non-land decisions, however, have either remained silent on the issue, or have ruled that the act does provide Indians with a separate cause of action.

For example, in an appended case to *Shabazz v. Barnauskas*, an Indian plaintiff incarcerated in the Florida State Penitentiary charged that the prison's regulation against long hair violated his First Amendment rights and AIRFA. The court acknowledged that Congress, by passing AIRFA, had recognized the existence of an American Indian religion and that the wearing of long hair was an important aspect of this religion. The First Amendment constitutionally and AIRFA statutorily protected the exercise of the inmates' religious rights. In the final analysis, however, the court ruled that the public's interest in maintaining penal security outweighed the plaintiff's First Amendment rights.

A Nebraska district court applied similar reasoning to dismiss Indian requests to use peyote during Native American Church services. In *Indian Inmates of Nebraska Penitentiary v. Grammer*, Indian prisoners charged that the warden's refusal to allow their use of peyote violated their First Amendment rights and AIRFA's provisions. The court accepted the central role of sacramental peyote in the inmates' religious services and acknowledged that AIRFA supported its use. Without further discussion of the act, the court deemed that the prison's security needs superseded the petitioners' First Amendment right to ingest peyote.

Indian inmates in Iowa were more successful in convincing a district court that prison regulations forbidding the wearing of headbands interfered with the exercise of their religious rights. In *Reinert v. Haas*, the court accepted the headband as the symbol of the sacred circle. This symbolism, the court reasoned, was analogous to the Christian cross or medal. The court ruled that the public's interest was best served by protecting the constitutional rights of all its members, including Indian inmates. Indian prisoners were also successful in two other district court cases, *Bear Ribs v. Taylor*, and *Marshno v. McMannus*. In these cases Indian inmates argued respectively that the warden's refusal of access to sweat lodges, and of access to sacred objects, religious leaders, and drum ceremonies violated their First Amendment rights. In all three cases above, the courts relied on AIRFA to support the plaintiffs' claims under the First Amendment.

In 1987, the Ninth Circuit divested AIRFA of even procedural obligations in yet another case (*Standing Deer*) brought by Indian prisoners. Eighteen inmates of the federal penitentiary at Lompoc, California, requested that the court set aside a prison regulation banning all headgear, including Indian headbands, as a violation of the inmates' First Amendment rights and AIRFA's regulations. The court refused, ruling that the penological interests in maintaining a headgear ban outweighed the prisoners' religious interests. To the argument that the federal prison authorities had not consulted with the Indian inmates as to the effect of the ban on their religious rights, the judges responded that AIRFA did not create procedural obligations. "An objective reading of the Act shows that Congress did no more than affirm the protection and preservation of Indian religions as a policy of the United States" (*Standing Deer*, 1530).[1]

As the *Reinert* case illustrates, Indians have proven most successful in protecting their religious practices when the courts can compare the tribal practice to a custom in one of the dominant religions. In *Frank v. Alaska*, the court ruled that an Athabascan Indian's arrest for killing moose out of season was an abridgment of the man's First Amendment rights. The moose meat, which was used in a funeral ceremony, was, according to the court, "the sacramental equivalent to the wine and wafer in Christianity" (*Frank*, 1072). Most importantly, the court ruled that allowing Indians to breach state game laws was a justifiable accommodation of religious practices. This accommodation did not violate the Establishment Clause, but reflected the government's "obligation of neutrality in the face of religious difference (*Frank*, 1075). The court did not analyze AIRFA's scope or intent, but simply noted its enactment as a support for its decision in the case.

The courts similarly noted, but did not discuss, the passage of AIRFA in three other conservation cases. In *The United States of America v. Buerk*, the court ordered the confiscation from a non-Indian of federally protected bird feathers, but ordered the charges dismissed given the individual's participation in Native religious ceremonies. In *dicta*, the court observed that AIRFA's passage had softened federal policy in regard to Indians' use of endangered species in religious practices. In *United States v. Dion*, the court mentioned AIRFA in conjunction with the plaintiff's First Amendment rights, but held that Dion had killed "protected" birds for "commercial gain not religious purposes." Hence, Dion's First Amendment claim was without merit.

The following year, a Nevada district court spoke specifically to AIRFA's scope in upholding the forfeiture of eagle parts by Chippewa Indians who had violated the Eagle Protection Act. In response to the claimants' argument that such a forfeiture would violate their AIRFA rights, the court, citing *Crow v. Gullet*, ruled that AIRFA created no private cause of action. The act, according to the judges, provided Indians with only those rights guaranteed by the First Amendment. To provide Indians with greater protections or rights, the court wrote, "could involve an excessive entanglement of the state and religion" (*Thirty-Eight Golden Eagles*, 279).

In 1986 the United States Supreme Court handed down the first of two decisions to discuss AIRFA. In *Bowen v. Roy*, the Court held that requiring a father to obtain a Social Security number for his daughter did not violate the Free Exercise Clause, "notwithstanding belief that use of numbers would impair the child's spirit" (*Bowen*, 2152). The First Amendment, according to the Court, could not be interpreted "to require the Government *itself* to behave in ways that the individual believes will further his or her spiritual development or that of his or her family." The Court did not discuss whether AIRFA provided the plaintiff with a statutory cause of action, but simply noted in its discussion of the First Amendment that AIRFA, "provides guidance ... by accurately identifying the mission of the Free Exercise Clause itself [to protect the] 'freedom to believe, express and exercise'" a religion.

The judiciary's most expansive reading of AIRFA has occurred in cases involving non-Indian plaintiffs. The district court in Texas used AIRFA in *Peyote Way Church of God v. Smith* to justify special protections afforded to American Indians in their religious use of peyote. Texas state law allowed religious consumption of peyote by Indians, but proscribed its use by non-Indians and those of less than 25 percent Indian blood. The Peyote Way Church of God, a non-Indian organization, challenged the state's law as violating the Establishment Clause of the First Amendment and the Equal Protection Clause of the Fourteenth Amendment.

The court ruled that the defendants' religious rights were not violated by their arrests for possession of peyote and that the government's separate treatment of Indian and non-Indian use of peyote was permissible. The court emphasized that the United States maintains a special political relationship with tribes. Congress has "a power or duty to the Indians to preserve our Native American Indians ... as a cohesive culture. ... In the AIRFA, Congress has recognized this duty" (*Peyote Way*, 639).

Two later decisions by lower courts expressed a similar view that AIRFA represented a legislative fulfillment of the government's fiduciary responsibility to tribes. Citing the *Peyote Way* decision, the court in *United States v. Warner*, reiterated that the Indian peyote exemption, supported by AIRFA, helped to preserve the Indians' culture and status as dependent nations. In *United States v. Rush*, the First Circuit similarly held that the state law forbidding marijuana use did not violate Ethiopian Zion Coptic Church members' First Amendment rights. In distinguishing the right of Indians to consume peyote from the prohibition against non-Indians to use peyote and marijuana, the court pointed out that AIRFA's legislative history supported the peyote exception for Indians, "finding that religion is an integral part of Indian culture and that the use of . . . peyote [is] necessary to the survival of Indian religion and culture" (*Rush*, 513).

Land Development and Exploitation Cases

Indians have faced their most serious First Amendment and AIRFA defeats in cases involving land development, access, and exploitation. In *Sequoyah v. Tennessee Valley Authority*, two bands and several members of the Cherokee Nation filed suit to obtain an injunction against the completion of the Tellico Dam on the Little Tennessee River. The plaintiffs argued that the flooding produced by the dam would prevent access to their sacred birthplace, Chota, their ancestral burial grounds, and a ceremonial area important for collecting medicinal herbs, thereby interfering with their religious practices. The Cherokees lost at the district level on the grounds that their lack of title to the area precluded their advancement of a First Amendment right.

The Sixth Circuit affirmed the decision in 1980 but for substantially different reasons. A proprietary interest was unnecessary to the Cherokees' claim. The plaintiffs, however, had failed to prove that the geographical location was imperative to the practice of their religion. Rather, the court ruled, the Cherokees were expressing a "personal preference"; their concern was with the "historical beginnings of the Cherokees and their cultural development, rather than religious practice . . . (*Sequoyah* 1980, 1164). The court also held that relief under AIRFA was immaterial given congressional legislation that directed the TVA to complete the dam notwithstanding the existence of any other federal laws.

The same year, in *Badoni v. Higginson*, Navajo religious leaders sued federal officials, claiming that the government's mismanagement of Rainbow Bridge National Monument violated their First Amendment rights. A 1910 executive order had withdrawn Rainbow Bridge National Monument from the Navajo Reservation without tribal consent or compensation. In 1977 the Bureau of Land Reclamation completed Glen Canyon Dam, thereby creating a large recreational lake around the monument. Pursuant to this recreational endeavor, federal officials licensed concessionaires to run boat services to the monument and to sell alcoholic beverages.

These actions struck at the heart of Navajo religious practice. The plaintiffs had long regarded the bridge as the incarnation of a deity. Navajo belief further held that if the earth is altered, the deities will not hear the petitioners' prayers, making their ceremonies ineffective. Inaccessibility to the religious site and the loud drunkenness of obnoxious tourists interfered with religious ceremonies. As remedies, the Navajos requested a prohibition on beer drinking at the monument and asked that the Park Service close the area periodically to visitors.

The district court granted the government's motion for summary judgment on grounds that the Navajos' lack of property interests precluded remedies and that the public's interest outweighed the Navajos' free exercise rights. The Tenth Circuit in 1980 rejected the requirement of proprietorship, but remained in agreement with the lower court's finding that the public's interest in low-cost electricity and tourism superseded Indian religious rights. The court acknowledged that Rainbow Bridge was of central importance to the Navajo religion and that Park Service regulations hindered Navajo religious practices. Despite this inconvenience, the court ruled, the Park Service's actions did not compel the Navajos to violate tenets of their religion. Furthermore, agreeing to the plaintiffs' request to exclude tourists from the area during religious ceremonies would constitute the creation of a religious shrine and violate the Establishment Clause. The court dismissed the plaintiffs' reliance on AIRFA with the statement that "we do not have before us the constitutionality of those laws or regulations" (*Badoni* 1980, 180).

The Hopi and Navajo met with similar defeat in the consolidated cases of *Wilson v. Block*, *Hopi Indian Tribe v. Block*, and *Navajo Medicinemen Ass'n. v. Block*. In the first case initiated after the passage of AIRFA, Navajo and Hopi religious leaders sought to prevent expansion by the Forest Service and Department of Agriculture of a ski area in the San Francisco Peaks. Located on federal lands, the area was of critical religious significance to both tribes. The court accepted the Peaks' importance, stating, "The Navajos pray directly to the Peaks and regard them as a living deity" (*Wilson*, 738). The Hopis, who believe the Peaks to be home to their kachinas, "have many shrines on the Peaks and collect herbs, plants and animals from the Peaks for use in religious ceremonies." In spite of the Peaks' religious importance, the district court held that the spiritual inconveniences caused by the ski bowl expansion did not constitute a violation of the plaintiffs' free exercise right. In fact, the court reasoned, to prohibit development would violate the Establishment Clause.

The District of Columbia Circuit Court affirmed the ruling on appeal. The court agreed that the Peaks played an important role in the religious life of the Navajo and Hopi, but distinguished between "offending" and "penalizing" adherence to religious beliefs. Since the plaintiffs had not proven the "indispensability" of the area to their religious practices, the government's actions had only offended their religious practices and was therefore permissible.

According to the court, AIRFA required only that the government fulfill three duties: to evaluate policies and procedures for protecting religious freedoms; to refrain from prohibiting access, performance of religious ceremonies, and the possession and use of religious objects; and to consult with Indian groups. The Forest Service, the court stated, had fulfilled these obligations by including the testimony of religious leaders in the preparation of the project's Environmental Impact Statement.

Religious leaders from the Lakota and Tsistsistas were equally unsuccessful in their attempts in *Fools Crow v. Gullet* to halt the development of additional tourist facilities at Bear Butte in the Black Hills. As a 1980 Supreme Court decision affirmed, Congress had illegally confiscated the Black Hills from the Lakota Nation in 1877. In 1962 South Dakota purchased the land for the development of a state park. Religious leaders argued that over the last several years Department of Game, Fish and Park projects and regulations had seriously affected the tribes' ability to conduct religious services. The department had constructed access roads and parking spaces which defaced the land and diminished the power of the Butte as a ceremonial ground. Viewing platforms for tourists to watch sacred rituals disrupted the ceremonies. Ongoing construction prevented the tribes from camping in traditional grounds and newly implemented regulations required them to obtain a permit before conducting religious ceremonies.

Although the court accepted that Bear Butte was for the Lakota and Tsistsistas the most sacred of all ceremonial sites in the Black Hills, the department's actions did not violate the tribes' First Amendment rights. Observing first that the tribes held no property interest in the Butte, the court dealt with their First Amendment claims by positing a distinction between religious belief and religious practice. The developments at Bear Butte, the district court held, with the circuit court in complete agreement, did not force the Indian practitioners to relinquish their religious beliefs or prevent them from conducting their religious practices. As one of the department's objectives was to inform tourists of the "traditional Indian religious experience," the improvements were in the public's interest. The roads allowed all people to reach the site more easily and the viewing platforms helped to ensure privacy by keeping the tourists in one location. Citing *Sequoyah* and *Badoni*, the court pointed out that if the Cherokees and Navajos' bar of access to lands permanently under water had not violated their First Amendment rights, then certainly the state had not violated the Lakotas' rights. Hinting that the department had already extensively accommodated the tribes' religious needs, the court warned that if the department complied with the Indians' demands, it could violate the Establishment Clause.

The court also rejected a statutory claim under AIRFA. The act, the court pointed out, did not cover state action. Citing *Wilson*, the court ruled that the act did not provide Indians with a separate cause of action. The act was merely a statement of federal policy toward Indian religious rights; it did not intend to vest Indians with more rights than they had under the First Amendment.

The lower court decisions in *New Mexico Navajo Ranchers' Assoc. v. I.C.C.*, and *United States v. Means* initially offered some hope that the courts, at a minimum, would interpret AIRFA as requiring federal agencies to balance Indian religious rights carefully with those of their respective agencies. In the *I.C.C.* case Navajo property owners requested the circuit court to order the Interstate Commerce Commission to review its approval for the building of a railroad line over their lands by the Star Lake and Santa Fe Railroads. The court, finding that the I.C.C. had failed to ensure adequately that the railroad company would comply with the requirements of AIRFA and the National Historic Preservation Act, remanded the case to the I.C.C. Suggesting the importance of the government's obligations under its trust responsibility, the court stated, "The I.C.C. is bound to consider the extent to which the proposed construction is consistent with the public interest in preserving the status of the Navajo tribe as a 'quasi-sovereign nation' and in preserving the tribe's ability 'to maintain itself as a culturally and politically distinct entity'" (*New Mexico Navajo Ranchers*).

The court's decision upon rehearing the case in 1988 reflected the uncertainty surrounding AIRFA's scope following the *Lyng* ruling discussed below. Although the Supreme Court had ruled in the *Lyng* case that AIRFA created no separate rights or cause of action, the court held that AIRFA still required federal agencies (as stated in *Wilson*) to consult with Indian leaders before approving projects that would affect religious practices. Hence, the pertinent issue before the court was to determine if the I.C.C. had fulfilled this requirement. Citing the *Standing Deer v. Carlson* ruling that required only that federal officials should seek to inform themselves of religious beliefs and practices, the court held that consultation with secular leaders and future talks with archeologists fulfilled AIRFA's requirements. The I.C.C.'s failure to consult with Navajo religious leaders was not a violation of AIRFA.

Members of the Lakota Nation were also initially successful in asserting their rights at the lower court level in *United States v. Means*. In this case participants from the Yellow Thunder Camp, located on eight hundred acres in the Black Hills, charged that the Forest Service's refusal to provide them with a special use permit for their camp violated the First Amendment and AIRFA. The court agreed, finding that the Forest Service had not properly and in good faith reviewed the Indians' request nor balanced their needs with Forest Service policy as mandated by AIRFA.

The case, however, met with resounding defeat on appeal. Citing the Supreme Court's decision in the *Lyng* case, discussed below, the Eighth Circuit ruled that the government's actions did not "burden" or "prohibit" the Indians' right to exercise their religious beliefs and practices. Indians could not impose a "religious servitude" upon public lands (*Means* 1988, 407).

The decision in the *Means* case relied on the Supreme Court's ruling in *Lyng v. Northwest Indian Cemetery Protective Assn.* In 1986, Indians appeared to have won a significant victory in the Ninth Circuit in *Northwest Indian Cemetery Protective Assn. v. Peterson*. Members of the Yurok, Karok, and Tolowa Tribes sought to halt the U.S. Forest Service from constructing a six-mile road (known as the G-O Road) near Chimney Rock and from authorizing logging in the surrounding sacred area, which the tribe used for religious practices.

Ruling in the tribes' favor, the court accepted the "central and indispensable" nature of ceremonies at Chimney Rock. The necessity to conduct ceremonies in isolation and without interference was vital to the tribes' exercise of their religious rights. The government's interest in revenue and increased recreational activities, the court found, did not outweigh the tribes' free exercise rights. Whereas in previous Indian religious freedom cases the courts had equated any form of accommodation as entanglement with the Establishment Clause, the court in the *Northwest* case stated, "The Constitution encourages accommodation, not merely tolerance, of all religions and forbids hostility toward any" (*Northwest*, 694). Congress had passed AIRFA, the court emphasized, for the protection and preservation of traditional Indian religious beliefs.

In a devastating decision for Indian religious rights, the Supreme Court overturned the circuit court's decision in 1988. Writing for a four-person majority, Justice Sandra Day O'Connor agreed that " . . . the Indian respondents' beliefs are sincere and that the Government's proposed actions will have severe adverse effects on the practice of their religion" (*Lyng*, 1326, citing 795 F.2, 693). Despite this admission and an additional statement that the government's actions in this case "could have devastating effects on traditional Indian religious practices," the Court concluded that the government's activities did not prohibit the tribes from exercising their religious beliefs.

The majority's decision is surprising in light of its own admission that previous First Amendment cases had "held that indirect coercion or penalties on the free exercise of religion, not just outright prohibitions, are subject to scrutiny under the First Amendment." Citing *Roy*, however, the majority ruled that "the Free Exercise Clause simply cannot be understood to require the Government to conduct its own internal affairs in ways that comport with the religious beliefs of particular citizens" (*Lyng*, 1325, citing 476 U.S., 699–700). "Whatever rights the Indians may have to the use of the area those rights do not divest the Government of its right to use what is, after all, *its* land" (*Lyng*, 1327, emphasis in the original).

In response to the argument put forth by the respondents that AIRFA created enforceable statutory rights, Justice O'Connor, quoting from Udall's remarks in the House that the "bill would not 'confer special religious rights on Indians,'" replied that there was not "so much as a hint of any intent to create a cause of action" (*Lyng*, 1328). The act did speak of consultation with Native religious leaders, but the Forestry Service had met this requirement by consulting with religious leaders and including their remarks in its final report.

In March 1989, Representative Morris Udall of Arizona, in response to the Supreme Court's decision in the *Lyng* case, introduced a bill to amend AIRFA. Noting that Justice O'Connor had referred in the decision to his speech in the House that AIRFA "has no teeth in it," Udall proposed an amendment "to ensure that the management of federal lands does not undermine and frustrate traditional Native American religious practices."[2]

Conclusions: Judicial Impediments to the Protection of Indian Religious Freedoms under AIRFA and the First Amendment

As the preceding discussion indicates, Indians face a number of barriers in obtaining recognition and protection of their religious rights under AIRFA and the First Amendment. The primary obstacles include the government's limited, and prior to the *Lyng* decision, inconsistent interpretation and application of AIRFA; the courts' application of more stringent requirements in Indian First Amendment cases; and the judicial system's ignorance of Indian religions.

The lower courts have enunciated at least three different interpretations, with minor variations, of AIRFA's scope, function, and guarantees. The most restrictive view interprets the act as merely a policy statement and directive. The act's scope is procedural, requiring only that agencies consider Indian religious needs within the parameters of their operations. Given the Supreme Court silence on this aspect of the issue, the degree of consultation required by the act remains unclear. The *Wilson* court was satisfied with the Forest Service's perfunctory consultation with Indian leaders prior to its initiation of the project. The appeals courts in the *Standing Deer* and the *New Mexico Navajo Ranchers' Association* decisions ruled that consultation with Indians was not obligatory, that knowledge of Indian religious beliefs and practices was sufficient. The district court opinions in *Means* and *New Mexico Navajo Ranchers' Asso-*

ciation decisions and the circuit court opinion in the *Northwest* decision imposed a higher standard of review on federal agencies, requiring them to consider seriously and balance Indian religious needs with those of the larger society.

A second interpretation is that the act provides substantive rights. Prior to the *Lyng* decision, the lower courts had disagreed as to whether AIRFA simply lent substantive weight to already existing constitutional First Amendment claims or provided Indians with a separate statutory claim. The courts in the *Oneida, Crow,* and *Thirty-Eight Golden Eagles* decisions clearly stated that the act did not provide American Indians with an independent statutory claim. Several cases, including *Nebraska Inmates, Reinert,* and *Bowen,* discussed the act as supportive of First Amendment rights. In contrast, the *Shabazz* case construed AIRFA as providing a cause of action for religious freedom violations in addition to that provided by the First Amendment.

A few lower court decisions, mostly involving non-Indians, have provided the most expansive interpretation of the act — that the federal government possesses a trust obligation to protect Indian culture and religion. AIRFA, according to the courts in the *Peyote Way, Warner,* and *Rush* decisions, represented a statutory discharge of this commitment. The courts expressed a similar idea in *dicta* in *S. of Fla. D. of Bus. Reg. v. U.S. D. of Interior,* a case in which local governments questioned the secretary of interior's decision to take a tract of land into trust for the Seminole Tribe. The court, citing AIRFA as support for the secretary's decision, emphasized, " . . . Congress has directed [that] the preservation of the American Indians' religious and cultural heritage is a national objective" (*S. of Fla.,* 1250). A similar notion is contained in *Ute Indian Tribe v. State of Utah,* a case in which the act is cited in a footnote as support for the federal government's trust responsibility in the management of Indian forest lands.

The judiciary's initial interpretation of AIRFA as simply lending support to First Amendment claims and the subsequent decision by the Supreme Court in the *Lyng* case that AIRFA "has no teeth" have forced Indian people back to a reliance on the First Amendment clause. Because of the manner, however, in which the judicial system has applied First Amendment tests to Indian cases, Indian plaintiffs have found it virtually impossible to convince the courts of a First Amendment infringement.

In judging whether a violation of the Free Exercise Clause has occurred, the courts consider, first, if the belief is religious in nature; second, whether the belief is sincerely held; third, if the government action in question burdens religious practice; and, fourth, whether a compelling state interest justifies the interference with free exercise rights. In determining a violation of the Establishment Clause, the courts inquire whether the action advocates or is "excessively entangled" with religion.

The courts have unfairly and inconsistently applied these tests to Indian religion cases. The courts have generally accepted that a particular practice is based on religious belief. (*Sequoyah* is an exception given the court decision that the religious beliefs in question were more an aspect of culture and history.) In regard to the second test, the courts have required Indian plaintiffs to prove not just sincerity, but centrality and indispensability. Plaintiffs in the *Sequoyah, Badoni, Crow,* and *Wilson* cases, for example, were in part denied their First Amendment claims because they had not proven that their sacred areas were central and indispensable to their religious beliefs.

First Amendment case law holds that a government action is suspect if it *indirectly* impedes religious practice. In the Indian cases discussed above, e.g., the *Lyng* decision, the courts have demanded more than an indirect burden; they have required that the tribes be prohibited from exercising their beliefs. Since the plaintiffs were only inconvenienced, the courts have ruled that the "impediments" incurred by government action were permissible.

In those few instances when the courts have inferred that the government action in question may have unduly burdened tribal religious practice, the courts have ruled that compelling state action justified this "burden." The Supreme Court has held in other instances that such state interests must be "of the highest order" such as national defense or public safety. When the courts have balanced Indian religious rights against those of the dominant population, the courts judged tourism, water development, and commercial development to outweigh the plaintiffs' First Amendment rights.

Whereas the Free Exercise Clause forbids unwarranted intrusion, the Establishment Clause forbids religious advocacy by the federal government. The courts in a number of situations involving non-Indians have determined that some governmental accommodation is necessary to provide governmental neutrality in the face of religious differences. The courts have rarely adopted (the peyote cases being exceptions) this view in deciding Indian religious pleas. In all other cases, the courts have strictly interpreted any governmental involvement as a violation of the Establishment Clause.

Why the courts have chosen to apply more stringent tests to Indian religious cases is unclear. What is evident is the judicial system's inability to understand and properly assess Indian religious beliefs, especially regarding the importance of land. Indian religious beliefs are integrated with all aspects of life, the earth, the community, and one's relationship within the universe. Unlike Judeo-Christian beliefs, which are linear in conception and revere religious personages and events, Indian religious beliefs and practices are spatial with emphasis placed on an ongoing process of spiritual renewal. For each tribe there are designated areas of spiritual renewal, where worship, ceremonials, and communication with the Great Spirit occur.

For the dominant society, land is not sacred, but is a commodity to be subdued and developed. This perception is evident in the *Lyng* decision and in the three decisions that initially ruled (later overturned) that the tribes' lack of title to the lands in question precluded their right to advance a First Amendment claim. Failing to understand correctly that traditional religious beliefs pervade all aspects of culture, the courts have either separated out religion from culture as in *Sequoyah*, or required a centrality and indispensability that is inappropriate in assessing Indian religions. The courts are obviously most comfortable in guaranteeing Indian religious rights when the practices in question can be made analogous to Christian beliefs or practices. For example, the sacred nature of peyote or moose meat is understandable to the courts when compared with the significance of the wafer and wine in Christianity.

More than ten years have passed since the passage of the American Indian Religious Freedom Act. The act has focused needed attention on the distinctive nature of Indian religions and on the lack of understanding of Indian religious beliefs and practices. It has promoted some administrative changes, but no legislative modifications, and generated distressingly ineffective judicial protection. Indian religions, which have experienced a revitalization within the last decade, remain at the core of Indian culture, identity, and tradition. Simultaneously, the United States remains morally and legally committed to the preservation of Indian culture and religious rights.

Sharon O'Brien is Associate Professor of Government and International Studies at the University of Notre Dame.

2

Peyote and the Law

OMER C. STEWART

A number of different types of law have impinged upon the Peyote religion. The earliest one of historic record was the theocratic law of the Roman Catholic Church, which was proclaimed in 1620 by the Inquisitors of New Spain to stop the use of peyote (Leonard 1942). Except for the peyote cases at Santa Fe in 1632 and at Taos in 1720, brought before Inquisitors (Slotkin 1951 and 1955), legal activity in the United States involved with Peyotism has been secular. Laws affecting Peyotists in the U.S. have been of several types: federal, state, and reservation. Under each of these were both administrative and statute laws.

Federal Attempts to Prohibit Peyotism

To present the legal history of Peyotism in the United States, reference must be made to the Rules Governing the Court of Indian Offenses recommended by Secretary of the Interior H. M. Teller to Commissioner of Indian Affairs Hiram Price in December 1882. The detailed rules were finally approved by Secretary Teller in April 1883. Each Court of Indian Offenses was authorized to stop "old heathenish dances" or ceremonies, plural marriage, usual practices of so-called medicine men, destruction of property at a burial, and use of any intoxicants, and to punish those Indians who practiced these "offenses."

Although not citing the above rules, in 1888 Special Agent E. E. White in charge of the Kiowa, Comanche, and Wichita Agency, posted an order that reads in part: "... all Indians on this Reservation are hereby forbidden to eat ... [peyote] or to drink any decoction ... or liquor distilled therefrom.... Any Indian convicted of violating this order will be punished by cutting off of his annuity goods and rations.... In extreme cases the grass money will be cut off." In his annual report, White recommended "legislation to prohibit traffic in Peyote" (White 1888, 99). In 1890, Commissioner of Indian Affairs T. J. Morgan instructed other Indian agents in Oklahoma to "seize and destroy" peyote and to classify it as an "intoxicating liquor." This type of administrative law was used on almost all Indian reservations from time to time until 1934 when Secretary of the Interior Harold C. Ickes approved the order of Commissioner of Indian Affairs John Collier, entitled "Indian Religious Freedom and Indian Culture," which was sent to all Indian Agencies as Circular No. 2970. The circular ordered, in part, that "no interference with Indian religious life or ceremonial expression will hereafter be tolerated."

Statute law against peyote was first enacted by the Oklahoma Territorial Legislature in 1899 upon the request of the superintendent of the Cheyenne and Arapaho Agency (Woodson 1899, 284). The law prohibited "medicine men from practicing their incantations" and authorized fines up to two hundred dollars and imprisonment up to six months. Part of the statute read, "Section 2652 — That it shall be unlawful for any person to introduce on any Indian reservation or Indian allotment situated within this Territory or to have in possession, barter, sell, give or otherwise dispose of, any 'Mescal Bean,' or the product of any such drug, to any allotted Indian in this Territory." No arrests were made under the law until 1907. In court it was demonstrated that mescal beans were distinct from peyote buttons and so the Indian defendants were dismissed.

Also in 1907, Comanche Chief Quanah Parker and ten other Indian leaders who were also Peyotists met with the Medical Committee of the Oklahoma State Constitutional Convention and convinced that committee that peyote was not harmful and was necessary for their Indian religious service. A year later the same chiefs and headmen were joined by Peyotists who were also tribal leaders of other tribes to testify against anti-peyote legislation sponsored by nearly all the Bureau of Indian Affairs reservation superintendents in Oklahoma. The Indians won and the new state legislature repealed the anti-"mescal bean" law and failed to enact any anti-peyote legislation. Numerous attempts in Oklahoma to enact laws prohibiting use of peyote have failed to this day.

Notwithstanding the defeat of the anti-peyote groups and individuals in the courts and in the legislature of Oklahoma in 1907 and 1908, some federal officials continued their efforts to stop the Peyote religion in Oklahoma and in other states where Indians accepted Peyotism. Bureau of Indian Affairs special officers who were hired to stop the illegal sale of liquor to the Indians frequently directed their energy toward stopping the sale and distribution of peyote. The first chief special officer hired to suppress the liquor traffic was W. E. "Pussyfoot" Johnson, a prohibitionist zealot who expended great talent and courage against alcohol and peyote from 1907 to 1911. He operated under recognized but questionable authority by interpreting peyote as an intoxicant, Congress having prohibited to Indians in 1897 any article whatsoever that produced intoxication (29 Stat. L., 506). Without specific authorization Special Officer Johnson purchased and destroyed the entire stock of peyote available in Laredo, Texas, the only center for the collecting, drying, and shipping of peyote. For $443 Johnson bought wholesale 176,000 peyote buttons (Johnson 1909). Bureau of Indian Affairs Special Officers seized and destroyed peyote taken from Indians on several reservations.

The transparent fiction that peyote was outlawed by the Indian liquor prohibition of 1897 was finally tested in two cases that the Indians won easily. The first was the trial of Mitchell Nick, a Menominee. It was charged that he "did unlawfully introduce on the Menominee Indian Reservation and give to certain Indians — Peyote in violation of act of Congress January 30, 1897, thereby causing intoxication of [five members of the Necomish family]" (Warrant to Apprehend April 2, 1914, U.S. District Court, Milwaukee, Wis.). In May 1914, the jury found the defendant "not guilty." From notes supplied by Dr. Francis P. Morgan of the Bureau of Chemistry, Washington, D.C., who was summoned to Milwaukee as a government expert, W. E. Safford (1915, 306) wrote: "The defendant was acquitted on the ground that the [peyote] was one of a religious nature." The principal defense witness was a Winnebago Indian, Thomas Prescott, of Wittenberg, Wisconsin. Although it was not mentioned, there is a strong implication that the act of 1897 did not cover peyote.

The next important case was decided on September 8, 1916, in the U.S. District Court of South Dakota, at Deadwood, South Dakota. In that year a Sioux Indian named Harry Black Bear had furnished peyote to a number of Indians on the Pine Ridge Reservation during a peyote ceremony. The reservation superintendent signed the complaint under the act of January 30, 1897 (29 Stat. L., 506), which prohibits "Sale of Intoxicating Drinks to Indians." The jury reached a verdict of guilty as charged. Upon the "motion in arrest of judgment" on the grounds that the statute did not apply, Judge Elliott granted the motion in arrest of judgment and dismissed the charges against Black Bear. Part of his opinion read as follows: "I am clearly of the opinion that this prosecution is not within the purview of this statute. . . . [Peyote] is neither an intoxicating liquor nor a drug." One of the attorneys for the defense was Hastings Robinson of the Sisseton Sioux Tribe, and the major defense witness and legal advisor was Thomas L. Sloan of the Omaha Tribe, an active Peyotist and an attorney.

Judge Elliott made it explicit that a new law by Congress would be needed to prosecute in federal court those using or selling peyote. Opponents of the Peyote Church had in fact expected such a decision in the event of a real test case, and they had ready a bill even before the Sioux case had come to trial.

On February 2, 1916, Harry L. Gandy, Representative from South Dakota, submitted H.R. 10669, "A bill to prohibit the traffic in Peyote...." On April 24, 1916, Senator Thompson of Kansas attempted to amend his bill to control narcotics by adding "analonium (mescal or mescal buttons, pellote)" to opium and other drugs to be controlled by S. 3526. This was the beginning of a futile forty-seven-year effort to outlaw peyote federally. Twelve different bills were introduced into Congress to prohibit the use of peyote in the United States from the 1916 Gandy bill to the 1963 Fascell bill. No federal bill ever resulted.

In February 1915, a year before the submittal of the Gandy bill, the Board of Indian Commissioners held hearings in reference to peyote at which Indian Peyotists from Oklahoma and Nebraska as well as ethnologists James Mooney and Frances LaFlesche of the Smithsonian Institution testified that peyote was neither habit-forming nor harmful and that it was used in connection with serious and admirable religious services. Indian leaders effectively carried the burden of protecting their own religious freedom whenever they were warned early enough that legal barriers against their religion were proposed.

Peyotism and the States

Whereas Congress never passed a law prohibiting Indian use of peyote, the same cannot be said for a number of western states. As soon as it was certain that the Gandy bill would not be enacted, both governmental and denominational opponents of Peyotism turned their efforts to obtaining state laws against peyote. The most active and persistent enemies of Peyotism were Sioux Indian activists Raymond T. and Gertrude Bonnin, who began to oppose the Peyote religion when it was introduced by a Sioux Peyote missionary to the Ute Indians of Utah, where Mr. and Mrs. Bonnin were employed by the Bureau of Indian Affairs. In 1916, the Bonnins moved to Washington, D.C., where Mrs. Bonnin worked against peyote, first as secretary of the Society of American Indians (1916–19), then also as editor of the *American Indian Magazine*, the journal of the society (Hertzberg 1971, 153–88). She was chief witness in support of the anti-peyote Hayden bill, H.R. 2614, in February 1918. Although the office of C.I.A. Chief Special Officer Henry A. Larson, in Denver, Colorado, was the source for an article in the *Denver Times*, December 2, 1916, which had a headline, "Peyote Replaces Whisky on Reservation" (Humphreys 1916), the evidence is convincing that Gertrude Bonnin personally was responsible for the passage of a law prohibiting use of peyote in Colorado. The evidence is in her own testimony in favor of the Hayden bill,

H.R. 2614 (Peyote Hearings Subcommittee of the Committee on Indian Affairs, 64th Cong. 2d Sess. Feb. 1918, 131–36). In January 1917 the Colorado, Nevada, and Utah legislatures almost simultaneously outlawed peyote.

Subjected to campaigns by B.I.A. officials, missionary societies, and some non-Peyotist Indians such as Gertrude Bonnin, other states enacted peyote prohibition laws as follows: Kansas in 1920; Arizona, Montana, North Dakota, and South Dakota in 1923; Iowa in 1924; New Mexico and Wyoming in 1929; Idaho in 1933; Texas in 1937 (Slotkin 1956, 52) and California in 1959 (Mosk 1962, 277). The New York State legislature outlawed peyote, July 1965 (Laws of New York, 1965 chap. 332, 17472).

In spite of the enactment of anti-peyote laws by fifteen state legislatures in the western states where most Indians lived, very few Peyotists were brought to trial under the laws. One reason few arrests were made to enforce the laws was the recognized fact that the state laws had no force on Indian reservations or upon Indian allotments. Another reason was the recognition by attorneys that laws might be unconstitutionally interfering with religious freedom.

Because Peyotism had been recognized as a bona fide religion by the Oklahoma legislature in 1908 following the testimony of the several Peyotist tribal chiefs and headmen and because the issue of religious freedom appeared to have restrained the U.S. Congress from passing laws against peyote, state laws were seldom enforced.

Slotkin (1956, 60–61) listed twenty-eight charters for Peyote churches issued in thirteen states and one in Canada. In most instances the states allowing the Peyotists to incorporate their churches had laws prohibiting sale or use of peyote. The incorporation of Peyotist churches started in 1914 in Oklahoma, but most took the name "Native American Church," which was first incorporated in Oklahoma in 1918. Subsequent to the publication of the Slotkin list cited above, the Native American Church was incorporated in Nevada and in California in 1958. Only in Arizona has there been a question about incorporating the Native American Church while an anti-peyote law was in force, and that action only on March 18, 1970. Members of the Native American Church of Arizona, mostly Navajo Indians, had allowed their charter obtained February 28, 1946, to be inoperative. Upon application for renewal of the date above the charter was refused and that action was confirmed by the full Arizona Corporation Commission on May 19, 1970.

The numerous state laws prohibiting the possession, sale, use, etc. of peyote did little to interfere with the Peyote religion practiced in those states. The laws could be used to discourage some shipments by the U.S. Postal Service and by express companies, yet many packages were mailed. That some reached the reservations is known from reports that they were confiscated. State laws allowed the Indians to be harassed by zealous law enforcement officers, usually encouraged by missionaries or reservation superintendents. Judge James M. Noland (1961) told the writer of his experience as a district attorney in Cortez, Colorado, where he would confiscate shipments of peyote, but would not bring the cases to trial because he thought he could not get a conviction. Records of cases in lower courts that were not appealed are difficult to locate. In one case a Peyotist was convicted and spent fifteen days in a Grand Junction, Colorado, jail (Larson 1919). In northern Utah a case against a Peyotist was dismissed in 1936, but in southeastern Utah Peyotists were convicted and placed on probation in 1938. A Nevada case was dismissed on a legal technicality in 1941.

Nearly all the court cases resulting from arrests under state laws that have become known take on the appearance of deliberate test cases. The earliest date is November 1924, when Big Sheep, a Crow Indian, arranged to be arrested near Hardin, Montana, to test the Montana state anti-peyote law enacted in 1923. Through appeals it reached the Montana Supreme Court, from which a ruling came down in January 1926 (75 Mont. 219; 243, 1067). The court upheld the constitutionality of the anti-peyote law, but reversed the conviction of Big Sheep and ordered a new trial. Both the Crow and Northern Cheyenne Peyotists in 1928 started campaigning to have the Montana law amended to allow the religious use of peyote, a campaign that was successful in 1957. The 1929 anti-peyote law of New Mexico was repealed in 1959 as a result of education of the legislature by members of the Native American Church.

Frank Takes Gun (Crow), an official of the Native American Church from 1944 to 1974 who stimulated a number of tribal groups to incorporate their congregations under the laws of various states, was also responsible for getting charges under state laws moved up from justice or police courts to county or superior courts. His first success was in Arizona in 1960, when the case of Mary Attakai, a Navajo Indian living off the Navajo Reservation, resulting from a complaint and charge in Williams, Arizona, was transferred from the Williams city court to the Superior Court of the State of Arizona in and for the County of Coconino, Flagstaff, Arizona (No. 4908). Besides testifying himself, Native American Church President Frank Takes Gun had arranged with the American Civil Liberties Union to furnish an attorney, Herbert L. Ely of Phoenix, Arizona, and expert witnesses, anthropologist Omer C. Stewart, University of Colorado, and Bernard C. Gordon, M.D (psychiatrist and neurologist) of Phoenix, Arizona. The opinion of Judge Yale McFate, widely cited, declared the anti-peyote statute "unconstitutional as applied to this defendant in the conduct and practice of her religious beliefs." As a lower court ruling, however, it did not affect the status of Arizona's anti-peyote law.

The Arizona statute was again enforced in October 1969, at Parks,

Arizona, resulting in the arrest of about forty persons, the majority of whom were non-Indians. The Indians, mostly Navajos, were allowed to be separated from the case, No. 5650 in the Superior Court of the State of Arizona in and for the County of Coconino, *State v. Janice Whittingham and Greg Whittingham*. The Whittinghams and their guests, mostly from Los Angeles, California, were at the Parks Peyote service to receive a wedding blessing according to the rites of the Native American Church. Although they were convicted in the Superior Court, the conviction was reversed in the Court of Appeals, State of Arizona, Division One, 1 CA-CR 443, in January 1973. After accepting the case for study, the Arizona State Supreme Court denied the petition for review that was filed by the state.

California, the state with the most recent anti-peyote statute, 1959, conducted peyote trials, the results of which have had the greatest national impact. The defendants were Navajo Indians, Jack Woody, Leon B. Anderson, and Dan Dee Nez, who were arrested while attending a peyote meeting near Needles, San Bernardino County, California, in April 1962. As in Flagstaff two years before, for the trial in Superior Court, San Bernardino, California, November 1962 (No. Cr. 15985), Frank Takes Gun testified as president of the Native American Church and arranged for Omer C. Stewart and pharmacologist Dr. Gordon A. Alles to testify under auspices of the American Civil Liberties Union. Before the hearing in Superior Court, Attorney General of California Stanley Mosk prepared an opinion (No. 62/93, May 18, 1962) justifying the anti-peyote law, and his opinion was followed by the judge in San Bernardino (No. CR15985, Memorandum Decision, Nov. 29, 1962), who convicted Woody et al.; and a similar opinion was handed down by the California District Court of Appeal (4th Crim., No. 1794, Dec. 6, 1963) when it upheld the conviction. It was the California Supreme Court decision of August 1964 (Crim. 7788), written by J. Tobriner and concurred in by five of the six other justices, reversing the other courts' rulings in Woody et al., which has been so important. A section of the twenty-one page opinion follows:

> We know that some will urge that it is more important to subserve the rigorous enforcement of the narcotics laws than to carve out of them an exception for a few believers in a strange faith. They will say that the exception may produce problems of enforcement and that the dictate of the state must overcome the beliefs of a minority of Indians. But the problems of enforcement here do not inherently differ from those of other situations which call for the detection of fraud. On the other hand, the right to free religious expression embodies a precious heritage of our history. In a mass society, which presses at every point toward conformity, the protection of a self-expression, however unique, of the individual and the group becomes ever more important. The varying currents of the subcultures that flow into

the mainstream of our national life give it depth and beauty. We preserve
a greater value than an ancient tradition when we protect the rights of the
Indians who honestly practiced an old religion in using peyote . . . (People
v. Woody, 40 Cal. Rptr.; 394 P. 2 813, 1964).

To a layperson it appears strange that such a strong opinion from a
state supreme court would not stimulate a state legislature to amend its
narcotic law to reflect that opinion. Such is not the case in California so
that, as of the passage of AIRFA in 1978, the anti-peyote statute remained
the same and Indians were being arrested and charged with violating the
narcotics code and sometimes remained in jail until a district attorney
or a court discovered the *Woody* decision (People v. Lee Roy Anstine,
D.A. File No. 96945, Bakersfield, Calif., and People v. Red Elk, 2 D.
Crim. 17157 California Court of Appeal Second District, Los Angeles,
May 1970). The above cases document the fact that Peyotists can still
be harassed for carrying on an American Indian religion approved by
a state supreme court.

Another court test of the constitutionality of anti-peyote state laws
occurred in Denver in 1967. Although Colorado in 1917 was the first
state to enact a law against peyote following the 1908 repeal of the
1899 Oklahoma peyote prohibition, there appears to have been only one
conviction under that 1917 law. That was a 1917 sentence of fifteen days
in jail in Grand Junction of Sam Lone Bear, Sioux Peyote missionary to the
Utah Ute, who received packages of peyote in that town (Larson, 1919).
Indians were harassed by having shipments of peyote confiscated, even
when no arrests were made (Noland, 1961). In 1919, the B.I.A. received
reports of peyote being confiscated in Wisconsin, Minnesota, Kansas,
Nebraska, and Montana (Replies to Circular 1522, National Archive).
One thousand pounds were confiscated in Sheridan, Wyoming, in 1933
from Northern Cheyenne Indians (Shreve 1937) and four Cheyenne
Indians spent two weeks in jail.

Most peyote services were conducted on Indian reservations and
were thus beyond the reach of state laws, but some peyote ceremonies
were held in or near Denver, more or less publicly, without interference
from law enforcement agencies (Baker, 1964, in the *Denver Post*). Yet
in 1967 self-proclaimed Apache Indian Mana Pardeahtan was arrested
for possessing peyote. Judge William Conley of Denver County Court
found Pardeahtan not guilty and declared the Colorado anti-peyote law
unconstitutional when applied to use of peyote in the Native American
Church (Conley, 1967, Finding, Criminal Action No. 9454, June 27).
It was not until 1969 that the Colorado state legislature amended its
narcotics statute to allow use of peyote in religious services.

Texas state laws regarding peyote are important for all members of the
Native American Church because the peyote cactus, *Lophophora william-*

sii, grows in abundance in the United States only in extreme southeastern Texas. Laredo is the distribution center. Although the Texas legislature passed an anti-peyote law in 1937, it appears to have had little effect on the peyote trade until 1953, when a Mirando City, Texas, dealer had his peyote confiscated and was charged under the 1937 law. Following discussions with Native American Church President Allen Dale of Venita, Oklahoma, E. James Kazen, District Attorney, dropped the charge. The next year by means of Texas House Bill No. 78, the words "peyote" and "mescal bean" were struck out of the Texas narcotic law (Letter, M. J. Raymond to Allen P. Dale, May 5, 1954).

The supplies of peyote essential for services of the Native American Church were again threatened by the Texas state legislature with the passage of Article 726-d, Penal Code, in 1967, which forbade the possession of peyote after August 28, 1967. Although the law was impossible to enforce, the Indians started immediately to have it changed or declared unconstitutional. Dozens of officials of the Native American Church from as far away as Montana, Wisconsin, and Arizona, as well as those from Oklahoma visited Texas state legislators as well as Texas and federal officials responsible for administrating narcotics laws. The first concrete result of the activities of the Indians was a test case arranged by the arrest of Navajo Peyotist David S. Clark in Laredo, Texas. The hearing before Judge E. James Kazen, who as district attorney had dismissed charges against a peyote dealer in 1954, was case No. 12,879 in the District Court, 49 Judicial District, Webb County, Texas, March Term, 1968. Clark, as chairman of the Native American Church of Navajoland, testified in his own defense; his testimony was supported by that of Native American Church past President Allen Dale and NAC President Frank Takes Gun. Judge Kazen cited the *Mary Attakai*, the *Woody et al.*, and the *Mana Pardeahtan* cases in reaching his own opinion that "Article 726-d of the Penal Code of the State of Texas is unconstitutional as it applies to this defendant herein, who possessed and used peyote in good faith in the sincere and honest practice of Peyotism, a bona fide religion; and therefore, the defendant herein is found not guilty." But the opinion of a district court judge cannot change a state law.

Tribal leaders and officials of several of the different incorporated Native American churches from nearly all western states continued their efforts to amend the Texas narcotics law to allow the collection, purchase, transportation, and use of peyote for religious purposes. The Indian goal was achieved in March 1969, when the Texas Senate Bill 189 was approved. About fifty Indians talked with Texas legislators and several testified in hearings. As before the Oklahoma legislature in 1908 when the anti-peyote law of that state was repealed, so also before the Texas legislature in 1969, the Indian members of the Native American Church helped themselves better than any non-Indians could help them, even though expert testimony from Whites was also useful.

In October 1941 in Reno, Nevada, Peyotist Ben Lancaster was arrested for possession of peyote, which was a mistake because the Nevada 1917 anti-peyote law had been repealed before 1941. In 1942, charges against Lancaster were dismissed (*Washington Daily News*, March 19, 1942). In 1965 a bill to prohibit use of peyote in Nevada was introduced in the state assembly. When hearings were held by the judiciary committee, Washo Indian Peyotist and tribal leader Earl James was among Indians who appeared to testify, and the Indians were supported by anthropologist Warren d'Azevedo of the University of Nevada (*Nevada State Journal*, 1965).

Reservation Laws Regarding Peyotism

As of the passage of AIRFA in 1978 all state laws of western United States where Indians practice the Peyote religion had been adjusted to allow Peyotism either by Supreme Court action, as in Arizona and California, or by legislative action. Yet the legal position of Peyotism on some reservations was still murky.

Reservation or tribal laws dealing with peyote were made in general after 1933 because only with the Indian Reorganization Act of the Collier era did most tribes assume active law making for their reservations. The records of tribal laws are not easily discovered, so that it is probable that information on a number of reservation or tribal laws dealing with peyote have not become known. A letter in this regard (Dickens 1917) may be interpreted as a reservation law:

> In reply to your letter . . . in which [you] make inquiry relative to the law prohibiting the introduction of peyote on this reservation. . . . I wish to advise that the Red Lake [Chippewa] Indian Reservation is a closed reservation, that we have an Indian Court, and have construed the introduction of peyote into this reservation as an act of disorderly conduct, and under the rules and regulations a jail sentence of not more than 90 days can be imposed. . . . One of our Indians . . . did introduce peyote and had seven or eight converts. We confiscated his outfit. He then left the reservation and we have had absolutely no trouble since.

So little is known of Red Lake Chippewa Peyotism, one might attribute the strong action against peyote in 1917 to its subsequent absence from the Red Lake Reservation. Peyote was reported present among the Cass Lake Chippewa in 1919 (Newberne 1925).

In February 1937 the Sioux Indians of Pine Ridge Reservation, South Dakota, met with Tribal Judge William Randall to discuss Peyotism, which Judge Randall wished to have the Sioux Tribe declare illegal.

Other Indians doubted that peyote was harmful, which led Judge Randall to say: "Mrs. Bonnin several years ago took special study of this practice . . . and there was [sic] twenty (20) delegates of other different reservations . . . and I was there. . . . It was on account of this investigation . . . they enacted [1923] this Peyote law that the State has now. . . . " There is no evidence of additional Pine Ridge attempts to outlaw peyote. Nevertheless, in 1937 Joe Deckert was arrested in Pine Ridge and tried under the state anti-peyote law. He was convicted and sentenced to thirty days in jail.

In 1937, the superintendent of the Rosebud Agency reported that the Rosebud Sioux Tribal Council wished to pass an ordinance to prohibit use of peyote on the Rosebud Reservation, except that a person could consume *one* button of peyote or have *one* glass of peyote tea during a service of the Native American Church. Following the advice of the Commissioner of Indian Affairs, John Collier, the ordinance was not enacted.

Indian tribal government may have enacted anti-peyote ordinances on other reservations that have escaped notice, but the two most famous were those imposed at Taos Pueblo and on the Navajo Reservation.

Between 1896 and 1910 Taos Indians periodically visited Cheyenne and Arapaho friends in Oklahoma and during these visits learned about peyote. When first officially reported to the Bureau of Indian Affairs in 1916, there were "12 Indians using Peyote. . . . They meet every two weeks. . . . " Taos Pueblo has been a theocracy since before the arrival of the Spanish in 1540 (Smith 1969), which may partly explain why Taos officials appear to have tried to stop Peyotism at Taos almost as early as it became established. Parsons (1936, 66) wrote: " . . . sometime before 1918 the hierarchy was bitterly opposed to it. . . . Three peyote men were turned out of their kiva membership." In August 1921 the Taos Pueblo Council informed the commissioner of Indian affairs that the council had decided upon "the necessity of suppressing the use . . . of Peyote" (Bergmans 1921). The letters reported that Peyotism had developed in about ten years and there were about twenty habitual users. In March 1922 the governor of Taos ordered the leading Peyotists before the council to answer "charges of misconduct while under the influence of Peyote as well as for violating the Pueblo law against . . . this drug" (Bolander 1922).

Elsie Clews Parsons (1936, 67) reported: "While I was in Taos in the summer of 1923 . . . two 'Peyote boys' were whipped by order of the Governor . . . one man getting twenty-five lashes . . . three Peyote Men were fined by the Council $700, $800, and $1,000 in land or personal property." The blankets, etc., were not returned to their owners until two Peyotists were elected governor and lieutenant governor in January 1934. Contrary to Taos Council wishes, the Peyotist officials returned the property confiscated more than ten years before. For this act and otherwise supporting Peyotism, the two officials were forced out of office and fined in June 1934. Anti-peyote officials at Taos Pueblo took a stronger position against the Native American Church after the state of New Mexico enacted a bill prohibiting peyote in 1929 at the request of the superintendent of the Northern Pueblos Agency (McCormick 1929).

Following the 1934 incident the Taos Pueblo officials continued their unfriendly attitude until February 1936, when the cacique, Tony Mirabal, acting as town marshall, arrested and jailed fifteen Peyotists as they were about to start a Peyote curing ceremony. Tony Mirabal then acting as judge fined each $100. Since they had no money, land was forfeited by most, but it appears to have been quietly returned in 1937, under pressure from the secretary of the interior and a Peyotist governor, Albert Martinez, although Fenton (1957, 328) reported that "the lands were returned when the Peyote Church got its charter" in 1945.

Since the Taos arrests in 1936, Peyotists in that pueblo appear to have enjoyed religious freedom and civil rights, exemplified by the fact that into the 1970s, Peyotists had been elected governor at least ten times, with almost as many serving as lieutenant governor and secretary (Stewart 1972 and Smith 1969).

The Navajo Tribe was thought to be immune to Peyotism until two Navajo members of the Native American Church "were arrested and 'charged with the offense of possessing dope [peyote] on the Navajo Reservation' and sentenced to serve 60 days in jail, on January 25, 1938" (Aberle and Stewart 1957, 58). A few weeks earlier, on January 8, 1938, Anselm G. Davis wrote to Collier to report "a new form of religion is being considered by some Navajos of this section," and to inquire if peyote "is detrimental to one's health" (Gorman 1940, 2). When he submitted his official report to the Navajo Tribal Council in 1940, Vice-chairman Howard Gorman introduced his remarks by saying: "A few weeks ago the Washington Office requested a report on the growing use of the weed called Peyote" (Proc. of the meeting of the Navajo Tribal Council 1940, 11). Gorman came to the conclusion that peyote was used regularly within the northern limit of the reservation by 1935 (Gorman 1940, 3), near the Ute Mountain Ute Reservation from which the Peyote religion had come.

The strong criticism levelled at Commissioner of Indian Affairs John Collier by Taos Pueblo officials when he attempted to protect the religious freedom of Taos Peyotists in 1936–37 may have prompted him to approve an anti-peyote ordinance that was part of Resolution No. CJ-1-40, passed June 3, 1940. The Law and Order Code of the Navajo Reservation came to read: "Sec. 161.87NH *Peyote violations*":

> Any Indian who shall introduce into the Navajo country, sell, use or have
> in his possession within said Navajo country, the bean known as Peyote,
> shall be deemed guilty of an offense and upon conviction thereof shall be
> sentenced to labor for a period not to exceed 9 months, or a fine not to
> exceed $100, or both.

Navajo tribal police started arresting Peyotists as soon as the anti-peyote ordinance was announced as approved, which took place on January 15, 1941 (National Archives). There is no full record of arrests available, but the Navajo yearbook for 1961 (Young 1961, 277–78) summarized the years 1941 and 1952 to 1960. Three arrests occurred in 1941; 96 in 1952; 89 in 1953; 102 in 1954; 99 in 1955; 86 in 1956; 91 in 1957; 97 in 1958; 70 in 1959; and 32 in 1960. Thus the Navajo Tribe arrested 768 Peyotists during the eight-year period 1952–60. Aberle (1966, 114–15) recorded eight additional scattered arrests, 1944–50. It is doubtful that the rate of arrests of the Navajos was as great as that of the Taos, but it is clear from these incomplete figures that the Navajo tribal government won the top place among the various governmental agencies in the United States that have harassed members of the Peyote religion, 1888 to 1989. Local political pressures as well as variations in subtle influences from the B.I.A. in Washington caused the anti-peyote law to be enforced with greater or lesser vigor before it was finally amended to permit the use of peyote for religious purposes on the Navajo Reservation in 1967 (*Navajo Times*, Oct. 19, 1967).

From 1940 to 1967 the Navajo members of the Native American Church were very active with their time and money working to protect their religious rites. Mention has been made of their efforts to have the Native American Church incorporated in the various states they lived. Navajos energetically fought to nullify state laws against peyote in state courts and state legislatures. The struggle against the Navajo tribal anti-peyote law had to be attacked in federal courts, and the struggle was long and unsuccessful.

The first trials in federal court were two test cases organized in 1956 by Peyotists Hola Tso, Navajo councilman, and Dudley Yazzie, employee of the Bellemont, Arizona, army base, for which the Flagstaff firm of attorneys Mangum, Christiansen, and Anderson was retained. In October 1956 Yazzie reported to J. Sidney Slotkin that the Navajo Peyotists had paid the attorneys $1,000 as a retainer fee and that a sum of $620 was on hand to support the cases as they developed. The first action was brought in the United States District Court for Arizona by the Native American Church of Arizona against the Navajo Indian Tribe, Fred A. Seaton, et al. Civil No. 488 Pct. In November 1956 the suit was dismissed, primarily on jurisdictional grounds.

In December 1956 Mike Kayonnie was arrested and jailed at Ft. Defiance on the Navajo Reservation. A hearing was arranged in Prescott, Arizona, before Federal Judge James A. Walsh, in the U.S. District Court, Civil No. 507. NAC President Frank Takes Gun (Crow) flew down from Lodge Grass, Montana, and Dr. J. Sidney Slotkin went from Chicago to testify. The attorneys asked for a writ of habeas corpus freeing Kayonnie and attacked the ordinance as a bar to religious freedom and hence unconstitutional. Judge Walsh dismissed the case and confirmed the anti-peyote ordinance while upholding the rights of the Navajo tribal council to enact such a ban. There is no record that this case was appealed.

In April 1958 a Native American Church service in Shiprock, New Mexico, was raided, and Shorty Duncan, William P. Tsosie, and Frank Hann, Jr., were arrested and assessed a fine and jail penalty by a judge of the Navajo tribal court under the 1940 anti-peyote ordinance. The Peyotists took their complaints to the U.S. District Court of New Mexico against the Navajo tribal council, Paul Jones, individually and as chairman of said tribal council, Joe Duncan, and Sam Garnez. Garnez was the arresting Navajo policeman and Duncan was the tribal judge who sentenced the Peyotists. On February 13, 1959, Waldo H. Rogers, United States district judge, dismissed the complaint, and on March 13, 1959 a notice of appeal was filed. In the United States Court of Appeals, Tenth Circuit, the case was assigned No. 6146 and arguments were presented in September 1959 in Denver. The opinion written by Judge Walter A. Huxman came down in November 1959 denying the appeal and saying: "It follows that neither, under the Constitution or the laws of Congress, do the Federal Courts have jurisdiction of tribal laws or regulations, even though they may have an impact . . . on forms of religious worship" (272 R.2d 131; 10th Cir. 1959).

In June 1960 American Civil Liberties Union Attorney David I. Shapiro, representing Navajo Peyotists Hola Tso, Dudley Yazzie, and three others from Arizona, as well as Ambrose Lee and James and Della Oliver of New Mexico, requested Fred A. Seaton, secretary of the interior, to "rescind and revoke the action of the Acting Secretary of the Interior dated December 18, 1940 in approving Resolution No. CJ-1-40, adopted by the Navajo Tribal Council June 3, 1940." The letter, a necessary first step, became Exhibit B of Civil Action No. 2180-60 in the United States District Court for the District of Columbia, filed July 12, 1960, in *Oliver, et al. v. Seaton*. The district court ruled against the Navajo Native American Church, and the ACLU took the case to the U.S. Court of Appeals for the District of Columbia Circuit where it became No. 16613. By the time the case reached the D.C. court of appeals Stewart L. Udall had become secretary of the interior, so that the dismissal of the appeal in 1963 came under the name *Oliver v. Udall* (306 F. 2d 819; D.C. Cir. 1962). When the Supreme Court denied the writ of certiorari in 1963, that refusal to review the case came to be cited as 372 U.S. 908.

Not all of the litigation in which the Navajo members of the Native American Church have become involved has been cited, but from what has been reviewed it is clear that members of that tribe have done a great service to the church as a whole by their vigorous effort to preserve religious freedom for all. The Crow Indian vice-president (1944–54) and president (1956–74) of the Native American Church, Frank Takes Gun, deserves much of the credit for protecting the church by legal means during the thirty years of his tenure in the highest offices.

The final solution to the local problems of Navajo Peyotists had to await the growth of the NAC in Navajoland so that the Navajo tribal council would vote to allow "any member of the Native American Church to transport Peyote into Navajo country or buy, sell, possess or use Peyote in any form in connection with the religious practices, sacraments or services of the Native American Church." This special exemption for religious use of peyote may not have been necessary since the Navajo Bill of Rights had been passed a few days before (*Navajo Times*, October 19, 1967). The U.S. Congress also enacted legislation to extend the Bill of Rights to all Indians in 1968.

Conclusion: Employment Division v. Smith

The bills passed by the U.S. Congress since 1965, together entitled the Drug Abuse Control Acts, list peyote along with other psychedelic drugs, but regulations for control published in the Federal Register have specified that peyote could be used in Indian religious ceremonies. Most states have adjusted their laws to comply, so that the use of peyote at the time of AIRFA's passage in 1978 was legal for use as a sacrament in the Peyote religion almost everywhere in the United States.

In the last decade, however, AIRFA has not served as protection for peyote users in Oregon, where peyote use is still regarded as a felony punishable by up to ten years in prison, with no exemption for Native American Church members who use peyote as a sacrament. In 1984 two Indians were fired from their jobs when their employer — a private drug and alcohol abuse treatment agency with a policy that prohibits employees from using "controlled substances" — learned of their participation in Peyote rituals. Subsequently the two men were denied unemployment insurance payments because the Oregon Employment Division ruled their firing to be justified by the fact that the men were drug-users.

The Oregon Supreme Court, and then the U.S. Supreme Court in 1990 (in a 6-to-3 decision in *Employment Division v. Smith*), upheld the refusal of benefits. In the majority opinion Justice Antonin Scalia wrote that peyote's sacramental character could carry no weight against "neutral" laws passed by the state against "criminal" activities. If such a ruling were to curtail the practice of American Indian (and other minority) religions, so be it.

Dozens of constitutional scholars, religious organizations, and Indian lobbyists protested the Supreme Court decision; however, it remains to be seen if the legal gains made by Peyotists over the century, and supposedly strengthened by the passage of AIRFA, are in any way secure against such a powerful judgment.

Table I
Laws and Official Orders against Peyote

1. Inquisitors of New Spain, 1620 (Leonard 1942).

2. Order by U.S. Special Agent E. E. White, Kiowa, Comanche and Wichita Agency (White, 1888).

3. Order by Commissioner of Indian Affairs T. J. Morgan to Agents in Oklahoma to "seize and destroy" peyote, 1890 (National Archives).

4. Oklahoma territorial legislature prohibited use of "mescal bean," 1899; repealed 1908.

5. Colorado, 1917; repealed 1969.

6. Utah, 1917; repealed 1935.

7. Nevada, 1917.

8. Kansas, 1920.

9. Arizona, 1923.

10. North Dakota, 1923.

11. Montana 1923; repealed 1957.

12. South Dakota, 1923.

13. Iowa, 1925; repealed 1937.

14. New Mexico, 1929; repealed 1959.

15. Wyoming, 1929.

16. Idaho, 1933; repealed 1937.

17. Texas, 1937, 1967, 1969.

18. Lower Brule Sioux Ordinance, 1938.

19. California, 1959.

20. New York, 1965.

21. Navajo Tribal Ordinance, 1940; repealed 1967.

Table II
Important Court Cases Involving State and Federal Laws
Dealing with Peyote

1. Santa Fe, New Mexico, 1632 (Slotkin 1951 and 1955).

2. Taos, New Mexico, 1720 (Slotkin 1951 and 1955).

3. Kingfisher, Oklahoma, 1907 (District Court, No. 1021).

4. Milwaukee, Wisconsin, 1914 (Safford 1915).

5. Deadwood, South Dakota, 1916 (*Deadwood Daily Pioneer Times*, Sept. 7–8, 1916).

6. Grand Junction, Colorado, 1917 (Larson 1919).

7. Hardin, Montana, 1924 (75 Mont. 219:243).

8. Sheridan, Wyoming, 1933 (Shrepe, 1937).

9. Duchesne, Utah, 1936 (Dart, 1936).

10. Pine Ridge, South Dakota, 1937.

11. Monticello, Utah, 1938 (Collier, July 27, 1938).

12. Reno, Nevada, 1941 (*Washington Daily News*, 1942).

13. Flagstaff, Arizona, 1960 (O. C. Stewart, witness 1961a).

14. San Bernardino, California, 1962 (O. C. Stewart, witness. Tobriner, 1964, California Supreme Court, *Woody et al.*).

15. Denver, Colorado, 1967 (Conley, 1967) (O. C. Stewart, witness).

16. Laredo, Texas, 1968 (Kazen, 1908).

17. Parks, Arizona, 1969 (Court of Appeals ICA-CR 443, January 9, 1973; O. C. Stewart, witness).

18. Phoenix, Arizona, 1970 (U.S. District Court of Arizona No. CIU 70-401 PHX-WPC, July 10, 1970).

19. Los Angeles, California, 1970 (Red Elk, 2DCrim 17157 California Court of Appeals, Second District, May 1970).

20. Washington, D.C. 1974 (U.S. Supreme Court denied Petition for Certiorari in Parks, Arizona, Case of 1969, thus leaving in force the reversal of the Whittingham convictions).

21. State v. Bullard (1966) 267 NC 599, 148 SE 2d565, cert den 386 US-917, 17LEd 2d789, 87 S. Ct. 876.

22. United States v. Kuch (1968, DC Dist Col) 288 F Supp. 439, 35 ALR 3d 922.

23. Kennedy v. B.N.DD., 459 F. 2d415 (9 Cir 1972), cert den 93 S. Ct. 901. reli den 93 S. Ct. 1414.

24. State of New Mexico v. Robert Dan Pedro, Court of Appeals of the State of New Mexico, No. 660 (October 15, 1971).

25. Golden Eagle, also known as Leo Roy Austin, Appellant, v. Deputy Sheriff Johnson et al., Appellees, No. 72-1820 (9 Cir 1974), 493 F. 2d 1179 (1974).

26. State of Oregon, Respondent v. Reginald Soto, Appellant, Court of Appeals of Oregon, Decided June 23, 1975. Or. App., 537 P. 2d 142.

27. George L. Whitehorn, Jr., Appellant, v. the State of Oklahoma, Appellee. No. F-75-476, Court of Criminal Appeals of Oklahoma, February 23, 1977 (Oklahoma Cr. 561 P. 2d 539).

28. State of Washington v. Kenny M. Little Brave, Robin H. Gunshows, and Roger J. Eagle Elk. In the Superior Court of the State of Washington in and for the County of Ferry No. 6535, 6536, and 6537. Findings of Fact, Conclusions of Law and Order of Dismissal and Expungement, January 8, 1979 (O. C. Stewart, witness).

29. State of Washington v. Thomas Cole, a/k/a Thomas Carson. In Superior Court of the State of Washington in and for Yakima County, before the Honorable Lloyd Wiehl. Case dismissed with prejudice, June 29, 1982 (O. C. Stewart, witness).

30. Superior Court, Vista, California v. Timothy Redbird (Kiowa from Oklahoma). Charges dismissed by Judge Daniel J. Kremer, March 27, 1984 (O. C. Stewart, witness).

31. U.S. District Court, Grand Forks, North Dakota, October 23–29, 1984. John and Frances Warner, non-Indians, acquitted (O. C. Stewart, University of Colorado, anthropologist, and George Morgan, Chadren College, Nebraska, anthropologist, witnesses for Warners).

Omer C. Stewart is Professor Emeritus of Anthropology at the University of Colorado with a lifetime of publications regarding the Peyote Religion.

3

Repatriation, Reburial, and Religious Rights

WALTER R. ECHO-HAWK and ROGER C. ECHO-HAWK

Collisions have occurred with increasing regularity in recent years between federal agencies, U.S. museums, and other non-Indian institutions, on the one hand, and American Indian communities, on the other, over issues related to Native religious freedom. One such issue concerns the treatment of human skeletal remains. This chapter considers how museums and other public and private institutions have dealt with Indian remains and explores some of the circumstances under which Indian bodies have entered the basements and display cases of museums throughout the United States. In addition, as a case study in contemporary problems for Indian religious freedom, this chapter describes the efforts of the Pawnee Tribe to repatriate and rebury their tribal ancestors exhumed from graves in Nebraska and Kansas.

The free exercise of Indian religious belief and practice in the United States has historically been undermined, regulated, obstructed, and suppressed in a broad array of contexts — from the slaughter of Ghost Dancers at Wounded Knee to the denial of unemployment benefits to members of the Native American Church in the state of Oregon. The passage in 1978 of the American Indian Religious Freedom Act represents an acknowledgment of this history and a symbolic affirmation that constitutional protections under the First Amendment extend to Indian people. Nevertheless, a fundamental reality of Indian religious life is that Indians must at times deal with a variety of agencies, institutions, legislatures, and courts if they wish to conduct their religious affairs in accordance with what the First Amendment promises.

In recent years this reality has dominated relations between Indian communities and federal agencies, museums, and many other institutions — particularly with regard to the treatment of Indian dead. When non-Indian institutions possess Indian sacred objects and living gods and when they control the disposition of the dead, they become little more than quasi-church facilities imposed upon Indian communities, regulating the "free" exercise of religion for dispossessed Indian worshipers. First Amendment religious freedoms are clearly controlled from the pulpit of science when museums elevate scientific curiosity over Indian religious belief in the treatment of the dead. Should Indians protest, some scientists are quick to raise the specter of research censorship, comparing such protesters to "book-burners" and referring to Indian plans for the disposition of their deceased ancestors as the "destruction of data." The inner sanctums of many museums and institutions throughout the United States have been troubled places in recent years, as administrators have struggled with the fact that — all predictions to the contrary — Indians have not died out, and now there is the problem of explaining to living Indians how so many tribal ancestors ended up as scientific and commercial "property."

While many of the present controversies involve a wide array of federal agencies, tourist attractions, and other institutions, much of this chapter focuses on the issue as it relates to museums. Since their inception, American museums have maintained an interest in American Indians that has been both beneficial and antagonistic — Lurie (1976) summarizes this as a "love-hate" relationship. On the beneficial side, museums serve as a bridge between cultures by addressing the heritage and history of Indian societies for the benefit and enjoyment of both the tribes and the public at large. Indeed, museums can effectively convey to American society a broader understanding and respect for Native peoples and their tribal religions. This would offer a meaningful benefit to tribes beleaguered by very substantial contemporary threats to their religious freedom. This potential role for contemporary museums resembles earlier assistance rendered to Indian tribes during crisis periods in American Indian history when the federal government practiced actual genocide and sought to assimilate Indians by force into mainstream American society. To some extent, perhaps, museums could be viewed as historical places of refuge for important tribal religious symbols threatened by oppressive pressures exerted by U.S. missionaries and government officials (Lurie 1976, 239). For their part, museums are also beneficiaries of positive Native relationships: they stand to gain a deeper understanding of their collections from close working ties with the cultures they portray and preserve. There is optimism that the beneficial aspect of the "love-hate" relationship can be fulfilled to its utmost potential. Indeed, it should be entirely possible for museums to educate the public about Indians without violating the cultural or religious integrity of the people concerned.

Unfortunately, present-day museums are heirs to massive collections of dead Indian people and to staggering amounts of Indian cultural patrimony; and they have inherited a number of serious social problems that must be solved before the Indian/museum relationship can reach its fullest potential. These problems draw upon a larger historical context not entirely of the museum community's making, and their resolution must be found by recognizing the basic character of this inheritance as a problem of religious rights and ethical responsibilities.

The Plundering of Native North America

An understanding of the historical context for the present crisis in American Indian religious freedom helps to clarify the origins and nature of the problem. A defining factor of Indian/White race relations in the United States has been the systematic transfer of the material possessions of Native Americans to non-Indian control. Under any definition of this relationship, Indian tribes have been virtually "picked clean" by the dominant society: land, natural resources, personal possessions, and even the dead left Native hands in surprisingly massive amounts within a relatively short time span.

By the 1870s, vast amounts of Indian lands had been swallowed up by the federal government; and the tribes had been successfully relocated onto ever diminishing reservations. Hunger for Indian possessions did not stop at real estate. Between 1875 and 1925, trainloads of Native artifacts left Indian hands for American and European museums and mansions. One wealthy collector, George Heye, managed to acquire over one million artifacts; statistically, he collected more than one object from every American Indian who was alive during that time! This remarkable, massive one-way transfer of material possessions has been summarized by Douglas Cole:

> During the half-century or so after 1875, a staggering quantity of material, both secular and sacred — from spindle whorls to soul-catchers — left the hands of their Native creators and users for the private and public collections of the European world. The scramble for skulls and skeletons, for poles and paddles, for baskets and bowls, for masks and mummies, was pursued sometimes with respect, occasionally with rapacity, often with avarice. By the time it ended there was more Kwakiutl material in Milwaukee than in Mamalillikulla, more Salish pieces in Cambridge than in Comox. The city of Washington contained more Northwest Coast material than the state of Washington and New York City probably housed more British Columbia material than British Columbia itself....

In retrospect it is clear that the goods flowed irrevocably from Native hands to Euro-American ones until little was left in possession of the descendants of the people who had invented, made, and used them. This situation, often regretted and sometimes deplored, in which Natives are divorced from the products of their heritage, has created some demands for repatriation, demands like those of the Greeks for the return of the Elgin Marbles (Cole 1985, 286, 310–11).

The "need" for such massive transfers of Native property and even dead bodies was predicated at the time upon the "Vanishing Red Man" social theory and spurred by the demand for collections made by newly founded American museums (Bieder 1986; Gould 1981; Cole 1985).

As to the collecting process itself, much was done under normal trade and intercourse with the tribes. However, some museum collecting crews conducted their work in fierce competition with each other; and many operations have been better described as "rip and run" raids, rather than as scientific expeditions (Cole 1985, 191, 248–54). In other instances, Native sacred objects were stolen, taken as spoils of war, improperly sold by Indians who did not have title, or illegally expropriated from federal lands by pothunters. The manner in which sacred objects left Indian hands and found their way into federal museums was reviewed in 1978 by a federal task force convened to carry out Section 2 of the American Indian Religious Freedom Act:

Museum records show that some sacred objects were sold by their original Native owner or owners. In many instances, however, the chain of title does not lead to the original owners. Some religious property left original ownership during military confrontations, was included in the spoils of war and eventually fell to the control of museums.[1] Also in times past, sacred objects were lost by Native owners as a result of less violent pressures exerted by federally sponsored missionaries and Indian agents.[2]

Most sacred objects were stolen from their original owners. In other cases, religious property was converted and sold by Native people who did not have ownership or title to the sacred object.

Today in many parts of the country, it is common for "pothunters" to enter Indian and public lands for the purpose of illegally expropriating sacred objects. Interstate trafficking in and exporting of such property flourishes, with some of these sacred objects eventually entering into the possession of museums.[3] (Department of Interior 1979, 77)

The deleterious impacts of the expropriation of Native religious property upon the practice of traditional Indian religion in the United States has been much discussed in the literature (Horse Capture 1989; Blair 1979; Davis 1980). In addition, competing property rights in this sacred material have also been analyzed (Echo-Hawk 1986). This chapter will focus on the problem in American Indian religious freedom caused by the digging up and carrying away of dead bodies.

Invasion of the Body Snatchers

It has been estimated that museums, federal agencies, other institutions, and private collectors retain between 300,000 and 2.5 million dead bodies taken from Indian graves, battlefields, and POW camps by soldiers, museum collectors, scientists, and pothunters. Examples of contemporary insensitivity in the treatment of Native dead in the United States abound. The Smithsonian Institution alone, for example, presently displays about 150 dead Indians in its showcases and warehouses over 18,500 Indian remains, and this does not even rank as the nation's largest "collection" of dead people. Many of the Smithsonian's dead bodies were taken from fresh graves and battlefields by army personnel under an 1867 order of the U.S. surgeon general to procure Indian crania for government sponsored studies.[4] In such a context, the racial slur "the only good Indian is a dead Indian" takes on a stark reality in the lives of Indian people today. In Montana for example, when the government failed to provide much needed rations during the early 1890s and Blackfeet Indians were dying from starvation, an army surgeon surreptitiously dug up more than a dozen graves and decapitated the remains in order to provide the Army Medical Museum with examples of Blackfeet crania. Last year, on the Island of Maui, Hawaii, a private developer dug up one thousand dead bodies from a Native Hawaiian burial ground in order to build a hotel. In 1987, two men paid a landowner $10,000 for the "right" to loot Indian graves located on his Kentucky farm and literally mined the dead in order to dig up 650 graves. In 1986, the Louisiana Court of Appeals decided a bizarre case in which an amateur archeologist dug up 150 Indian graves and then tried to sell 2.5 tons of "goods" looted from these burials to the Peabody Museum.[5] Even federal agencies, such as the U.S. Park Service, claim dead Indian bodies as their "property" under existing federal law and have issued permits to dig up and carry away untold thousands of deceased Indian people.[6] Motives for Indian body snatching range from interests in race biology, to museum competition for anthropological "collections," to commercial exploitation, to just "carrying out orders."

Non-Indians have methodically exhumed untold thousands of dead bodies and literally hundreds of thousands of associated burial offerings from Native graves. All tribes throughout Indian country, including Alaska and Hawaiian Natives, have been victimized by what has become the most grisly and frightening problem confronting Native Americans today. The impact of this activity upon Native people, regardless of the motive, is always the same: emotional trauma and spiritual distress.

The reburial issue, as illustrated by the following case study, raises two basic human rights issues. First, Natives are confronted with a discriminatory denial of equal protection of the laws. Systematic disturbances of non-Indian graves, on one hand, are abhorred and avoided at all costs, while Indian people are actively searched out, dug up, and placed in museum storage. Criminal statutes in all fifty states very strictly prohibit grave desecration, grave robbing, and mutilation of the dead — yet they are not applied to protect Indian dead. Instead, the laws and social policy, to the extent that they affect Native dead, do not treat this class of decedents as human, but rather define them as "non-renewable archaeological resources" to be treated like dinosaurs or snails, "federal property" to be used as chattels in the academic marketplace, "pathological specimens" to be studied by those interested in racial biology, or simple "trophies or booty" to enrich private collectors. The huge collections of dead Indians are compelling testimony that Indians have been singled out for markedly disparate treatment.

Second, the refusal of agencies or institutions to allow tribes to bury their desecrated dead undermines basic religious freedom rights of living Native Americans. Native religious beliefs regarding the sanctity of the dead are not idiosyncratic beliefs peculiar only to American tribal peoples. On the contrary, humans have *always* treated their dead with reverence, religion, and respect. These are universal values that have been held by all societies in all ages, including the United States, where the sanctity of the dead is firmly ingrained in the common law and statutes of all fifty states. Aside from these basic human rights issues, the problem also affects political rights of Indian tribes that are based upon treaties and inherent sovereign powers of tribal governments to repatriate tribal or ancestral dead (Echo-Hawk 1988).

Case Study:
The Disinterment and Reburial of Pawnee Remains

As with other American Indians, the Pawnee Tribe of Oklahoma has suffered harm from massive grave looting and desecration by non-Indians of every description: through the mutilation of their dead by soldiers, from the commercial exploitation of tribal ancestors, and from museum expropriation of deceased tribal citizens that have been exhumed from cemeteries located throughout the Pawnee Central Plains homeland. This case study will briefly describe the mortuary traditions and history of the Pawnee Indians, recount the history of non-Indian desecration and expropriation of tribal dead that came to the attention of the tribe in recent years, and then summarize the repatriation and reburial efforts of the tribal government to correct this problem.

Pawnee History and Mortuary Traditions

The Pawnee Tribe of Oklahoma is a federally recognized Indian tribe with a citizenship of about 2,500 persons. The tribe includes four confederated bands of Northern Caddoan Indians (Skidi, Chaui, Kitkahahki, and Pitahawirata), located on a small reservation in northern Oklahoma. The cultural traditions of the Pawnee Tribe draw upon an ancient and complex human heritage; and the Pawnees today continue to value those traditions in spite of a more recent history of religious suppression and other destructive pressures directed at Pawnee culture by the United States.

Human history in the Central Great Plains extends back in time for at least several thousand years, and this history is dominated by the Pawnee people and their northern Caddoan relatives and ancestors, who resided in earthlodge towns and settlements along the streams of Nebraska and Kansas. Recognized as accomplished warriors and agriculturalists by neighboring tribes, the Pawnee also enjoyed a complex ceremonial and religious life. The people relied upon the great herds of buffalo and crops of corn, squash, and beans for their subsistence. They also took advantage of diverse plant and animal life, together with other natural resources; and they traded extensively with other tribes and peoples (Gilmore 1912; White 1983).

Treaties made by the Pawnees with the United States between 1833 and 1857 dramatically reduced the Pawnee land base until all the bands were consolidated upon one small reservation on the Loup River near present-day Genoa, Nebraska. The lack of protection from White encroachment and the threat of war with local settlers ultimately made reservation life for the Pawnees in Nebraska intolerable, and during the mid-1870s the tribe was forced to leave its Central Plains homeland (Riding In 1985). The federal government moved the entire tribe four hundred miles south to its present reservation in Oklahoma. One consequence of this "Trail of Tears," of course, was that the Pawnees were forced to leave behind tribal cemeteries filled with their deceased relatives and ancestors.

The Pawnees have historically buried their dead in cemeteries and graves located near their tribal communities. According to one description in 1851: "On the highest mounds in the prairie, we often observed little hillocks of earth, which we were informed were the places of sepulture [sic] of their chiefs and others of their tribe" (Oehler and Smith 1974). The Pawnees have always responded to the occurrence of death by following well-established religious beliefs and practices regarding the appropriate treatment of the dead. These traditions guide the preparation of remains, interment procedures, graveside observances, and other customary activities associated with the disposition of human remains.

The general purpose of these practices is to influence the spiritual condition of both the dead and the living. Nevertheless, death evokes deep sorrow in all human communities, and the Pawnee people are no exception. One traveler witnessed the funeral of a young Pawnee man at Fort Kearney in 1858 and reported: "They placed him in the grave amid the acclamations and lamentations of the whole tribe" (De Smet 1863, 74).

Pawnee funerals are traditionally conducted by priests who exercise the authority to hold such services by hereditary right and training. Superficial differences have apparently distinguished the "way of burial" of each priest according to the mandates of the various traditions handed down within their families. Other factors can influence funeral arrangements as well, including the reputation and position of the deceased, circumstances of death, age, and gender. No substantive differences occur between the four Pawnee bands in mortuary practices.

The dead are prepared for burial through a variety of ritual activities, during which the body of the deceased is consecrated and then "considered holy" (Dorsey and Murie 1940). Following a period of public visitation, the remains are conducted by procession to a burial site within a nearby tribal cemetery and interred with further ceremony, together with a variety of offerings designed to provide for the spiritual benefit of the dead. During the days, months, and years following interment, additional activities at the graveside and within the community include the funeral feast, ceremonial sacrifices, the offering of more gifts, and mourning visits. An example of one form of offering was described by a Pawnee agency school teacher who attended the funeral of a Chaui elder during the 1860s or early 1870s:

> At his death the agent and many of the employees followed him to his burial overlooking the beautiful valley of the Loup. A most remarkable phenomenon occurred as we awaited the burning of the dried buffalo meat which his wife had drawn aside to offer for his support as he traveled to the distant land of the dead. As the smoke of the offering ascended, from out of the clear azure above us came a long roll of distant thunder. (Platt 1918, 792)

The improper disposition or handling of grave offerings can have serious repercussions for the living. A Pawnee historical tradition mentions the occurrence of drought and the absence of buffalo when grave offerings were not properly positioned on one occasion; but with the correction of this problem "there came a great rain storm accompanied by thunder" (Dorsey and Murie 1940, 107). The spirits of the dead become restless when their possessions are disturbed. Spiritual danger is also associated with the theft of grave offerings; one Echo-Hawk family elder recalls a childhood friend who took some articles out of a partially exposed grave and fell sick. When attempts to spiritually purify the boy failed, he soon died. This tragic incident serves as a stern warning concerning the sanctity of Pawnee graves and associated funerary objects.

This overview briefly summarizes the array of religious observances that surround the traditional Pawnee treatment of the dead.[7] Human bodies are regarded as holy remains to be interred with dignity in a permanent resting place. Associated grave offerings are sanctified as the spiritual possessions of the dead. The total assemblage of elements associated with Pawnee burials is closely related to the spiritual condition of the deceased; the strong proscriptions serve to protect the grave from future disturbance. In short, burials among the Pawnee represent the outcome of highly religious (and emotional) events in the life of the community.

The Spoils of Conquest

Following the removal of the Pawnees to a new reservation in the south, non-Indian settlers began an unrestrained plundering of tribal cemeteries in Nebraska, opening graves to search for grave offerings of any apparent value or interest. One Pawnee caught a troubling glimpse of this cavalier treatment of Pawnee graves in 1898, when he visited the site of the last Pawnee town in Nebraska: "Where my sisters graves were is now cornfield what few graves I did find were open and robbed of what little — if any trinkets were found on the dead [sic]" (Wilson 1984, 326). According to research commissioned by the Pawnee Tribe, the looting of Pawnee graves by private citizens also extended to human remains, as archeologists later found in 1940 at the site of a Kitkahahki Pawnee cemetery:

> At the site 25HM2, archeologists noted that extensive looting had occurred. Of the seven burial pits excavated at the site, only two retained burials. Archeologist Robert B. Cumming observed that Field Burial #7 lacked a skull and stated that "the region had been potted before and the owner of the land remembers digging up skulls here 55 years ago." (Svingen 1989, 10–11)

But these disturbances of Pawnee graves were not the first instances of American interest in the dead of the Pawnee Nation. In 1820, the United States organized the Long Expedition, a military and scientific reconnaissance party, and sent it through Pawnee country into the Central Great Plains. This party of American scientists acquired the skull of a man whom their guides described as a Pawnee killed two years earlier. Several years later, Samuel Morton apparently included this skull in his comparative study of human crania, which demonstrated a "scientific" basis for perceiving the intellectual inferiority of Indians and Blacks to White Americans (Svingen 1989, Gould 1981).

Other Pawnee bodies fell into the hands of U.S. scientists before the tribe left Nebraska; these wound up in Washington, D.C. in the Army Medical Museum and the Smithsonian. Among these individuals are at least six skulls of Pawnees who were killed by the army in January 1869 and beheaded in compliance with the 1867 order of the surgeon general, which requested the submission of Indian heads from army surgeons in the field for a new collection of crania at the Army Medical Museum.

These Pawnees were themselves veterans of the Pawnee Scouts, a military unit that operated in alliance with the U.S. Army against other Indian tribes (Riding In 1989). The post surgeon at Fort Harker, Kansas — an avid collector of Indian heads — directed the decapitation of these former Pawnee Scouts for the Army Medical Museum. Surgeon B. E. Fryer described his initial difficulties in "collecting" the Pawnee heads: "I had already obtained for the Museum the skull of one of the Pawnees, killed in the fight you speak of, & would have had all had it not been that immediately after the engagement, the Indians lurked about their dead & watched them so closely, that the guide I sent out was unable to secure but the one."[8]

Reminiscing about the killing of these Pawnees years later, a former Pawnee agency teacher wrote that the federal government "had taken no notice of the foul deed" (Platt 1918, 793); but the army had indeed taken notice. Unknown to the Pawnee Tribe, the skulls were carefully measured by government scientists as a contribution to the "progress of anthropological science"; and from the measuring of seven or eight hundred Indian crania, the curator of the Army Medical Museum was able to determine in 1870 that "American Indians must be assigned a lower position in the human scale than has been believed heretofore" (Sledzik and Murphy 1987). These Pawnee skulls later underwent the scrutiny of Ales Hrdlicka, a Smithsonian anthropologist who believed that his research could be used to justify White supremacism in the United States (Blakey 1987). Ignorant of the circumstances under which these Pawnee skulls entered the keeping of the Army Medical Museum, Hrdlicka concluded that several of the crania might be White; and in 1989, Smithsonian anthropologists cited Hrdlicka's work to Pawnee tribal leaders in an effort to cast doubt upon the Pawnee identity of these remains.

Archeologists entered the hunt for Pawnee bodies and grave offerings during the 1920s. By this time, recognizable Pawnee cemeteries had been thoroughly rifled and the graves plundered. Still, the search for graves continued. Asa T. Hill was a used car salesman and amateur archeologist who became known as the "father" of Nebraska archeology and served as the director of the Nebraska State Historical Society Museum. He referred to himself — at least in correspondence with his

White friends — as Nebraska's "champion pothunter" (Svingen 1989, 16). During the 1920s Hill managed to locate a Pawnee town that scholars now agree is the earthlodge town that Zebulon Pike visited in 1806; Hill immediately began to hunt for graves. Referring to the exhumation of Pawnee bodies, Hill described his activities to the press as a form of recreation and compared the Pawnee cemetery to a golf course for the pleasure it brought him (Ryan 1925). Between 1920 and 1950 hundreds of Pawnee bodies were disinterred by archeologists for scientific study — all without the knowledge or approval of the Pawnee Tribe.

Near Salina, Kansas, during the 1930s, the remains of Pawnee tribal ancestors were exposed in their graves and placed on public display for commercial profit by a farmer and a police sergeant, who later acknowledged the "scientific help" of A. T. Hill of the Nebraska State Historical Society and Waldo Wedel of the Smithsonian Institution (Whiteford 1937, 10–11). This business enterprise took advantage of tourist traffic on the nearby interstate and served for over fifty years as Salina's primary "tourist attraction" — one that featured the public viewing of open graves for a "modest fee." Few cities can lay claim to such a distinction. Had another enterprising Depression-era family opened the Topeka city cemetery in a similar fashion, public outcry would have demanded swift punishment. Instead, elementary school teachers brought their classes to view the Indian remains near Salina, and the cemetery was designated by the National Park Service as a National Historic Landmark in 1964 (McPhilimy 1989; Witty 1984).

The Pawnee Struggle for Reburial

During the mid-1980s, Pawnee tribal leaders became involved in Indian repatriation and reburial issues when they learned that the human bodies on display at the "Salina Indian Burial Pit" were ancestral to the Pawnee people. Tribal leaders called for the closure of this "tourist attraction" and joined in efforts to devise legislation that would shut down the "Burial Pit" as a commercial enterprise and offer protection for unmarked graves in Kansas. The Kansas State Historical Society cooperated with Indian representatives in forming a writing committee that would produce a bill for the state legislature (Witty 1989). The resulting legislation was introduced in 1988, and the Pawnee Business Council endorsed it by resolution in January. This legislation, however, foundered on the issue of compensation for the operator-owners of the Indian cemetery near Salina. The Kansas attorney general subsequently issued an opinion holding that landowners were not entitled to compensation when the state exercised its police power to regulate the disposition and protection of dead bodies.

In that same year the Pawnee Tribe also learned that the Nebraska State Historical Society (NSHS) had a "collection" of Pawnee dead bodies; in March, the tribe was formally notified by the NSHS that it had from five hundred to one thousand human remains, together with associated funerary objects, and that some of these could be identified as Pawnee. The tribal government immediately requested the return of these people for proper reburial according to Pawnee religious traditions, but this request was soon denied. Tribal attorneys at the Native American Rights Fund (NARF) were directed to continue negotiations with the NSHS. As in Kansas, a writing committee was formed by the Nebraska Indian Commission to develop state-level legislation, and this committee was composed of Indian and NSHS representatives. The attorneys for the Pawnee Tribe also requested more information from the society about the Pawnee remains; but access to documents concerning the acquisition and identity of these human remains was denied by the NSHS until society researchers could respond to NARF's request for information.

The Pawnees also initiated negotiations with the Smithsonian Institution for the return of tribal ancestors held at the National Museum of Natural History after receiving information from the Smithsonian regarding its collection of dead Pawnee Indians. In August 1988 the tribe submitted a formal repatriation demand to the Smithsonian for "all Pawnee Indian remains and associated burial goods" and in late September followed with a request for a response to this demand. In late January 1989, the Smithsonian finally responded with a letter that asserted that only two remains out of a total of nine possible candidates could be reasonably identified as Pawnee. However, based upon the analysis of a 1988 Smithsonian "Master List of Specimens," Pawnee tribal historians suspected that many more individuals might prove to be ancestral to the Pawnees. Those suspicions were subsequently confirmed by tribal researchers.

Through the spring and summer of 1988, the Pawnee Tribe could only wonder how Pawnee bodies had entered the keeping of the NSHS. In late August, the society finally responded to NARF attorneys. They reported that approximately 204 remains could be reasonably identified as Pawnee, and that these bodies had been acquired during the 1930s and 1940s in the course of federally funded archeological excavations in Pawnee cemeteries dated "between A.D. 1750 to 1870 or later." The NSHS defined remains from earlier sites as "prehistoric, that is they originate from archeological sites created before written records were made in the Nebraska region," and asserted that due to periodic population "disruptions," these "prehistoric" remains could not be assigned an ethnic identity. The NSHS archeologists advised the Pawnee Tribe that all such remains "must remain objectively anonymous and the subject of skeptical enquiry." But the tribe felt that the NSHS might have Pawnee bodies from sites dating before 1750, since tribal traditions suggest a lengthy residence in the Central Plains. However, until full access to

NSHS archives could be obtained, the Pawnees were forced to rely on NSHS census information.

When tribal researchers were again denied access to NSHS archives in September, the attorneys for the tribe filed a motion to Nebraska's attorney general, Robert Spire, under the state public records law for an order opening the society's files, and on October 6, he ordered the NSHS to cooperate with the Pawnees. A second order on October 21 was required before the tribe's researchers could gain access to archival records.

Tribal attorneys prepared lengthy memoranda for the NSHS, clarifying the society's legal and ethical obligations for the return of identifiable Pawnee human remains and associated grave offerings. The tribe's legal research was supplemented by the Nebraska attorney general, who issued an opinion holding that in litigation the First Amendment rights of the Pawnees would take precedence over the state interest in withholding tribal remains from burial. The NSHS director responded to this legal authority by citing a federal regulation that allegedly prohibited compliance with the Pawnee request; but NARF subsequently found that this law *did not exist.*

In September, members of the writing committee for Nebraska legislation learned that the NSHS — in spite of the fact that it had a representative on the committee — had secretly produced its own bill, without any Indian input. Efforts to meet with the NSHS and merge the two versions of human remains legislation proved futile, and the Nebraska Indian Commission and Indian tribal representatives went ahead with their version. Both bills were eventually introduced in January of 1989, but the NSHS version failed to generate any support and died in committee.

In November, the tribe rejected a proposal circulated by a member of the NSHS board of directors that would have arbitrarily limited repatriation of Pawnee ancestral remains to bodies dated after 1750 C.E. — but only if the Pawnee Tribe would agree to place the skeletal remains in a protective vault designed to prevent decomposition, preserving the skeletal remains for future scientific interest. This plan also postponed any decision on the return of burial offerings — the NSHS would keep them for yet further rounds of negotiation. With this wholly inadequate proposal, the board of directors hoped that the Pawnee Tribe would endorse a plan already known by the board to be completely repugnant to tribal religious traditions and spiritual beliefs — a plan that called for the Pawnees to compromise away a substantial portion of their heritage and history. In December, good faith negotiations broke down completely when the board of directors rejected a reburial policy proposed by the Pawnee Tribe and adopted its own proposal. The NSHS director also contended that an ownership interest by the federal government prevented return of any skeletal remains; but the Department of Interior immediately disclaimed any alleged federal ownership. Even so, the NSHS board of directors still refused to reconsider its decision. The Pawnee Tribe and its representatives had conducted lengthy and expensive negotiations with the NSHS to no avail. Pawnee government officials, religious leaders, elders, historians, and tribal attorneys all failed to sway the NSHS — the board remained unmoved even by letters from numerous Pawnee schoolchildren. The tribe then turned its efforts to the Nebraska legislature, where Senator Ernie Chambers introduced LB 340, the Nebraska Unmarked Burial Sites and Skeletal Remains Protection Act, on behalf of Nebraska's Indian people and the Pawnee Tribe.

The tribal researchers, headed by Dr. Orlan Svingen, released a preliminary report on their initial research in January 1989. This report described the manner in which the NSHS acquired its "collection" of Pawnee bodies and burial offerings. Dr. Svingen estimated that the NSHS had exhumed about 304 Pawnee men, women, and children from tribal cemeteries dated between 1500 and 1875. A more complete census of NSHS human remains ancestral to the Pawnee Tribe was later begun under yet a third order from the state attorney general, overruling the continuing objections of NSHS director James Hanson.

The Pawnee Tribe moved to support new Kansas legislation in 1989, developed under the auspices of the Kansas State Historical Society: House Bill 2144, the Kansas Unmarked Burial Sites Protection Act. That effort was supported by tribal attorneys who negotiated an agreement between the owners of the "Salina Indian Burial Pit," state officials, and the Pawnee, Arikara, and Wichita tribal governments. The "Treaty of Smoky Hill" of January 1989 called for the reburial of the 146 exposed human remains at the "Burial Pit" and promised support for state compensation to the owners. The state legislature subsequently passed the burial protection bill, together with appropriations to fund the purchase of the Salina Indian cemetery and to carry out the "Treaty of Smoky Hill." As a result of these successful efforts, the Pawnee, Arikara, and Wichita tribes began planning the reinterment of these 146 deceased tribal ancestors.

The passage of LB 340 in Nebraska, mandating the return of all reasonably identifiable human remains and associated grave offerings to tribes of origin upon request, was bitterly opposed in Nebraska by the NSHS and a small group of anthropologists associated with the University of Nebraska and the National Park Service. Nevertheless, the Nebraska Unicameral eventually passed LB 340 and it was signed into law. By the end of spring 1989, the Pawnee Tribe stood before the one-way mirror of Nebraska anthropology to view documents filled with accounts of desecration and anguish; but the reburial of their restless ancestors in the Central Plains was at last in sight.

Dissatisfied with Smithsonian inaction, the Pawnees and other tribes with similar requests decided to seek federal legislation directing the National Museum to repatriate Indian remains to tribes of origin on request. At a July 1989 congressional hearing on the National Museum of the American Indian Act (H.R. 2668), the NARF Pawnee tribal attorney was joined by other tribes and national Indian organizations in insisting that appropriate repatriation language be included in the bill. Subsequently, negotiations with the secretary of the Smithsonian were held in an effort to find a solution for the national moral crisis surrounding the treatment of Native dead. These negotiations produced the historic "Smithsonian Agreement," which directs the return of human remains and funerary objects to tribes where a cultural affiliation is shown to exist by the preponderance of available evidence. That agreement was incorporated into the bill before Congress, and despite the active opposition of the Society for American Archaeology (which consistently resists tribal reburial efforts at the national level), Congress passed the bill, and it was signed into law. Under this new repatriation law — which hopefully marks a turning point in federal policy — all culturally affiliated human remains and associated funerary objects will be identified and repatriated.

This case study describes prolonged and vigorous repatriation efforts by one small Indian tribe to rebury its desecrated dead — ultimately requiring extensive lobby efforts, several attorney general orders and opinions, negotiated agreements, four pieces of state legislation, and one act of Congress. Throughout the time in question, while Pawnee bodies were being dug up, state law spelled out very stringent conditions for exhuming the dead, but those statutory requirements for court orders, permits, etc., which are intended to safeguard the sanctity of the dead and the rights of the living, were simply not followed when it came to Indians. Thus, hundreds of dead bodies were dug up without any regard for the feelings or rights of the Pawnee people, providing a clear denial of equal protection of the laws. In Kansas, open commercial exploitation of an entire Indian burial ground existed for years because of a "loophole" in Kansas statutes, despite systematic efforts by the legislature to comprehensively protect burial grounds and cemeteries of every conceivable description. And, of course, the 1867 order of the U.S. Army surgeon general, under which the heads of slain Pawnees were taken, was racially motivated conduct patently discriminatory against American Indians under any interpretation of the Equal Protection Clause.

However, the Pawnee struggle for repatriation was motivated by the adverse impact of this disparate racial treatment upon longstanding tribal religious traditions, which require that Pawnee dead be respected and properly laid to rest. The unfolding facts of this history were met with shock and outrage among the Pawnee people. The spiritual implications of such vast disturbances of the dead required that the government of the Pawnee Tribe take immediate action. As such, the case study reveals the deep impact that grave desecration and body snatching can have upon living communities of American Indians and their religious beliefs and mortuary traditions. Under these circumstances, the withholding of the dead from proper burial by the government, acting through its museums and federal agencies, directly infringes upon very clear religious beliefs and practices that require Indians to lay their dead to rest properly.

Conclusion: Implications for Indian Religious Freedom

As we have seen, tribal repatriation to rebury the dead is religiously impelled action taken by tribal governments to protect basic religious freedoms and the sensibilities of their citizenry. Indian religious obligations, such as those embraced by Pawnee mortuary traditions, often exist between living Indians and the spirits of deceased ancestors. This relationship imposes a duty upon the living to bury the dead properly and to ensure that the spirits and sanctity of the dead are not disturbed. Such religiously motivated conduct is readily understandable, because death and burial have always been deeply held religious matters for all peoples. As one commentator notes, "[No] system of jurisprudence permits exhumation for less than what are considered weighty, and sometimes compelling reasons."[9]

Thus, denial of sepulcher to deceased Indians, when done by the state acting through its museums, agencies, or other public institutions, directly burdens the free exercise of Indian religion by preventing Native people from burying their dead. Government interference with Native religion through the withholding of the dead infringes upon fundamental beliefs and practices of the universal type mentioned above.

The federal government recognized in 1979 that Native American sepulcher involves basic religious liberty of Native people. As found by the federal task force in the *American Indian Religious Freedom Act Report*:

Native American religions, along with most other religions, provide standards for the care and treatment of cemeteries and human remains. Tribal customary laws generally include standards of conduct for the care and treatment of all cemeteries encountered and human remains uncovered, as well as for the burial sites and bodies of their own ancestors. Grounded in Native American religious beliefs, these laws may, for example, require the performance of certain types of rituals at the burial site, specify who may visit the site or prescribe the proper disposition of burial offerings.

The prevalent view in the society of applicable disciplines is that Native American human remains are public property and artifacts for study, display, and cultural investment. It is understandable that this view is in conflict with and repugnant to those Native people whose ancestors and near relatives are considered the property at issue.

Most Native American religious beliefs dictate that burial sites once completed are not to be disturbed or displaced except by natural circumstances. (Department of Interior, 64)

The courts have not been called upon to decide whether the withholding of the dead by the state violates the First Amendment rights of kin to bury the deceased in accordance with their religious beliefs. This is presumably the case because it would be an extremely rare situation indeed, given the strong public policy that all persons are entitled to a decent burial, for the state to withhold the dead permanently from burial over the objection of the closest relatives. However, in *Fuller v. Marx*, 724 F.2d 717 (8th Cor. 1984), the court suggested the obvious when it intimated that a failure by the state to return human remains to next-of-kin for burial can indeed violate a First Amendment right to bury a decedent as required by the religious beliefs of the next-of-kin. There, a civil rights action was brought by a widow against a doctor who performed an autopsy on her deceased husband and failed to return certain organs. The widow asserted that the failure to return all organs with the body violated her "First Amendment right to bury her husband in a manner consistent with her religious beliefs" (ibid., 719). The court did not doubt that such a First Amendment right exists, but ruled that the widow failed to show that her right had been infringed upon under the facts of that case, because she could have retrieved all of the organs had she followed procedures that were available to her (ibid., 720).

Under *Fuller*, should Indian tribes prove in particular cases that denial of sepulcher by the state impairs religious practices, then the burden of proof under the traditional First Amendment test shifts to the state to prove that its withholding of the dead is necessary to serve materially some compelling state interest — one that cannot be served in a manner less restrictive of religious liberty than a permanent withholding of the dead from burial.[10] In regard to the state's burden of proof under the test, the Nebraska attorney general issued an opinion in 1988 upholding the Pawnee religious rights involved in that case and stated in part: "I am not convinced that scientific curiosity, or the possibility that future scientific advances will permit further study of the remains, are sufficient reasons to overcome the strong impulses in the law to allow human remains to rest in peace in a grave or other proper sepulcher."[11]

Although other constitutional, common law, and federal Indian law rights are at stake,[12] it is the protection of Indian religious liberty that cries out the loudest. Felix S. Cohen, a noted scholar and father of the field of federal Indian law, once noted that society's treatment of America's Native people is a social barometer for the basic freedoms and well-being of all Americans:

> the Indian plays much the same role in our American society that the Jews played in Germany. Like the miner's canary, the Indian marks the shift from fresh air to poison gas in our political atmosphere; and our treatment of Indians, even more than our treatment of other minorities, reflects the rise and fall in our democratic faith.[13]

Similarly, the way in which society treats the dead, especially the dead of minority cultures, is also a social barometer for the respect and well-being it accords to the living. Museums and other institutions that have inherited a legacy of insensitivity and oppression toward Native communities must address this heritage as a major priority if they wish to open their halls to living people with as much enthusiasm as they have for the dead. The formation of productive and positive relationships between culturally diverse people should be based upon bonds of mutual respect — not chains of religious oppression. Indians have long been yoked to museums, historical societies, universities, and federal agencies by such chains. But through repatriation, reburial, and the recognition of fundamental religious rights, Indian people hope to be free to visit such places as equal partners in the sharing of human traditions, rather than as dispossessed victims and humiliated plaintiffs in court proceedings.

Walter R. Echo-Hawk is senior staff attorney for the Native American Rights Fund. His brother, Roger C. Echo-Hawk, is a student of Pawnee tribal history. Both are members of the Pawnee Tribe of Oklahoma.

4

Sacred Sites and Public Lands

STEVEN C. MOORE

The American Indian Religious Freedom Act became law in 1978, creating hope among American Indians that a new, more understanding, and thus tolerant era of relations with the federal government had begun both generally on the subject of Indian religion, and specifically on the issue of the protection of sacred sites on public lands. Now, over a decade later, it is apt that we pause to take stock of the gains or setbacks made for and by Indian people in this area. Do Indian people enjoy greater religious freedom today than ten years ago? To phrase the question another way: if understanding is a necessary predicate to tolerance and accommodation, does the federal government through its agency officials and decision makers today better understand Indian religion and the needs of its practitioners than it did in 1978?

The thesis of this chapter is that the federal government, while making very small strides under AIRFA to improve its record concerning sacred site protection in isolated areas and instances, by and large has not made the kinds of changes — as a matter of law, policy, and practice — necessary to provide meaningful accommodation for the religious needs of Indian peoples. In fact, as will be demonstrated in the sections that follow, agencies have exhibited outright resistance and hostility to efforts by Native people to protect sacred sites on public lands. Such efforts by agencies include aggressive litigation against accommodation and, recently, opposition to strengthening amendments to AIRFA. Indeed, in light of the 1988 decision of the United States Supreme Court in *Lyng v. Northwest Indian Cemetery Protective Association*, the forthcoming decade threatens even greater persecution of Indian religion, if not as a matter of outright intentional coercion, then as a consequence of the "incidental effects" of government activity.

Given the past decade of continued abuse by federal agencies and the recent *Lyng* decision of the Supreme Court, the antipathy of the federal executive and judicial branches is likely to continue. It thus remains for Congress to chart a new course for Indian religious tolerance.[1] Congress from time to time investigates the effectiveness of previously enacted legislation and by way of legislative amendments takes corrective action. Now is the time for the Congress to initiate a broadscale investigation of AIRFA, with a view toward making it a more useful and effective federal law, one that fairly and equitably balances the divergent views of traditional Indian people and the broader American public, paying special attention to unique needs of Indian religion.

Background and Context for Understanding AIRFA

There was optimism a decade ago that the enactment of AIRFA would chart a new course in America concerning respect for Indian religious and cultural traditions. The civil rights movement of the 1960s, with its component American Indian Movement, President Johnson's War on Poverty, the Vietnam War protests, the Watergate scandal, and other similar occurrences on the national scene helped fracture the joints of the "root paradigm" of White American society. The seeds of the revitalization of traditional Indian culture, planted in this era, grew and blossomed in the relative civil liberalism of the latter half of the 1970s.

Any optimism felt in 1978, however, has been dampened in the years since AIRFA's enactment. Federal departments and agencies have worked actively *against* accommodation of Native religions, in direct contravention of AIRFA's findings and policy pronouncements. This includes litigation defending against changes in agency policies and practices. AIRFA has proven to be of little real utility in protecting Indian religion.

The power and intransigence of the dominant society, embodied in its economic, political, and legal institutions, are largely responsible for this decade of frustration. White cultural resistance has been fostered and fueled over the past decade by the conservatism of the Reagan and Bush administrations. In retrospect, AIRFA represents a critical first step in a tremendously difficult effort to change federal law and policy to respect and deal responsibly with Indian religious and cultural issues. But ultimately, the dominant society will have to increase substantially its understanding of and tolerance for Indian religious beliefs and practices. Effective and meaningful amendments to AIRFA can assist in the process of creating a means or mechanism for directing such change in the collective American psyche.

AIRFA is noteworthy, however, because it represents the first attempt by the Congress (or for that matter any governmental body on any level) to investigate comprehensively the history of intolerance of Indian religion in the United States. The preamble, or "whereas" clauses, of the act expressly recognize that this country was *not* founded with any consideration for the principle of religious freedom for its Native people, and that the government of the United States has, both deliberately and through ignorance and inadvertence, infringed upon the free exercise of Indian religion. Through AIRFA, Congress made a number of legislative fact-findings that evince this history of persecution:

> Whereas the traditional American Indian religions, as an integral part of Indian life, are indispensable and irreplaceable;
> Whereas the lack of a clear, comprehensive, and consistent Federal policy has often resulted in the abridgment of religious freedom for traditional American Indians;
> Whereas such religious infringements result from the lack of knowledge or the insensitive and inflexible enforcement of Federal policies and regulations premised on a variety of laws;
> Whereas such laws and policies often deny American Indians access to sacred sites required in their religions, including cemeteries; ...

AIRFA traced the history of the federal government's insensitive treatment, indeed outright persecution, of Indian people in matters of traditional religion and culture. Such matters included the protection of sacred sites on public lands, performance of ceremonies and rituals, and the collection and transportation of sacred objects and materials. It traced the evolution of federal environmental, natural resource, and wildlife laws and policies that, although unquestionably well-intentioned, failed to account for Indian access to and use of federal lands and resources for religious, ceremonial, and gathering purposes. With this history as backdrop, it established that henceforth the policy of the United States was:

> to protect and preserve for American Indians their inherent rights to believe, express and exercise [their] traditional religions ... including but not limited to access to sites, use and possession of sacred objects, and the freedom to worship through ceremonials and traditional rites.

Section 2 of AIRFA directed federal departments and agencies to review their policies, procedures, and practices, in consultation with traditional Indian religious leaders, with an eye toward making changes to correct this historical legacy of persecution, intolerance, and insensitivity. The 1979 Federal Agencies Task Force Report, prepared as part of AIRFA's Section 2 mandate, identified minimal changes in the day-today affairs and activities of the executive branch necessary to bring the bureaucracy into compliance with AIRFA and the First Amendment to the Constitution. Have such changes in fact occurred? Sadly, the answer is a resounding "No."

Again, in reviewing the course of AIRFA compliance, one must keep in mind the forces working against traditional Indian culture. First, Indians face an entrenched federal bureaucracy, with an engrained resistance to *any* change, much less the profound changes necessary to provide real accommodation for Indian religious practices. The attitude of the entrenched bureaucracy exemplifies that of the dominant society, which on an institutional level provides very little, if any, real accommodation for traditional Indian culture. Generally speaking, the dominant, largely White society and its economic, political, legal, and social institutions embrace and foster an ethnocentric view of America. Thus, AIRFA, with its recognition of past and continuing injustice and insensitivity, represents little more than a brief, temporary fracture of the American psyche or consciousness.

One cynical view is that AIRFA has done nothing more for Indian people than to whet their appetite, to allow them to feed momentarily on the guilt of the American conscience. The social "window" of opportunity which had opened briefly between the mid-1960s and the mid-1970s was but a false hope or promise for traditional Indian religions. There are examples of Congress's sensitivity to Indian religion — Blue Lake (Taos) and Mount Adams (Yakima) — but these are unusual exceptions. What of Rainbow Bridge, San Francisco Peaks, the Little Tennessee River Valley, Bear Butte, the Black Hills, the Puna Rainforest area of the Big Island of Hawaii, the Sweet Grass Hills and the Crazy Mountains of Montana, the Pipestone Quarry in Minnesota, and others?

AIRFA: An Examination of the Implications of Federal Law and Policy on Indian Religion

Section 2 of AIRFA mandated that federal departments and agencies take a close look at their organic laws and the various regulations, policies, and practices that effectuated their interpretation of the will of Congress, with an eye toward making changes in these enactments so as to bring their affairs into conformance with AIRFA and the Constitution. In this section of the chapter, particular attention is paid to the various federal agencies that have jurisdiction over public lands, lands in the public domain owned by the United States. Only one conclusion can be drawn from the past decade: federal land management agencies have made no real, meaningful regulatory or policy changes in response to AIRFA. The record, examined below, speaks for itself.

Federal Land Management Agencies: Response to AIRFA

United States Forest Service (Department of Agriculture)

In response to AIRFA, in 1978 the Forest Service formed an internal task force to review and evaluate existing policies and procedures and to recommend necessary changes. That task force identified no policies or procedures that, in its view, would abridge the religious free exercise rights of Indian people. In the agency's view, AIRFA gave Indians no greater right of access or input to the agency decision-making process than would be extended to any member of the public. Such a policy decision has had the effect of subordinating the religious free exercise rights of Indian people to nothing more than one of the several "multiple uses" for which Forest Service lands are administered. Presently, the Forest Service has no published regulations on AIRFA. The Department of Agriculture has codified a generic set of regulations for its Office of Environmental Quality. Only brief, passing reference is made to AIRFA in these regulations. The only Forest Service regulation citing AIRFA pertains to Archaeological Resources Protection Act (ARPA) compliance. The conflict between the values expressed by ARPA and AIRFA has been completely ignored as a matter of federal law and policy. Again, the net effect is to subordinate the religious beliefs and needs of the Indian community to those of the professional archeological and physical anthropological communities.

More telling than anything of the Forest Service's attitude is the fact that it, more than any other agency, has fought aggressively against Indian religious interests in the federal court system. See, e.g., *United States v. Means* (Forest Service denial of permit to construct spiritual camp — Yellow Thunder Camp); *Wilson v. Block* (improvements to ski area in San Francisco Peaks of Arizona that violated Navajo and Hopi religions); *Lyng v. Northwest Indian Cemetery Protective Association* (construction of Forest Service road in "high country" of northern California violated religions of Yurok, Karok and Tolowa Tribes; see extended discussion of *Lyng* below). Presently, ongoing disputes involving Native sacred sites include efforts by several Rocky Mountain area tribes to protect the Medicine Wheel in Wyoming, and efforts by Crow Indians to protect sites in the Crazy Mountains, Montana, from destruction through Forest Service development activities.

The Forest Service has a new policy on Native American issues. Entitled "Forest Service Native American Policy: Friends and Partners." It portends a new, more open, and cooperative relationship on cultural and religious matters. The policy encourages agency officials to "walk the land with Native Americans to gain an understanding and appreciation of their culture, religions, beliefs and practices. We must identify and acknowledge these cultural needs in our activities. We consider these

values to be an important part of management of the National Forests."
While the policy addresses the need to *understand* Indian religions and
cultures, it is only a vague statement of policy, and, like AIRFA, is not
enforceable by Indian people. Ironically, while espousing this new, limited policy, the Forest Service has simultaneously used it as the basis for
opposing any new amendments to AIRFA.[2]

National Park Service (Department of the Interior)

As part of the AIRFA process, the Park Service in 1978 agreed to commit
itself to "a policy of concern with, informed awareness of and sensitivity
to Native American issues, resources and sacred sites. This directive has
served as an impetus to develop implementing guidelines, which is an
on-going process" (*AIRFA Report* 1979). In part as a follow-up to its 1978
promises, on September 22, 1987, the National Park Service published
in the Federal Register its Native American Relationships Policy. Having
taken nine years to produce, the policy represents the first effort by any
federal agency to explore by way of published policy or regulation the
conceptual parameters of a means for integrating the needs of Indian
religious practitioners into agency management functions.[3]

Several general statements in the policy are laudable. It mandates
that Park Service programs be developed and executed "in a manner that
reflects knowledge of and respect for the cultures of Native American
tribes or groups" (35675). And it requires service managers to "establish
and maintain effective consulting relationships with potentially affected
Native American tribes and groups" (35675).

The most revealing and troublesome aspect of the policy, however,
is that it allows Native religion claims to be subordinated to all other service management priorities. The policy, for example, carefully instructs
service managers and other personnel that while AIRFA bespeaks a need
to be more sensitive to the cultural/religious concerns of Native people
by seeking to accommodate their requests to use Park System lands,
"such uses must be within the bounds of existing legislation as well
as NPS rules and policies that implement legislative mandates to protect and preserve the system's resources" (35674). Such caveats appear
throughout the policy.[4] The final passage in the section entitled "Native American Involvement and Consultation" renders the final blow to
AIRFA and Native religion: "Although final decisions in all cases shall
consider the results of consultations, the authority and the responsibility for the decision rests with the Service."[5] The policy is that the Park
Service is the only maker of policy. As such, Park Service policy is for the
most part subject to varying interpretation, largely unenforceable, and
implemented by service personnel committed to other service priorities.
It is, simply, no substitute for legislation.

Particularly revealing is that, like its agency counterpart, the Forest

Service, the National Park Service has aggressively fought Indian religion in the federal court system (see *Badoni v. Higginson*, flooding of Rainbow Bridge, which violated Navajo religion). And in 1989, Jerry Rogers, the service's associate director for cultural resources, testified in opposition to S. 1124, which would strengthen AIRFA, on the basis that sufficient protection for Indian religion exists through existing federal statutes.

Bureau of Land Management (Interior Department)

Like the Forest Service, the Bureau of Land Management responded to the dictates of AIRFA by *promising* to integrate Indian religious needs into its land management planning process, under the Federal Land Policy and Management Act of 1976 (FLPMA). In the view of the BLM, FLPMA invested it with the necessary "policy and direction to incorporate socio-cultural values, such as Native American religious concerns, into its land use planning and management systems" (*AIRFA Report*, 33). BLM was confident that "many of the potential impacts upon Native American religious freedom can be avoided through use of these existing systems" (FLPMA).

And like other agencies, the BLM presently has no AIRFA regulations published in the Code of Federal Regulations. Despite its rhetoric of sensitivity to Indian religions, the BLM testified in opposition to both S. 2250, Senator Cranston's 1988 bill to amend AIRFA, and H.R. 1546, Congressman Udall's bill. In both instances the BLM testified that existing statutes gave Indians sufficient standing to protect their religious interests.[6] The BLM has also recently resisted efforts by the Blackfeet Tribe of Montana to protect sacred sites in the Sweetgrass Hills of eastern Montana from disturbance by gold prospectors and miners.

Concluding Remarks on the 1978 AIRFA

The record from recent history speaks for itself. AIRFA's preamble unequivocally documents both the legacy of Indian religious persecution in America and the multitude of otherwise well-intentioned federal laws and policies that have unintentionally produced religious infringement. Another record of more recent vintage is becoming equally clear. By and large federal departments and agencies, despite some sophisticated rhetoric and lip service, have completely diverted Congress's real intent in enacting AIRFA. To date, not one recommendation for legislative amendment has percolated out of the executive branch. *No* agency has promulgated AIRFA regulations. And at most *one* agency — the National Park Service — published a *policy* statement on Native American relationships, its "response to the policy guidance" of AIRFA.

What has gone wrong? First, an uninformed and timorous Congress must share some of the responsibility. Facing controversy on the House floor, which threatened to kill the joint resolution that became AIRFA, Congressman Udall spoke of AIRFA as nothing more than a statement of policy; the sense of the Congress: "it has no teeth in it." What good is an unenforceable policy statement to America's smallest minority population, its indigenous people? Litigation of disputes involving AIRFA has only reaffirmed its lack of enforceability.

Second, the Federal Agencies Task Force contributed to burying Indian expectations for real change through AIRFA. The *AIRFA Report* concluded that Indian religious concerns and needs, identified in AIRFA, could in part be met through *existing* laws. Other recommendations for statutory amendments were never acted on (see *AIRFA Report*, 62–63). The net effect has been of no real utility to Indian religion. At best the result of the task force process is typified by the National Park Service Native American Relationships Management Policy. That policy ignores AIRFA as federal law, as the solemn embodiment and expression of the constitutional free exercise rights of Native people, relegating it to a second-class law, to be considered only after all other federal laws and regulations implementing those laws.

Third, federal departments and agencies mistakenly believed existing laws and policies would fulfill the expectations and demands of Indians. In 1978 these agencies failed to understand, and continue to misunderstand, the distinction between cultural resource management and real religious accommodation. Their testimony opposing recent AIRFA amendments continues to repeat this mistake. Thus we have the situation today that most agencies believe they are fulfilling the mandates of AIRFA because they have archeological resource regulations! They ignore the broad range of Native religious needs and concerns — for instance, sacred site protection — that fall outside the ambit of archeological or cultural resource management.

Contributing to the problem is the fact that most agencies look, if at all, to their staff archeologists for guidance on AIRFA matters. Agencies generally do not have cultural anthropologists, or, for that matter, advisory groups of Native Americans, to assist them in ongoing AIRFA policy creation and review. Archeologists by training and by inclination misperceive the cultural and religious implications of agency planning and management activities, in favor of cultural resource implications. Unquestionably, there is more to understanding and accommodating the religious needs of a living Native culture than simply understanding the objects and artifacts of its ancestors.

Finally, there is a real agency or bureaucratic arrogance that emerges when one reads between the lines of a policy statement such as that adopted by the Park Service. There is also an unmistakable fear, paranoia, or distrust by federal agency personnel of the motives of Native people and their desire to protect the spiritual value of physical place. The net effect is to make clear to Native people that the agencies and their resource management "experts" ultimately call the shots. So while "they" will talk to "you," the import of the policy is that "they" define the process and "they" make the final decision by "their" rules. From the Native perspective, it is "business as usual."[7]

AIRFA Case Study:
Lyng v. Northwest Indian Cemetery Protective Association

On April 19, 1988, the United States Supreme Court handed down its decision in *Lyng v. Northwest Indian Cemetery Protective Association*. *Lyng* involved the challenge by members of three northern California Indian tribes of a decision by the United States Forest Service to construct a road (commonly referred to as the "G-O Road") and related development activities through a sacred area in the Six Rivers National Forest known as the "high country." For centuries Indians have used the high country for vision questing and other ceremonial and ritual purification purposes. After an extensive investigation of the ethnographic literature on the Yurok, Karok, and Tolowa Indians and scores of interviews of primary Indian religious informants, the Forest Service's own expert anthropologist, Dorothea Theodoratus, concluded that the proposed land development activities would destroy the "very core" of their religious beliefs and practices. Theodoratus recommended that *no* road be built.[8]

Notwithstanding the recommendations of its own expert witness, the Forest Service officials decided to proceed with construction of the road at one of several alternative sites. These bureaucrats ignored the factual evidence before them and determined that certain mitigative practices would suffice to ameliorate the harm to the Indians' religion. They refused to believe the Indians' claim.[9]

After a lengthy hearing on the Indians' motion, the federal district court in Northern California in 1983 permanently enjoined the Forest Service from constructing the G-O Road, on constitutional and federal environmental statutory grounds. The court applied the traditional test under the Free Exercise Clause of the First Amendment to the Constitution and held that the proposed activities impermissibly burdened the Indians' religious free exercise rights. The government interests in development of the G-O Road were grossly speculative and insufficient to outweigh the Indians' interest (*Northwest* 1983). The Ninth Circuit Court of Appeals subsequently upheld the lower courts' permanent injunction of the road's construction on constitutional free exercise grounds twice, first in 1985 and again on rehearing in 1986 (*Northwest* 1986).

In 1988, the Supreme Court reversed the decision of the Ninth Circuit. First, it held that the Free Exercise Clause of the First Amendment does not bar the federal government from conducting activities on public lands which violate the Indians' religion. The court ruled that *Lyng* was controlled by its earlier decision in *Bowen v. Roy*. *Bowen* held that a federal statute requiring states to use Social Security numbers did not violate Indian religious rights under the Free Exercise Clause (*Lyng*, 545–49). In *Bowen* the Court reasoned that an individual through the First Amendment could not block the government's conduct of its own internal affairs; it found the government's use of a Social Security number for administrative, record keeping purposes to be purely internal in nature. In the Court's opinion legal disputes involving decisions by federal land management agencies concerning land considered sacred to Indians were indistinguishable from *Roy*, involving nothing more than the government's internal affairs.

Justice Brennan, writing a stinging dissenting opinion joined by Justices Marshall and Blackmun, criticized as "remarkable" the majority's inability to distinguish the facts in *Lyng* from *Roy*. Brennan emphasized that Congress was well aware of the difference in 1978 when it enacted AIRFA:

> Federal land-use decisions, by contract, are likely to have substantial external effects that government decisions concerning office furniture and information storage obviously will not. . . . [AIRFA is] an express congressional determination that federal land management decisions are not "internal" government "procedure," but are instead governmental actions that can and indeed are likely to burden Native American religious practices. (*Lyng*, 560–61)

Justice Brennan also noted that in *Roy* the government's record keeping system did not impair the exercise of one's religion; in contrast, construction of the G-O Road would impair the Indians' "freedom to exercise their religion in the greatest degree imaginable" (561).

The Court in *Lyng*, however, did not stop there. As a second basis for the reversal it rejected what is known as the "effects" test, which essentially directs courts to assess the effect of government conduct on the religious free exercise rights of individuals. Writing for the majority, Justice O'Connor held that:

> Whatever may be the exact line between unconstitutional prohibitions on the free exercise of religion and the legitimate conduct by government of its own affairs, the location of the line cannot depend on measuring the effects of a government action on a religious objector's spiritual development. (548)

The rejection of the "effects" test represents a significant departure from well-established constitutional precedent (see, e.g., *Sherbert, Waltz, Yoder, Thomas, Hobbie*).

In lieu of the "effects" test, the Court adopted a strained interpretation of the Free Exercise Clause that limits the scope of cognizable free exercise claims against the government to circumstances of "coercion " or "penalty":

> individuals [would] be *coerced* by the Government's action into violating their religious beliefs; . . . [or *penalized* by being denied] . . . an equal share of the rights, benefits and privileges enjoyed by other citizens. . . .
>
> This does not and cannot imply that incidental effects of government programs, which may make it more difficult to practice certain religions but which have no tendency to coerce individuals into acting contrary to their religious beliefs, require government to bring forward a compelling justification for its otherwise lawful actions. (*Lyng*, 546, 547)

The Court necessarily had to attempt to articulate a principled difference between "indirect coercion or penalties on the free exercise of religion" and "incidental effects of government programs." Forms of "indirect coercion," the Court recognized, in keeping with precedent, are subject to First Amendment scrutiny; "incidental effects," following *Roy* and now *Lyng*, are not. In other words, in the Court's view government actions that compel affirmative conduct inconsistent with religious belief are coercive and, hence, unconstitutional. But those government actions that "merely" prevent conduct consistent with religious belief are "incidental" and thus not unconstitutional.

Citing the diverse nature of our society and the possibility that any government action might offend the religious sensibilities of some individual or religious sect, the Court sidestepped these difficult cases and dumped them off on Congress (548; cf. 562).

In dissent Justice Brennan spared no criticism of the majority's rejection of the effect's test:

> I thus cannot accept the Court's premise that the *form* of the Government's restraint on religious practice, rather than its *effect*, controls our constitutional analysis. . . . [C]onstruction of the G-O Road . . . will virtually destroy respondents' religion, and will necessarily force them into abandoning those practices altogether. Indeed, the Government's proposed activities will restrain religious practice to a far greater degree here than in any of the cases cited by the Court today. . . .
>
> Ultimately the Court's coercion test turns on a distinction between governmental actions that compel affirmative conduct inconsistent with religious belief, and those governmental actions that prevent conduct consistent with religious belief. In my view, such a distinction is without

constitutional significance. The crucial word in the constitutional text ... is "prohibit," ... a comprehensive term that in no way suggests that the intended protection is aimed only at governmental actions that coerce affirmative conduct. Nor does the Court's distinction comport with the principles animating the constitutional guarantee; religious freedom is threatened no less by governmental action that makes the practice of one's chosen faith impossible than by governmental programs that pressure one to engage in conduct inconsistent with religious beliefs. ...

Both common sense and our prior cases teach us, therefore, that governmental action that makes the practice of a given faith more difficult necessarily penalizes that practice and thereby tends to prevent adherence to religious beliefs. The harm to the practitioners is the same regardless of the manner in which the Government restrains their religious expression, and the Court's fear that an "effects" test will permit religious adherents to challenge governmental actions they merely find "offensive" in no way justifies its refusal to recognize the constitutional injury citizens suffer when governmental action not only offends but actually restrains their religious practices. (558–59)

Like the decision of the Forest Service to build the G-O Road over the objections of the Indians and its own expert anthropologist, the Supreme Court's decision in *Lyng* is both offensive and paternalistic. Like the Forest Service bureaucrat who decided to construct the G-O Road, five justices found the Indians' claims simply too incredible to believe, notwithstanding the Court's own admonition that it is *not* in a position to "determine the truth of the underlying beliefs that led to the religious objections ... " (551). The Court's disbelief is grounded in what it thought was a lack of unanimity in the record concerning religious impacts, as a basis for discrediting the Indians' claims:

To be sure, the Indians themselves were far from unanimous in opposing the G-O Road, see App. 180, and it seems less than certain that construction of the road will be so disruptive that it will doom their religion. (548)

Two criticisms of the Court's ethnocentric application of the First Amendment are in order. First, free exercise precedent does not require unanimity of belief.[10] Second, where in the Constitution or constitutional jurisprudence is it stated that proof of certainty of the destruction of one's religion is required as prerequisite to triggering the protections of the Free Exercise Clause? The Court itself has noted that "sincerity" is the key inquiry here:

If judicial inquiry into the truth of one's religious beliefs would violate the Free Exercise Clause, an inquiry into one's reasons for adopting those beliefs is similarly intrusive. So long as one's faith is religiously based at the time it is asserted, it should not matter, for constitutional purposes, whether that faith is derived from revelation, study, upbringing, gradual evolution, or some source that appears entirely incomprehensible (*Hobbie*, quoting *Callahan*).

In *Hobbie v. Unemployment Appeals Commission*, the state of Florida attempted to argue that Paula Hobbie's claim to unemployment compensation for being fired for refusing to work on Saturday, her Sabbath, were unfounded because she converted to the Seventh-Day Adventist faith after entering into a contract of employment. One of Florida's purported interests was in preventing fraud on its unemployment compensation fund by individuals feigning new-found religiosity or spirituality. The Supreme Court rejected such a notion by an 8–1 vote. "The First Amendment protects the free exercise rights of employees who adopt religious beliefs or convert from one faith to another after they are hired" (*Hobbie*, 199). In clear contrast to *Thomas* and *Hobbie*, the Court in *Lyng* regarded the Indians' religious claims as inferior by imposing a higher standard of factual proof. Why the singling out of Indian religion for disparate treatment? Religious claimants in previous Supreme Court cases could not have met such a rigorous proof standard.

By now the Supreme Court's interpretation of AIRFA in *Lyng* is well known, the same or similar conclusions regarding the act having been reached in most reported lower court decisions. First, it held that AIRFA is but a statement of policy by Congress; the *Lyng* Court was of the opinion that the Forest Service could not have been "more solicitous" in respecting Indian religion and AIRFA policy (*Lyng*, 550).

Second, the Court concluded that "[n]owhere in the law is there so much as a hint of any intent to create a cause of action or any judicially enforceable individual rights" (550).

Finally, the Court referred to unfortunate remarks by Congressman Udall, sponsor of H.R. 1546, that AIRFA was but a "sense of Congress's joint resolution," that it confers on Indians no "special religious rights," and that in fact it "has no teeth in it" (550–51). After *Lyng* Indians need not worry about special religious rights: the effect of the *Lyng* decision is to strip them of all constitutional religious rights for the protection of sacred sites.

Concerning AIRFA, Justice Brennan made two points in dissent. First, as mentioned earlier, he recognized that Congress made express findings, via AIRFA and its legislative history, that the federal government has left a legacy of persecution of Indian religion under the guise of "incidental effects." If the "incidental effects" of government actions are above constitutional scrutiny, that persecution will continue. Second, he castigated the Court's decision as making a "mockery" of AIRFA's policy to "protect and preserve for American Indians their inherent right of freedom to believe, express and exercise the[ir] traditional religion" (564).

The majority in *Lyng* reasoned that to accept the Indians' free exercise claims would amount to establishing a "religious servitude" on public lands, thereby divesting the government of its "right to use what is, after all, its land" (549). Such a servitude, which may perhaps be hard to establish legally, does exist historically and morally. Justice O'Connor and the Court majority ignored the centuries-old spiritual connection of Native people to the land, as if designating it as "government" property gave the United States license to sever this connection.

In dissent, Justice Brennan recognized that the Indians did not seek to exclude all human activity. Indeed, a number of environmental groups were co-parties to the litigation, an implicit recognition that certain non-religious uses of the high country are in fact harmonious with religious uses. Although in *Lyng* a case of exclusive Indian use was clearly not before the Court, the specter of one certainly appeared to be. But only under those circumstances, in Brennan's view, might legitimate Establishment Clause concerns be raised (see 562, 546).

Finally, Justice Brennan lamented the Court's "stripping" of Indians' constitutional protection against destruction of sacred lands:

> Ironically, the Court's apparent solicitude for the integrity of religious belief and its desire to forestall the possibility that courts might second guess the claims of religious adherents leads to far greater inequities than those the Court postulates: today's ruling sacrifices a religion at least as old as the Nation itself, . . . so that the Forest Service can build a six-mile segment of a road that two lower courts found had only most marginal and speculative utility. . . .
>
> Given today's ruling, [the Indians'] freedom [to maintain their religious *beliefs*] amounts to nothing more than the right to believe that their religion will be destroyed. (563–64)

A Decade of Disappointment: Lessons Learned and the Need for AIRFA Amendments

It has been over a decade since AIRFA's enactment. With the passage of time, Indians and Indian advocates have become experienced in terms of AIRFA's strengths and weaknesses. Even before the Supreme Court's decision in *Lyng*, the results of various administrative and court battles have demonstrated the need to change AIRFA in several ways. Now, because of the *Lyng* decision, Indians must look to and rely exclusively on Congress to strengthen AIRFA to re-establish an equitable balance between Indians and the federal government concerning land management matters. Below is a discussion of the critical elements of any effort to amend AIRFA.

Justice Brennan identified the essence of the dilemma created by the majority's decision in *Lyng* when he noted that federal bureaucrats have now been blessed with "unilateral authority to resolve all future disputes in [their] favor, subject only to the Court's toothless exhortation to be 'sensitive' to [Indian] religions" (562). Prior to the *Lyng* decision, Indians had the First Amendment as a means of ensuring *some* measure of protection for their religions. After *Lyng*, Congress must now shoulder the responsibility the Court shirked, that of allowing a fair measure of "mutual accommodation... tempered by compromise" (563).

As a first element, any amendment to AIRFA must include a mandate that all federal lands must be managed in such a manner so as not to violate AIRFA's statutory protections. The preamble to the 1978 AIRFA contained express findings that emphasized that AIRFA was necessary for the very reason that over the years Congress had enacted a number of laws, land management and otherwise, and federal land management agencies had implemented these laws through rules, regulations, and policies, without any consideration whatsoever as to their effect on Native religions and religious practices. Examples of such laws include the Wilderness Act, the National Forest Management Act, the Multiple Use and Sustained Yield Act, the Federal Land Management Policy Act, and the Endangered Species Act. The original AIRFA has had no effect whatsoever on the agencies' interpretations of these laws. While Congress did direct in Section 2 of AIRFA that agencies make recommendations for legislative changes, none were forthcoming, and Congress never has followed up on its mandate.

An example of the federal agencies' exploitation of AIRFA's vagueness is the National Park Service's Native American Relationships Policy, discussed earlier. The stated purpose of the policy is to implement AIRFA by executing its programs "in a manner that reflects knowledge of and respect for the cultures of Native American tribes or groups" (35675). Notwithstanding, the Park Service stated expressly in the policy that Native uses of Park Service lands "must be within the bounds of existing legislation as well as NPS rules and policies that implement legislative mandates to protect and preserve the system's resources" (35674). Similar restrictions appear throughout the policy.

This mandate effectively nullifies the original intent and purpose of AIRFA. The loophole must be closed the next time around. For AIRFA to affect the way these agencies operate, as it must if it is to provide any guidance and protection whatsoever, it must be made clear that these laws must be interpreted in such a way so as not to violate AIRFA. There are ways to harmonize the needs and interests of all diverse users of the public lands without sacrificing the legitimate rights of Native people.

Second, the AIRFA of 1978 did not require agencies to promulgate regulations to implement its directives. And no federal land management agency took the initiative to draft regulations to guide local officials in their land management and decisions processes. As a result, AIRFA is routinely criticized by agency officials as being "vague," "pie in the sky," and "meaningless" in providing any real direction.

In contrast, Congress, in the Archaeological Resources Protection Act of 1979, required certain federal land agencies to promulgate rules to implement ARPA. These agencies have done so. And as a result, when land management agencies encounter "archeological resources" on lands within their respective jurisdictions, they by and large understand their legal responsibilities and have in place administrative and policy means of implementing and executing those responsibilities. An analogous situation exists with respect to Section 106 of the National Historic Preservation Act of 1966, as amended. Consequently, while land management agencies have ARPA and Section 106 "clearance" procedures, no such clearance process exists for AIRFA.

In the summer of 1988 the Native American Rights Fund conducted a survey of federally recognized Indian tribes and Alaskan Native villages concerning their experiences with the 1978 AIRFA, canvassing their recommendations for change. Of the approximately fifty responses received, without exception AIRFA worked best only in circumstances where the villages and tribes had taken the initiative and forced federal agencies to implement it. In the majority of instances agencies made little real attempt, if any, to work out plans with tribes and villages to implement AIRFA. In many situations AIRFA was simply ignored by the agencies.

Most responding tribes and villages recommended mandatory consultation between the agencies and affected Native groups as the most important step in overcoming the ignorance of and noncompliance with the 1978 AIRFA policies. Also important was the need for agency officials to become sensitive to the worldview and religious and cultural needs of their Native constituencies — in effect, to have a change of attitude. While federal laws cannot change human attitudes, a required system of regulations and consultation can improve the level of AIRFA understanding and compliance and help to foster better relationships and attitudes between Native people and the federal bureaucrats.

As a final point on this issue, consultation must be meaningful. By requiring more attention to the details of the consultation process, as record keeping would accomplish, agencies and their key decision makers will be more familiar with the specific concerns and needs of the affected Native groups. A greater likelihood will develop that these decision makers fully *understand* and *be sensitive to* the needs of those affected by the proposed activity or decision. A major concern of Native groups that NARF polled last year was that agencies did not take the time to educate themselves as to the impacts of various activities on Native religious traditions and the exercise of those traditions. Requiring detailed records will not make insensitive agency officials more sensitive, but it will allow the development of a record to track the level of effort by officials to fully understand the ramifications of their decisions. Where agency officials fall short on their obligation to Native people, a record will exist of that shortfall.

Third, assurances of confidentiality to Native people disclosing intimate details of their religions are minimally necessary to foster the complete participation of Native groups in agency decision making. Native groups are particularly apprehensive about releasing intimate details concerning their religious beliefs and practices to total strangers. It has been our unfortunate history in the United States that once released from the control of a particular Native culture, information concerning religious practices has often times been exploited, with the result that the culture is thereby also exploited. Such abuse occurs whether the initial release of information was to an agent of the United States government or to some other party. This has led to a high level of mistrust by Native groups, groups that are already frustrated with and suspicious of the federal administrative bureaucracy. Required confidentiality, with harsh penalties for violations thereof, would add a positive step toward building improved relations between Native groups and federal agencies and their officials.

Finally, the Supreme Court expressed the sentiment in its 1988 decision in *Lyng* that what the Indians sought in that case might very well establish a "religious servitude" on federal public lands. Opponents to recent efforts to amend AIRFA over the past few years raised the same specter — that of an absolute "veto" by Indians over decisions of federal land management agencies and officials. These claims, while perhaps superficially attractive, are little more than hyperbole.

In all but the most exceptional of circumstances Native groups have never and will never seek exclusive use of a land area for religious purposes. The Indians in *Lyng*, in *United States v. Means*, or in other sacred site cases have never sought to tie up the sacred land areas for their exclusive use. In *Lyng*, for instance, the record was clear that several of the Forest Service's espoused "multiple uses" would be fostered by preservation of the high country, including recreation, watershed protection, fishery habitat protection and enhancement, scenic values, as well as cultural resource protection. Similarly, in *Means*, the Sioux traditionalists who sought an application to construct Yellow Thunder Camp in the Black Hills National Forest did not seek to exclude recreationists or the grazing of livestock.

Native groups usually find their interests in alignment with other important user groups who benefit from the preservation of the federal public land base and out of alignment with those interests who would seek to exploit the natural resources for private profit. Often the range of interests immediately served by private profit is narrow and not multidimensional. Such is not the case with respect to the other values with which Native interests are aligned.

Strengthening AIRFA to give it some teeth, especially after the Supreme Court's handiwork in *Lyng*, fosters religious plurality and diversity in America — the ultimate objective of the First Amendment. The promotion of cultural and religious diversity and freedom for Native peoples also serves broad federal land policies of multiple use. And because the preservation of traditional religions and cultures is an essential focus of the mission of Native governments, AIRFA amendments help fulfill the broad United States policy of Indian self-determination and the government-to-government relationship between the U.S. and Native government.

Congress, with power under the Indian Commerce Clause, Article I, §8, of the Constitution, and with asserted "plenary" authority over Indian affairs, can statutorily reinvest Indians with religious and cultural rights under AIRFA that prior to *Lyng* were taken for granted as *constitutional* rights. Religious diversity and free exercise are valid secular purposes of a constitutional democracy. Thus, contrary to the claims of some opponents, an amendment to AIRFA that fairly accommodates and insulates Indian religious free exercise from persecution by the executive branch of the federal government does not run afoul of the Establishment Clause. Congress can ground legislation in the area of Indian affairs that results in "special treatment" in its unique obligation to Indian people (*Morton*). The 1978 AIRFA establishes an unambiguous, unique obligation to Native people in the area of religious freedom.

AIRFA amendments foster and promote the 1978 AIRFA policies, which the record of the past decade makes clear have never been fulfilled. A "mid-course" correction in AIRFA is warranted by the past thirteen years of continued ignorance, insensitivity, and abuse of Native religions. Moreover, Native religious groups would not be given preferential treatment in the use of federal lands under a new AIRFA. The legal burdens and standards built into new legislation would insure only a fair balancing between the needs and interests of Native peoples and the government, a "fair accommodation" in Justice Brennan's view.

America's religious free exercise jurisprudence is built on a foundation of accommodation, recognizing that accommodation must vary in kind and degree if we are truly to be a diverse, plural religious society. Accordingly, the primary effect of AIRFA amendments would be to remove federal impediments to Native religious practices, i.e., to allow freedom for Native religious practices, without undue interference. In light of the past thirteen years of continued infringement of Native religion notwithstanding the 1978 AIRFA, and now *Lyng*, the situation becomes ever more compelling.

Steven C. Moore is a staff attorney for the Native American Rights Fund in Denver, Colorado.

5

Protection of American Indian Sacred Geography

DEWARD E. WALKER, JR.

Robert S. Michaelsen (1986) has reviewed many of the recent cases brought by American Indian groups to protect various aspects of their religious belief and practice, especially their access to geographical sites and areas that are sacred to them. In concluding his review, he states:

> Indeed, the time is at hand, if not past, for the development of concerted strategies for the American Indian first amendment rights generally, and more specifically, the protection of those rights in connection with sacred sites. (Michaelsen 1986, 76)

Elsewhere in the same review, Michaelsen concludes that the most significant losses of religious freedom for American Indian claimants so far have occurred in connection with protection of and access to sacred sites (Michaelsen 1986, 53).[1]

He notes that adoption by the courts of the centrality standard (ultimately stemming from the *Yoder* and *Sequoyah* cases) has placed a heavy burden on American Indian litigants (57), and that such litigation of centrality is difficult and can bring unexpected, negative results. He likens these trials to mine fields (61). In this chapter, I shall review major distinguishing features of American Indian religious practice and propose an alternative standard of integrity through which to seek better protection for American Indian sacred geography. While certain cases indicate that it is possible to use the centrality standard in gaining First Amendment protection for a few examples of American Indian sacred geography, the centrality standard is too strict to protect many others. Clearly sacred geography is a universal and essential feature of the practice of American Indian religions. Without continuing access to many sacred sites that maintain their physical integrity, most practitioners of traditional American Indian religions will be denied the opportunity to practice many vital ceremonies.

I have spent the last thirty-five years exploring the traditional religious life of the hunting cultures of the Northern Rockies, including portions of Oregon, Washington, Idaho, Montana, the Dakotas, Wyoming, British Columbia, and neighboring Alberta. This field research and attached bibliography of published research on relevant aspects of northwestern North America are the source of data for this chapter. Although their disappearance was widely predicted in the last century, American Indian cultures and their religions have survived widely in the Americas. Of great importance to this chapter is the equally impressive, ongoing revitalization of traditional non-Christian religions taking place among American Indians of the United States and Canada. Many Christian converts are returning to the religions of their ancestors, which have been preserved by those who rejected the Christian missionaries. This revitalization became widely noted in the 1930s and its legitimacy and validity cannot be questioned. Nevertheless, it has continued to encounter opposition by the social, economic, and legal institutions of the United States. These institutions must be made to recognize the legitimate needs of Indian religious practitioners in ways that preserve the integrity of both their religious practice and the sacred geography that is so essential to that practice.

Hunting and Agricultural Religions

Although this chapter discusses primarily religions of hunting groups (so called archaic religions) in Native America, not all American Indian religions are of purely hunting peoples. For example, in the Southwest, Southeast, and in the Mississippi Valley and its tributaries, religious influences stemming ultimately from Mexico and Meso-America are also found. They bear a close connection to the religious beliefs and practices of pre-European Mexico in their emphasis on an economic communalism or collectivism that is rationalized by a complex religious life that stressed collective dependence on fertility, rain, and related spirits and gods. The introduction of corn, beans, and squash had profound consequences, for it changed the basic cultural orientation of many groups. There were many dimensions to this change, including a concentration of populations in sedentary villages, a preoccupation with sowing, planting, and harvesting, an enhanced economic importance for women (from food collectors to food producers), and new forms of matrilineal social organization. Typical of these agricultural religions were concern for crops and fertility, the rise of priestly organizations, the creation of temples and shrines, and the appearance of new deities to represent such vital plants as corn, beans, and squash, or the rain and seasons. Rituals, in turn, grew more complex. Nevertheless, nowhere did agriculture entirely supplant hunting, because the rituals encouraging the growth of corn, beans, and squash remained basically the same as the rituals of thanksgiving for fish and game animals. Such religions are led by specialists who have the attributes of true priests, including their various types that often play a prominent role in the political and other social affairs of the group. Despite these changes, sacred geography continues to be a vital part of ceremonial life in the agricultural groups of Native America.

From my own field work and a review of the available research, I believe it is possible to describe such traditional religions in terms of a number of core features, which include:

1. A body of mythic accounts explaining cultural origins and cultural development as distinctive peoples.

2. A special sense of the sacred that is centered in natural time and natural geography.

3. A set of critical and calendrical rituals that give social form and expression to religious beliefs and permit the groups and their members to experience their mythology.

4. A group of individuals normally described as shamans (medicine men and medicine women) who teach and lead group(s) in the conduct of their ritual life.

5. A set of prescriptive and proscriptive (ethical) guidelines establishing appropriate behavior associated with the sacred.

6. A means of communicating (dreams and visions) with sacred spirits and forces.

7. A belief in dreams and visions as the principal sources of religious knowledge.

8. A belief that harmony must be maintained with the sacred through the satisfactory conduct of rituals and adherence to sacred prescriptions and proscriptions.

9. A belief that while all aspects of nature and culture are potentially sacred, there are certain times and geographical locations that together possess great sacredness.

10. The major goal of religious life is gaining the spiritual power and understanding necessary for a successful life, by entering into the sacred at certain sacred times/places.

The more archaic or hunting groups possess what is commonly regarded as a more ancient set of religious beliefs and practices. For example:

1. In their religious life, hunting tribes are not very hierarchically organized; nor do they favor tightly constructed hierarchical mythologies or religious philosophies.

2. Hunting tribes in Native America do not seem to rely on pilgrimage routes along networks of shrines to a central point, such as Jerusalem. They do not commemorate the lives of great prophets or saints in the manner of the so-called world religions.

3. The sacred sites of hunting tribes are not so confined or precisely located as they are among agricultural tribes in either the New or Old World; such sacred sites are more numerous, more diverse, and less geometrically patterned than is seen among agricultural religions.

4. Mountains and other points of geographical sacredness are not commonly in the center of cultic developments as is so frequently seen in the Old World or in Meso-America. Nor are mountains identified so frequently with the state or with society as in Meso-America and the Old World.

5. Generally, hunting tribes in Native America seek the *intrinsic* sacredness of nature and do not force their notions of sacredness onto the land in the manner of the pyramid builders and temple builders that we see in agricultural religions of both the Old and New World; this difference I have described as a *reactive* approach to sacred geography, rather than a *proactive* approach typical of agricultural religions.

The Sacred

In order to understand the religious conceptions of American Indians, it is first necessary to examine their ideas concerning the sacred. Durkheim (1915) has defined the sacred as follows:

> A religion is a unified system of beliefs and practices relative to sacred things, that is to say, things set apart and forbidden — beliefs and practices which unite into one single moral community called a Church, all those who adhere to them. (Durkheim 1915, 62)

It is generally agreed among scholars that all known religious beliefs, whether simple or complex, possess *some* sense of the sacred, although American Indian notions of the sacred may diverge somewhat from Durkheim's definition given above. This division of the world into two domains, the one containing all that is sacred, the other all that is profane, is a distinctive trait of most religious traditions.

Among American Indians the sacred is more founded on the idea that it is an embedded attribute of all phenomena. For example, among the Lakota this attribute is *wakan*, whereas among the Algonkians it is *manitou*. Accessing this sacred attribute is a major ritual goal found in all American Indian cultures and entails actually entering sacredness rather than merely praying to it or propitiating it. Whereas Judeo-Christian religion tends to create its own sacred space and times arbitrarily by special rituals of sacralization, American Indians attempt to discover "access points" or "portals" to the sacred that are often impossible to know before the dreams or visions that reveal them. Despite this, there are underlying regularities concerning where such access points to the sacred are most often located.

These access points to the sacred in American Indian religious beliefs and practices have received relatively little attention by scholars. As noted above, they are not only points in space, but also points in time, best described as sacred "time/spaces." For example, especially sacred times are at dawn, at dusk, and during the equinoxes and solstices. Given this, certain geographical spaces or points may be used rarely but can still be very valuable at appropriate times. It is such "time/spaces" where entry into the sacred is most common, although not guaranteed. It is believed that the ultimate control of this process is in the hands of the spirits, who must decide if the supplicant or petitioners are worthy of admission to the sacred.

Spiritual Beings

In addition to being divided into agricultural and hunting religions, American Indian religions are distinguished by a strong dependence on visions, dreams, and a very exacting and demanding ceremonialism, all of which are concerned primarily with communicating with various spirits and maintaining the natural and cultural orders. In many tribes, prayers are directed to a collectivity of divine or spiritual beings, as in the pipe ceremony of the Plains tribes. Belief in a supreme being is apparent among most groups, but the connection of a supreme being with creation is often minimized by the fact that in mythology there is another supernatural being, the culture hero, who is invested with creative powers. This hero's true mission is to deliver cultural institutions, including religious ceremonies, to human beings. Trickster tales occupy a major part of Native American mythologies. The tales usually portray the culture hero-trickster as an animal such as Coyote on the western Plains, in the Basin, the Plateau, and California. There are numerous other beings in the sacred world, varying from tribe to tribe.

Hunting tribes generally (but not in all cases) believe the dead are in the sky or somewhere beyond the horizon, but they are believed to play a continuing role in the lives of the living. Agriculturists may believe that the dead are in the ground, or at the place of emergence of humankind.

In stratified agricultural societies like those of the Mississippian culture, there are different abodes for different social categories of the dead. At the same time, there is everywhere in Native America belief in ghosts on earth, who often can be heard whistling at night. Independent of these beliefs is the widespread idea of human reincarnation or human transformation into animals.

The most important spirits among hunting tribes are the guardian spirits acquired in fasting visions by youths of such areas as the Plateau, the Northwest Coast, California, the Plains, and the Basin. These are mostly animal spirits and appear to the person during a vision quest, which consists of several days and nights of fasting and isolation at special sacred places. This spirit endows the person with a particular "medicine" (or "power"), a sacred song, sacred dance, sacred dress, and instructs the person to make a pouch or medicine bag in which is kept the sacred paraphernalia associated with the vision. "Power" often requires specific rituals as well as avoidances (e.g., food). The vision quest is basic to most American Indian hunting religions, but some of the agricultural tribes also follow this custom.

Shamans and Priests

Both in Asia and in North America, the shaman ("medicine man" or "medicine woman") is a visionary who has received power to cure people, but there are other types of visionaries with extraordinary powers, e.g., warrior and prophecy powers. Shamans customarily heal diseases that are ascribed to causes such as witchcraft or the breaking of a taboo. Normally the causes of disease are of two major types: a spirit or disease object is supposed to have intruded into the body, or the sick person's soul or power has been stolen. In the former case it is the medicine man's task to frighten the spirit away or to remove it from the body by sucking or drawing it out. If the latter cause is involved, he has to catch the lost soul through special ritual. The medicine man may also sink into a trance, release his own soul, and send it out after the stolen soul.

Among hunting groups, the medicine man is an essential part of most ritual activity. Principally, he conducts rituals and teaches their proper form, meaning, and use. Active practice of most aspects of religion would be impossible without this person. The medicine man is regarded as a sacred person because of his proximity and access to sacred beings and forces. He is especially instrumental in helping others establish, maintain, and utilize their relationships with the sacred.

The life of a medicine man or medicine woman is demanding and materially unrewarding. They are in constant demand and often must travel great distances to attend to the needs of the sick. They are also called upon to help correct behavioral and interpersonal problems. Family counseling and psychotherapy for individuals are acknowledged techniques of medicine men who use them to deal with many psychological and behavioral problems.

Although they are not usually in positions of political leadership, medicine men frequently influence the selection of political leaders. Their support is seen as a reliable indicator of a candidate's promise as a leader. Medicine men also are called on to serve as mediators in disputes, much as judges or magistrates are in other cultures.

Medicine men are arbiters of custom and are the authorities who determine the authenticity of cultural practices; they sometimes prescribe the appropriate ritual dress, ritual behavior, and ritual performance for communities and their members. It is not surprising, therefore, that they are also the principal teachers in matters of religion. As religious teachers, they exercise immense influence on the young, as they gradually acquire a step-by-step familiarity with the intricacies of their religion. Because there are no written "holy books," the medicine man as teacher is even more important for learning and teaching the religion than would be true of priests in literate cultures. It is rare that any serious ceremony is begun without a medicine man officiating. Each ceremonial performance is at least partly a lesson he teaches about the religion and its meaning. Teaching and learning about religion is a person-to-person experience, and each serious participant engages in a lifelong learning process.

In conducting rituals, most medicine men seek not only to strengthen and preserve the traditional religion, but to find new leaders who can be trained as medicine men to carry on this unwritten religious tradition. Once found, the neophyte medicine men are carefully guided through a series of steps of increasing complexity. Often they are guided by several senior medicine men of distinguished reputation developed over a period of many years. Because of their knowledge and influence, medicine men have often become the principal defenders of traditional culture and the beliefs and practices of traditionalists against the destructive assaults of missionaries and government agents. Medicine men have often been the understanding mediators of cultural conflict among those persons who suffer confusion and inner contradictions because of the frequently conflicting worlds (Indian and non-Indian) in which they have grown up.

In the agricultural religions of North America, medicine men (sometimes considered priests) join together, exchanging experiences and working out a common, secret ideology; or they may form societies of clergy into which neophytes are accepted after passing through a series of ritual requirements. In the Southwest, where collectivism is part of the cultural pattern, there are organizations of professional healers and ritualists who perform rituals in patterns of complex cooperation. In all areas, however, regaining the patient's health means that harmony has been restored between human beings and the sacred.

Other common rituals conducted by medicine men in Native North America include bear ceremonialism, the so-called shaking tent, the sweat bath, confession, fertility rites, and various thanksgiving ceremonies. In some groups the medicine man performs animal ceremonialism, usually intended to appease a particular spirit, but the primary purpose of such rituals is to ensure the return of the game by showing proper respect.

Rituals and Sacred Geography

There is a great deal of individual diversity in vision questing among most groups. A vision quest requires that an individual directly petition the sacred for spiritual aid. This ritual most commonly requires isolation from the community for a set period of time, fasting, praying, and offerings to the sacred. Commonly, and as a result of instructions from spirits received while isolated in this manner, an individual will make a medicine bundle. These bundles contain sacred objects, prepared as the spirits direct. Associated with these bundles will be clothing, songs, dances, and myths that are also considered part of this sacred power. Commonly most groups require that one be purified before engaging in this ritual, a process normally including fasting and the sweat bath. The sites used for vision quest rituals are among the most common forms of sacred geography in Native America. Such sites number in the thousands in the Northern Rocky Mountain region, where I have conducted most of my research into this area.

Group ceremonies designed to thank and/or petition the sacred are common throughout the area, e.g., the sun dance, the horse dance, and the various animal dances. Such group rituals include elaborate multi-day preparations by organized groups of religious specialists, the building of ceremonial structures, the reciting of important sacred stories and myths, the performance of preparatory sacred rituals and dances, and the presentation of offerings to the sacred at specific sacred sites at specific sacred times. These rituals can require months of preparation to accumulate the food and other supplies needed for the participants, and entire reservation communities will cooperate in the construction of ceremonial structures located at specific sacred grounds. Such sacred structures are generally left to become sites of pilgrimage and prayer.

As already noted, most ceremonies/rituals require performance at special times, e.g., calendrical rituals, such as the spring and fall equinoxes or the winter and summer solstices. Such sacred time/places are found in a bewildering variety, but major types include the following:

1. Vision quest sites.

2. Monumental geological features that have sacred (usually mythic) meaning — mountains, waterfalls, or unusual geological formations are frequent examples.

3. Rock art sites, such as pictographs and petroglyphs.

4. Burial areas and cemeteries.

5. Sites of ceremonial structures, such as medicine wheels or sun dance arbors.

6. Sweat bath sites.

7. Gathering areas where sacred plants, stones, and other natural materials are available.

8. Sites of historical significance, such as battlefields.

9. The points where a group is described in myth to have originated, or routes they hallowed in myth.

Following is a short list of some thirty (from my accumulating list of about three hundred) currently used sacred sites from the Northwestern United States that have been field-verified in my research. (In the following I have relied partly on a list compiled by Deaver 1986):

1. *Eagle Nest Butte*. This is a prominent topographic feature of the northeastern part of the Pine Ridge Reservation in South Dakota. It may have been used traditionally as a site for eagle-trapping. Today it is used for vision questing, memorials, and other rituals (Hassrick 1965, 233, and Powers 1982, 92–93).

2. *Buzzard Butte*. This site is near Eagle Nest Butte and is used for vision questing (Powers 1982, 92), memorials, and other rituals.

3. *Saddle Butte*. This is also near Eagle Nest Butte and is used for vision questing (Powers 1982, 92), memorials, and other rituals.

4. *Snake Butte*. This is also near Eagle Nest Butte and is used for vision questing (Powers 1982, 92), memorials, and other rituals.

5. *Black Hills*. These are located in South Dakota. Their various mountain tops are favored for vision quests (Feraca 1963, 25). The Black Hills are used for virtually all types of rituals, including the sun dance.

6. *Bear Butte*. This is a very sacred site, used today by Lakota and various other tribes (some coming from hundreds of miles away) for vision questing (Parks and Wedel 1985, 169), memorials, and other ceremonies.

7. *Paha Wakan* (Sacred Hill). This prominent hill is two miles southwest of Blunt, South Dakota, a traditional vision questing and ritual site (Howard 1972, 293). A snake effigy has been reported in this location (Howard 1972, 293), suggesting Mississippian cultural affinities.

8. *Paha Wakan* (Sacred Hill). This is another sacred hill near Reliance, South Dakota (Howard 1972, 293), widely used by the Lakota and certain other Plains tribes for vision questing and other rituals.

9. *Paha Wakan* (Sacred Hill). This is yet another sacred hill near Redfield, South Dakota, and is a site for vision questing and other rituals (Howard 1972, 295).

10. *Wanagi-Kaga*. This is located east of Choteau Creek along the Missouri River. It is known to the Lakota as "Imitates-a-Ghost" for a Yankton shaman who lived near there (Howard 1972, 295).

11. *Mounds*. These are near Fisher's Grove State Park, just west of Frankfort, South Dakota, and are used for vision quests, memorials, and other rituals (Howard 1972, 298).

12. *Turtle River Oracle*. This was located near the mouth of the sacred Turtle River (Howard 1972, 299). A boulder could communicate knowledge of the future to those who interpreted its movement; it was removed in 1892 (Howard 1972, 299–300) and its present location is a secret.

13. *Bede Wakan*. This first sacred lake is Lake Madison, and its name is derived from a phosphorescent light that appears there at night (Howard 1972, 301).

14. *Bede Wakan*. This second sacred lake is Spirit Lake, located north of De Smet, South Dakota. The calamus root, a sacred root, is dug near this lake (Howard 1972, 302).

15. *Bede Wakan*. This third sacred lake is located east of the Fort Peck Reservation in Montana. It is sacred in part because curative herbs and roots grow around its shores.

16. *Custer Battlefield*. This is one of many battlefields where many died in Montana; it is the locus of memorial and other ceremonies conducted by descendants of the warriors who participated in this battle.

17. *Wounded Knee Battlefield*. This battlefield is similar to the Custer Battlefield in Montana and is used in the same manner. Other well known Cheyenne battlefields are Summit Springs and Sand Creek, Colorado.

18. *Deer Medicine Rocks*. This is a pictograph site where Sitting Bull is believed to have had a vision, foretelling the outcome of the battle of the Little Big Horn (De Mallie 1982, Badhorse 1979, Niehardt 1961). Hundreds of pictograph and petroglyph sites dot the landscape of the Northern Plains and are used primarily for vision quests.

19. *Medicine Rock*. This is on the edge of the Northern Cheyenne Reservation in Montana. It is a site for sun dances, including the last one held before the Battle of the Little Big Horn (Badhorse 1979, 27).

20. *Big Horn Medicine Wheel*. Like Bear Butte, this is one of the most sacred sites in the Northern Plains and is used by many tribes, some from great distances. Many different kinds of rituals are conducted here.

21. *Cave Hills*. This South Dakota site is a pictograph site, sacred to both the Cheyenne (Parks and Wedel 1985, 171) and the Lakota.

22. *Sleeping Buffalo Monument*. This Montana site is identified with a well-known myth; it is used as a memorial site and may be used as a vision quest site.

23. *Kootenai Falls*. This Idaho site is a critical sacred site on which the entire Kootenai religious system is founded. Various other falls in this region are sacred to the Kootenai and other tribes.

24. *Elmo Pictographs*. This Montana site is a Kootenai and Flathead vision quest site. There are hundreds of such sites in Western Montana and neighboring Idaho and Wyoming.

25. *Chicago Peaks*. This site is sacred to the Kootenai of Idaho and Montana.

26. *Pilot Knob*. This Nez Percé vision quest site is also used for other rituals; it is very old, like Kootenai Falls. Like Kootenai Falls and the G-O Road "high country," it has been the subject of controversy between tribes and federal bureaucracies.

27. *Wallowa Lake*. This northeastern Oregon, Nez Percé vision quest and ceremonial ground was the home of Chief Joseph, whose descendants gather here to memorialize his life, death, and historical significance to the Tribe.

28. *Celilo Falls*. This former sacred fishing site near The Dalles, Oregon, now inundated, was the scene until the 1950s of numerous intertribal ceremonies of the Northwest, especially those associated with fertility, thanksgiving, and salmon.

29. *Mount Adams*. This mountain in Washington is the site of frequent vision questing and other ceremonies identified with Yakima, Klikitat, and other Sahaptian groups.

30. *Mount Rainier*. This mountain in Washington is the scene of various rituals conducted by Puget Sound and other tribes.

Functions of Sacred Geography

Throughout the Northern Rocky Mountain region, American Indian religious leaders attest that the geographical location of rituals is vital. Unless rituals are performed at the proper locations, they have little or no efficacy. In a literal sense, the natural environment becomes an altar or church in these religions. Similar conceptions are recorded for other American Indian groups throughout the Northwest, Southwest, Eastern Woodlands, Subarctic, and Arctic regions of North America. It is the rule rather than the exception that American Indian ritual life is inextricably tied to the natural environment.

In reviewing some three hundred sacred sites, I have noticed that all groups tend to hold sacred the boundaries between cultural life and

and geological zones. In addition, all groups possess a body of beliefs concerning the appropriate sacred times and rituals to be performed at such sites. It has also become apparent to me that sacred sites serve to identify fundamental symbols and patterns of American Indian cultures. They also project an image of the social order and lend concreteness to the less visible systems of human relationships. They create an organization. These sacred symbolic systems, when superimposed on geography, give it significance and intelligibility. The more central a place is in the religious life of a group, the more numerous the symbolic representations it will possess. Sacred divisions of time are customarily marked at sacred sites by the timing of rituals performed there. Sacred sites create a conceptual and emotional parallelism between the objective order of the universe, the realm of the spirits, and the constructs of human cultures. Sacred sites are places of communication with the spirits, portals where people enter the sacred. Thus, they are a link between the world of humans and the sacred, where spiritual power can be attained. For example, Black Elk, when describing the sweat lodge, spoke of the willows as being set up in such a way that they mark the four corners of the universe. The whole lodge symbolizes the universe, and all the things of the world are contained in it. He described the round hole, which holds the heated rocks for making steam in the center of the lodge, as the center of the universe in which dwells Wakantanka with his power that is the fire. Sacred sites are also natural maps that provide direction to life and shape to the world. They give order to both geographic and social space, and by ordering space they order all that exists within it.

There are yet other reasons why geography is so often sacred to American Indians. As I have noted above, points of geographical and other natural transition become access portals to the sacred. Natural and temporal discontinuities or transitions are portals; dreams and visions are access techniques used to enter the sacred through these portals. In observing these phenomena, I have been struck by the parallelism of these ideas with those of Arnold Van Gennep and others who have demonstrated that the rites of passage in the human life cycle are also sacred transitions. In many cultures, the sacred is entered by individuals during such life cycle transitions. Broadening this focus on life cycle transitions as portals to the sacred, I have also noted the customary celebration of annual seasonal transitions as times of great sacredness in many cultures, e.g., when the sacred domain is accessed during calendrical rituals. Examples would be the "first game" and "first fruits" thanksgiving and fertility rituals surrounding equinoxes and solstices in Native America. Also well known are transitions in the lunar cycle in which the first quarter, second quarter, third quarter, and full moon are seen as parallel to a human life in birth, adolescence, marriage, and death/renewal.

A conjunction of such transitions (simultaneous occurrences) normally provides even greater opportunities for access to the sacred. For example, most Northwestern tribes view such conjunctions of transitions as especially sacred times; at such times access to the sacred is virtually guaranteed for those conducting appropriate rituals in the appropriate places. Yet other transitions to be considered in the timing and location of rituals include dawn, noon, dusk, timber line, and other similar natural demarcations or transitions.

From this view, therefore, sacred sites and sacred geography function as fundamental ingredients of ritual in American Indian religions. Points of geographical transition are joined with the sacredness of the seasons, the sun, the moon, the life cycle of the individual, and the rhythm of community life to form a complex set of sacred transitions customarily celebrated in ritual.

Centrality or Integrity

As interpreted by the courts in the cases referenced by Michaelsen (1986), "central" has a meaning best described as indispensable, essential, or requisite. The courts have, therefore, introduced a very high standard that must be met for First Amendment protection of American Indian sacred geography. Under this interpretation of "central," preservation of a specific sacred site can be achieved only if it is deemed to be essential, indispensable, or requisite for the practice of a particular tribal religion. In its applications, this standard goes well beyond the meaning of "infringement" and borders on "extinction." In other words, to receive First Amendment protection, American Indians must demonstrate that a change will not merely infringe but virtually destroy a religious practice or belief. Judgments by courts as to centrality, therefore, are being made in terms of a standard of survival/extinction.

It is possible, I think, to construct an alternative standard that not only protects American Indian religious practice, but that does so before the brink of extinction is reached. Such a standard is also consistent with scholarly standards concerning what is essential for the practice of American Indian religions. I intend this alternative standard to protect religions rather than sanction the destruction of religions.

Integrity is proposed here as an alternative standard, because it refers to "the quality or state of being complete and undivided," or simply to "customary practice." Infringement then can be understood as a forced or undesired change in the customary practice of a religion. Under the present centrality standard, infringement is not reached until the very existence or continued survival of the religion is threatened; even at this point it is still not clear *exactly* what centrality means. A desirable feature of a standard of integrity is that it is more open to factual investigation than a standard of centrality. Determination of whether the integrity of a religious practice has been violated would rest on answers to factual questions.

Among the factual questions that could be raised concerning whether the integrity of a religion has been violated, the most important is whether its customary functioning has been altered. For example, if the normal requirements or conditions necessary for the performance of customary rituals are changed so the performance is prevented, then the integrity of the religion has clearly been infringed. Alternatively, if this happened, are there functional alternatives? If not, then the integrity has not only been infringed, but permanently.

Anthropologists and other scholars of American Indian religions rarely, if ever, describe the practice of religions in terms of the relative necessity of particular rituals. Instead, such descriptions normally include all aspects of the religion without interpretation or evaluation of this kind. More often, religions in all their complexity and detail are viewed functionally. No part is seen to be unnecessary; if it were unnecessary, it would not be part of the religion in the first place. Given this, how may a standard of integrity be applied when specific parts of a religion are threatened by change? Possible factual questions would be:

1. Is the affected practice held by members of the group to be an essential part of their religion? or,

2. Are there alternatives to the affected practice acceptable to members of the group? or,

3. Would removal or alteration of the affected practice impair or prevent other essential practices of the religion?

The alternative to a standard of integrity is to continue having the courts make dubious judgments about centrality. There are few factual inquiries or other research procedures that can provide unambiguous answers to questions of the relative centrality of religious practices. Most questions of centrality are not subject to factual inquiry. The only possible factual inquiries center on what changes would destroy a religion. Clearly, infringement is more effectively investigated from a perspective of integrity. This standard must replace the standard of centrality, a standard that has been far too limiting in providing protection for American Indian sacred geography.

Integrity and Sacred Geography

The integrity of religious practice in American Indian religions also entails consideration of sacred sites and sacred geography. In the preceding, I have demonstrated that sacred sites and sacred geography are fundamental ingredients of rituals. This finding is widely supported by the research literature I have consulted and by the field research I have described above.

A task remaining in this paper is to clarify the relations between a standard of integrity and the protection of American Indian sacred geography. I have suggested above several factual questions that may be raised concerning whether integrity has been violated or infringed.

In answering the first question, one must factually determine if a sacred site or space is held to be essential for the performance of rituals. In answering the second question, one must determine factually if there are acceptable alternatives to a sacred site or space. In answering the third question, one must determine factually if destruction or alteration of a sacred site or space will prevent other essential practices of the religion. Answers to these questions then provide the courts with not only a means of determining whether infringements of practice will occur, but also to what degree such infringements may impact other practices of the religion.

One of the most difficult factual questions to answer is the geographical extent of sacred sites and spaces. I would argue that a standard of integrity is a feasible and practical means of gaining factual answers to this question. In order to do so, however, one must understand that its context is a vital part of a sacred site. Context may include the relative remoteness of a sacred site from settlements and other disturbances, as well as positioning relative to one or more of the cardinal directions. For example, a common contextual requirement may be a view to the east of the first rays of dawn. Undisturbed views of other awe-inspiring scenes are frequently described as essential contexts for sacred sites. To the degree that such contexts are altered, they can erode or eliminate the ritual efficacy of sacred sites. In the words of one of my principal teachers, "The spirits may go away."

It is possible in some examples to argue that certain sacred sites are more important than others, but criteria must be established before such rankings are valid. For example, if a particular site is the scene of several rather than one required ritual, or if it is the only site where a ritual can be performed, or if it is used by more rather than fewer worshippers, or if it is used by several tribes rather than one, then there are grounds to argue that it may be relatively more important, *but not necessarily less dispensable than other sacred sites.*

Conclusion

In summary, decisions as to the integrity of religious practices and of sacred sites and how they may be infringed are fact-bound. My purpose here has been to suggest various means by which objective, informed decisions can be made concerning essential connections between American Indian religions and sacred geography. I believe that the judicial system can make more informed, sensitive judgments in these difficult cases by focusing their inquiries on the facts of Native religious practice, and through the use of the concept of integrity rather than centrality.

Deward E. Walker, Jr., is Professor of Anthropology at the University of Colorado, with many publications regarding Native American ethnohistory.

6

Law and the Limits of Liberty

ROBERT S. MICHAELSEN

Law as Bulwark

Numa Pompilius, legendary second king of Rome, was regarded in Roman mythology as the founder of Rome's religious system and as a significant law maker. (Typically, law and religion make compatible bedfellows.) Desiring to instill respect for property rights, Numa had *termini*, or boundary stones, made to mark dividing lines between neighbors. Property rights were further sanctified by Numa through the erection of a temple to Terminus, the god of boundaries. The temple had no roof, symbolizing the fact that the god of boundaries could not himself be bound, or, in more mundane terms, that property rights extend into the heavens. Further evidence of the characteristics and prowess of Terminus is shown in the story concerning the building of the Capitoline Temple. In order to build the temple it was necessary to remove the altars of the gods who already occupied the summit of the Capitol. Augurs sought the assent of the gods to this temporary dislocation. *Terminus* refused to be moved, and as the temple was built the roof was left open over the stone representing him. The stolidity of this deity is further indicated by the fact that in a late representation he appears armless atop a square pedestal. Scarcely a friendly presence. (See Keightly and Schmitz 1976 and King 1965.)

The legal scholar Milner Ball has suggested that Terminus is an appropriate figure to represent the law in America. The dominant metaphor pictures law as a bulwark. Law holds back chaos. It restrains and divides. It is "a system of rules and boundaries safeguarding property.... The law

116

purports to divide and defend." It is, therefore, protective and adversarial in nature (Ball 1985, 119).

Picturing law as bulwark is especially apt in understanding American approaches to land and to the Natives who occupied the land when the Europeans arrived. From their earliest encounters with the New World Europeans brought Roman influenced notions of property boundaries and rights with them. Pope Alexander VI divided the New World between Portuguese and Spanish monarchs in 1493. (The pope was something of a Christian Terminus, a boundary setter and enforcer.) A document called the "Requirement" was prepared in the sixteenth century for the Spanish conquistadores to proclaim to the Natives in taking their land from them. This statement traced the legitimacy of the Spanish crown's claim to the land to the pope and beyond him to God who had given the pope's predecessor, St. Peter, "the world for his kingdom and jurisdiction." One of Peter's successors, the statement declares, "made donation of these isles and terra-firme" to the king and queen of Spain. Failure to acknowledge that divinely sanctioned sovereignty, the statement concludes, would result in defeat and enslavement of the Native occupants (Hanke 1965, chap. 3).

Other symbolic acts were utilized in staking claims in the New World on behalf of Christian sovereigns. The act of planting a standard or marker such as a flag or a cross or a pillar on newly discovered land was a common one among representatives of the exploring and colonizing European powers, for example. It was assumed that such a rite established the sovereign's claims over the competing claims of any other Christian sovereign. The rite also served, in the minds of the Europeans at least, to impress the Natives in much the same way that it was expected the proclamation of the "Requirement" would do. (Planting the flag continues as a symbolic act. Note, e.g., the fact that Neil Armstrong planted Old Glory on the moon shortly after he had stepped on the surface.)

From the beginning, relationships between Europeans and Native Americans have been dominated by imposition of boundaries, limits, restrictions, and prohibitions. As Ball points, "When settlers came, they brought with them property law" whose "primary characteristic was bounded land and the fence" (Ball 1985, 96). They also brought with them definite views of what constituted appropriate behavior and, whenever possible or feasible, sought to impose such patterns of behavior on the Natives. This too is reflected in American law.

This is not to suggest that all European colonizers engaged in unrelieved predation. The notion of exchange was not uncommon. In some cases arrangements were made for purchase of land, but whether purchased or taken, the laws governing the subsequent rights to the land were suffused with the metaphor of bulwark. Fences and legal descriptions served as "termini."

Even where exchange characterized acquisition of land it was not likely to be a fair exchange. The Puritan preacher John Cotton suggested what was to become perhaps the most potent notion of fair exchange in the minds of the English colonizers when he urged a group of them about to depart from England for New England in 1630 to give the Natives their faith in exchange for the Natives' land: "Offend not the poor natives, but as you partake in their land, so make them partakers of your precious faith, as you reap their temporals, so feed them your spirituals" (Cotton 1634). Cotton's advice is not too far distant from that of Thomas Jefferson, given to American Indians over and over when he was president: "Become as we are." "Follow our example" (Jefferson 1801–9). This kind of advice was also embodied, in effect, in the Dawes Allotment Act of 1887, which promised individual Indians land ownership, with legally binding boundaries, in exchange for appropriate behavior.

Well before the passage of the Dawes Act land had become a commodity, an article of commerce to be bought and sold for profit. Even land that remained public was, as Ball points out, "generally rendered into commodities through extraction and marketing of the underlying minerals, timber sales, and leases of grazing ranges" (Ball 1985, 97). Hence the "multiple use" policy of the National Forest Service. Hence also multiple difficulties encountered by the Indians in their attempts to protect the sanctity of selected areas of public land. (More below.)

Terminus has not only survived but has thrived in relationships between Europeans and Natives, Whites and Indians, in the United States. And the law has generally been his ally. It has been used to impose limits, as a guardian imposes limits on a "ward," to reinforce that "civilizing" process pursued by Jefferson and his successors.

For much of American history it was assumed that the civilizing process would culminate in the absorption of the Indian into the larger, White-dominated culture and society. The boundaries would disappear. And yet that assumption was tugged by a strong undertow that questioned the capacity of Indians to become as Whites. It was more likely that the race would vanish from the earth.

Failure of the Indian to disappear has been cause for embarrassment. What to do? Continue to impose limits? Try new means of integration? Or acknowledge the validity of Indian ways and try to protect and encourage them?

In the meantime, American Indians, with full knowledge of the role of law as bulwark, have sought increasingly to enlist Terminus in their own cause. To change the metaphor, the law can be a double-edged sword. Why not use the other edge, cut the other way, for a change? (See Michaelsen 1985.)

AIRFA and Its Impact

Increasing Indian use of the law has coincided with a period when the governmental termination policy designed to absorb Indians into the general society has been replaced by a policy that acknowledges Indian distinctiveness and even seeks to encourage it. AIRFA is one of several pieces of legislation designed to acknowledge and even undergird Indian life and cultures.[1] At the time of its passage it was seen by some as a, if not *the*, significant culminating point in federal policy encouraging self-determination in repudiation of the tribal termination policy that had been in effect during the Eisenhower years, and, even more importantly, as a clear reversal of the animosity toward Indian religions that had informed federal policy and practice for so long. Whether it has been, in effect, that significant appears in retrospect to be questionable.

My discovery of AIRFA shortly after President Carter signed it into law in August 1978 was initially cause for puzzlement. Why a special act? Isn't the First Amendment's Free Exercise Clause sufficient? (The First Amendment begins "Congress shall make no law respecting an establishment of religion or prohibiting the free exercise thereof. . . . ") And, on second thought, didn't the Congress, by singling out traditional religions of Indians and other Native Americans, come close to violating the Establishment Clause of that amendment? Congress is precluded from establishing a religion. And the Supreme Court has generally held that any special governmental attention to religion or any governmental "entanglement" with religion constitutes "an establishment of religion" (Miller and Flowers 1987).

It soon became obvious to me that these were uninformed and naive questions. Indian religions had suffered much at the hands of the federal government, and some traditional practices continued to be under siege by representatives of governmental agencies. Given this fact and the unique relationship between the U.S. government and American Indians, it was about time that the U.S. made amends for past sins by taking steps to remove governmental barriers that impede Indian religious practices. Furthermore, the question of the Establishment Clause seemed beside the point. Given the unique legal status of Indian tribes, a status that Chief Justice Marshall had hopefully described as involving a fiduciary responsibility of the U.S. government for what he denominated as these "domestic dependent nations" (*Cherokee Nation* 1831, 17), and given the intimate connection between Indian religion and culture, there is no way completely to eliminate any entanglement between the government and American Indian religions. The question is not, therefore, whether the government will have anything to do with Indian religions but how the government and its agents will respond to Indian religious practices. Will the response be negative, as in the past, or positive, as AIRFA appeared to mandate?

The beginnings were hopeful. Many Native Americans who testified at the Senate hearings on AIRFA or sent communications to the committee expressed optimism that the law would finally put an end to governmental efforts to restrain or suppress Native religions (AIRFA *Hearings* 1978, 40, 71, 102). The Federal Agencies Task Force, chaired by Secretary of the Interior Cecil D. Andrus, carried out an extraordinary degree of fact finding, traditional religious leaders or elders were widely consulted, and an impressive series of recommendations was produced and published in the *AIRFA Report*, 1979. However, the impact of AIRFA since it became law has been minimal and disappointing. Possibly the act stimulated a degree of consciousness-raising among governmental bureaucrats. Under its influence some federal agencies did modify procedures that directly or indirectly affected Indian religious practices. But the substantive impact of the act on governmental practices has not been significant. Furthermore, courts have understood the act to apply primarily to procedures in dealing with Indians and not to add anything of substance to their free exercise rights under the First Amendment.

Perhaps the most decisive court language relative to AIRFA was that used by the federal district court in a case involving Hopi attempts to prevent the U.S. Department of Agriculture from allowing further development of recreational skiing facilities at the "Snow Bowl" in the Coconino National Forest in Arizona. AIRFA, the court declared, "was meant to insure that American Indians were given the protection that they are guaranteed under the First Amendment; it was not meant to in any way grant them rights in excess of those guarantees" (*Hopi* 1981, 3076). (The district court of South Dakota was even more explicit a year later when it held that "the Act does not create a cause of action in the federal courts for violations of rights of religious freedom" [*Crow* 1982, 793].) In response to the *Hopi* plaintiffs' claim that AIRFA created a fiduciary duty on the part of the federal agency to protect traditional Indian resources and communities as well as their religious beliefs and practices, the D.C. District Court declared that AIRFA "does not create a 'fiduciary relationship' as such, and the Court is not willing to imply one" (*Hopi* 1981, 3076). On appeal to the District of Columbia Circuit Court of Appeals, the district court's interpretation of AIRFA was approved. The circuit court found that the intention of the act was that any federal agency that proposed or carried out an action that had or could have an impact on Indian religious beliefs and practices was obligated to investigate the matter fully and to consult with Indian leaders about it. The court concluded, however, that while federal agencies must consider "Indian religious values," they need not defer to them

(*Wilson* 1983, 746). That interpretation became decisive in subsequent court cases in which Indian plaintiffs appealed to AIRFA in support of their efforts to preclude or discontinue governmental actions that, in their view, impinged negatively on their religious beliefs and practices (Craven 1983, Ensworth 1983, Gould 1986, Michaelsen 1983a, Sewell 1983).

Indian plaintiffs have been successful in their appeal to AIRFA in two cases in which courts found that governmental agencies had not adequately investigated the possible impact of proposed actions on Indian religious beliefs and practices or had not sufficiently consulted with Indian leaders about such matters. In both these cases the courts, in effect, sent the matter "back to the drawing board" for redoing with an eye to cleaning up the procedural irregularities (*New Mexico Navajo Ranchers' Assoc.* 1983 and *Means* 1985). Curiously and ironically, the one case in which a court implied that AIRFA reinforced an existing governmental fiduciary responsibility toward protecting American Indian religions did not involve Indian free exercise claims at all but involved an unsuccessful attempt by non-Indians to overthrow laws that allow an exemption for peyote use by Indians in services of the Native American Church (*Peyote Way* 1983).

A significant test of the possible substantive impact of AIRFA in the courts came with United States Supreme Court review of and decision on *Smith* during its 1989–90 term. Alfred L. Smith and Galen W. Black, drug counsellors with the Douglas County (Oregon) Council on Alcohol and Drug Abuse Prevention and Treatment (ADAPT) were fired because they ingested peyote while off duty during a ceremony of the Native American Church. They were subsequently denied unemployment compensation for the same reason. On appeal, the Oregon Supreme Court held that this denial violated their free exercise of religious rights (*Smith and Black* 1986). The state of Oregon appealed to the U.S. Supreme Court, which remanded to the Oregon Supreme Court for determination whether the possession and use of peyote violated Oregon law, without exception. The Oregon court found that the Oregon statute on controlled substances provides no exception for the possession and use of peyote under any circumstances. However, that court found further that the "outright prohibition of good-faith religious use of peyote by adult members of the Native American Church would violate the First Amendment directly as interpreted by Congress" (*Smith* 1988). AIRFA was appealed to by the Oregon Supreme Court in support of this conclusion. In the language of the act and in the reference to peyote in the accompanying House report on AIRFA (as well as in the congressional expression of intention in 1965, when peyote was included under the Drug Abuse Control statutes, that "it expected the implementing regulations to exempt the religious use of peyote") Congress has clearly indicated its intention to afford good-faith American Indian religious practices protection (*Smith* 1988, 149). The U.S. Supreme Court did not reach a similar conclusion and thus dashes the hopes of many Indians who hoped to witness a positive effect of AIRFA in the high court.

The U.S. Supreme Court had already responded to Indian free exercise claims based in part on AIRFA in two cases previous to *Smith*. In one, the Court found that the government's requirement that the Indian claimant's daughter have a Social Security number before the family could receive benefits under the Aid to Families with Dependent Children and Food Stamp programs "does not itself in any degree impair [the claimant's] 'freedom to believe, express, and exercise his religion'" (*Bowen* 1985, 700). (Stephen J. Roy, a Native American descended from the Abenaki Tribe, objected to the requirement on the ground that a Social Security number would violate his religious belief by depriving his daughter, Little Bird of the Snow, of her spirit [see *Roy* 1984].)

In *Lyng*, which involved Indian claims that the completion of a Forest Service road across an area of a high degree of sanctity for them would violate their free exercise rights under the First Amendment and the provisions of AIRFA, the Court concluded that, in fact, the government had been very solicitous regarding Indian religious beliefs and practices involving the area. "Such solicitude," the Court asserted, "accords with 'the policy of the United States to protect and preserve for American Indians their inherent right of freedom to believe, express, and exercise the traditional religions of the American Indian ... including but not limited to access to sites, use and possession of sacred objects, and the freedom to worship through ceremonials and traditional rites'" (*Lyng* 1988, 550, quoting from AIRFA). The Court reached this conclusion despite the fact that the proposed course of action by the Forest Service ran directly counter to the advice given by their own commissioned anthropologist to the effect that such a course of action would pose a serious threat to the continued vitality of the religion *and* culture of the Indians involved in the case (Falk 1989, Lupu 1989, and Michaelsen 1988). The Court's interpretation of AIRFA in *Lyng* reinforces and gives precedential power to the circuit court's view in *Wilson* that, while the government is required to consult with Indians regarding the impact of a proposed action, it need not "necessarily" defer to them or their understanding of their religion (*Wilson* 1983, 746). It also clearly demonstrates the truth of Representative Udall's description of the American Indian Religious Freedom Resolution as "merely a statement of policy" with "no teeth in it" (124 *Cong. Rec.* [1978], 21445–46). Udall apparently made this statement in an effort to head off resistance to the resolution in the House of Representatives, as O'Brien notes in her essay above.

American Indian Religious Freedom
and the Free Exercise Clause of the First Amendment

There is more than one irony evident in the fact that AIRFA has proved to be quite ineffectual in advancing Indian freedom of religion rights. While the courts have declared that AIRFA adds nothing to the Free Exercise Clause, they have also, to put it mildly, been quite minimalist in upholding Indian rights under *that* clause. AIRFA has gained little for Indian claimants and neither has the Free Exercise Clause. While Indians have prevailed in their free exercise claims in some lower courts, they have lost more than they have won (Michaelsen 1983b and 1984). Furthermore, and most significantly, the U.S. Supreme Court has recently nullified victories gained by Indian free exercise of religion claimants in lower courts. In *Roy* the trial court held that the use of the Social Security number assigned to Roy's daughter against his wishes was or would be in violation of his free exercise rights. The court held further that that use was not sufficiently essential to governmental operations to override Roy's rights (*Roy* 1984). The Supreme Court reversed in *Bowen*. The more significant of that Court's reversals in terms of long-range impact occurred, however, in *Lyng*. This was the one sacred site case in which the Indian claimants had won in both district and appellate courts (*Northwest* 1983). A Supreme Court decision for the Indians in that case would have meant a substantial step forward in the application of the Free Exercise Clause to beliefs and practices intimately related to land.

The dampening impact of *Lyng* on sacred site litigation — and hence on sacred site claims generally — is dramatically evident in the October 20, 1989, decision of the U.S. District Court for the District of Arizona in *Manybeads*. Jenny Manybeads, a Navajo who resides in what has been described by Congress in the Navajo-Hopi Land Settlement Act of 1974 as Hopi Partitioned Land, applied, together with forty-six other Navajo plaintiffs, for a preliminary injunction to stop the removal process mandated by the Land Settlement Act. Manybeads claimed that since her religion was intimately bound up with the land upon which her people had lived for more than a century, forced removal from that land would constitute an egregious violation of her free exercise of religion rights under the First Amendment and of the provisions of AIRFA. (A similar claim was made in *Attakai v. U.S.*, which was incorporated into the proceedings in *Manybeads*.)

The district court summarily denied the Manybeads motion for an injunction and granted the defendant's motion to dismiss the case. Resting its decision squarely on *Lyng*, the court held that (a) the plaintiffs had no First Amendment claims, and (b) there was no violation of AIRFA in this case. The court lifted from *Lyng* some of the most chilling language that the Supreme Court has used in free exercise of religion cases: "The fact that a person's ability to practice their religion will be virtually destroyed by a governmental program does not allow them to impose *a religious servitude* [sic] *on the property of the government*. . . . The nature of the religious rights claimed cannot create *a de facto beneficial ownership of public property*, in order to practice one's religion" (*Manybeads*, 4–5, my emphasis; see *Lyng*, 548–49). The prediction of virtual destruction of the religion of the Northwest Indians was made by the Ninth Circuit in *Northwest* 1986, 693). In effect, what courts have said to Indian claimants, then, is that AIRFA equals no more than the Free Exercise Clause of the First Amendment, and, in your case, that clause means very little. The further irony here is that a constitutional amendment clearly intended to maximize freedom (of religion, speech, etc.) has, as applied by the courts in most cases involving Indians (and in all cases involving sacred sites), actually severely restricted freedom and even threatened the vitality and possibly the actual existence of certain Indian religions. (Only those intimately involved in those religions can know the full extent of the damage.) Court decisions, as one legal scholar has put it,

> in place of a total victory for the Indians, have dictated a total loss for the Indians. The approaches used have set up a win all–lose all situation that does not comport with either the intent of the religion clauses to protect religion from governmental interference or the idea behind accommodation, i.e., to allow the broadest possible freedom for religious exercise without significantly undermining the present regulatory structure of American society. (Andreason 1984, 334, citations omitted)

Hence, while the federal government abandoned its official policy of terminating Indian tribes, and while the Congress has enacted several pieces of legislation designed to sustain and encourage tribal existence and identity, governmental erosion of the religious foundations of Indian culture continues apace. Terminus still lives.

Strategies

Why this bifurcation, this schizophrenia, in the governmental approach to American Indian religions? And what can be done about it? A reasonably full answer to these questions would require the rehearsal of a good deal of American history and no little probing of the American psyche, not to mention the American soul. A tempting short answer is that what is evident here, as in other aspects of Indian-White relations in this country, is an underlying bad will on the part of those who represent the American people, which reflects the outlook of a majority of that people. The solution in that case, as in any circumstance where one is under duress, would appear to be *fight or flight*. But one is reminded that the relationship between American Indians and other Americans (and especially the federal government) is like the relationship between the characters in Jean Paul Sartre's *No Exit*; history would suggest that there is no escape from it. Hence the option that remains is to fight and continues to be a fight from within. In more concrete terms that means to continue to pursue political and juridical means for effecting change while not neglecting the larger task of educating the majority regarding the nature and needs of American Indian religious traditions.

A variety of legislative enactments, mostly in the 1970s, suggest that that route is not entirely a dead-end.[2] Efforts to amend AIRFA so as to put teeth into it have not thus far been successful, but may be worth pursuing even more systematically and vigorously than they have been.[3] In the meantime, one legal analyst has suggested, "Native Americans who believe that their religious freedom has been violated should steer away from the first amendment and AIRFA as means to redress those alleged infringements. The Indians might be more successful if they argue that they are being denied equal protection of the laws with regard to the exercise of their religions" (Smith 1986, 185). Another scholar has suggested that in addition to the equal protection provisions in the Fifth and Fourteenth Amendments consideration be given to the Ninth Amendment, which "could be used to protect certain fundamental rights beyond those listed expressly in the Constitution" (Higginbotham 1982, 102). In other words, try other constitutional guarantees.

It may also be worth recalling and attempting to build upon the underlying motivation that led to the introduction by Senator Abourezk of the American Indian Religious Freedom Resolution in 1977 — i.e., the inherent value in protecting the religions of Native Americans. "America does not need to violate the religions of her native peoples," the Senator declared in urging the passage of the act. "There is room for and great value in cultural and religious diversity. We would all be poorer if these American Indian religions disappeared from the face of the Earth" (123 *Cong. Rec.* 39,300-39,301 [Dec. 15, 1977]). Sarah B. Gordon (1985) has pointed out that the legislative history of AIRFA parallels that of the Endangered Species Act of 1973 (ESA) in this kind of underlying motivation: It is eminently worthwhile to preserve something of inherent value and of value to the Republic generally through the fostering of diversity. In our scale of values such preservation should take precedence over courses of action that, on their face, appear to be more immediately valuable in material terms. Hence Justice Brennan, in his eloquent dissent in *Lyng*, stressed the irony evident in a Court decision that "sacrifices a religion at least as old as the Nation itself, along with the spiritual well-being of its approximately 5,000 adherents, so that the Forest Service can build a six-mile segment of road that two lower courts found had only marginal and speculative utility, both to the Government itself and to the private lumber interests that might conceivably use it" (*Lyng* 1988, 564).

Acknowledgement of values which in some cases may even override governmental property interests and rights is evident not only in the ESA but also, as Gordon suggests, in the concept of the *public forum*. Under this concept the Supreme Court has upheld free assembly and expression in public places even though that assembly and expression might not be acceptable to a majority or a significant number of the people. This "constitutional protection of First Amendment activity that has taken place on public land 'from time immemorial,'" Gordon asserts, "naturally includes within its ambit not only speech and assembly, but also provides a useful guide for analysis of traditional Indian religions and worship, which have been observed at sacred sites for thousands of years" (Gordon 1985, 1466).

Another legal scholar has suggested the possible utility of *common law* principle in the pursuit of free exercise of religion litigation and in free exercise adjudication. "Instead of viewing the problems of law and religion as divorced from the ordinary concerns of the legal system," Ira Lupu argues, "one may draw creatively on the entire Anglo-American legal tradition in service of the free exercise clause" (Lupu 1989, 966). Lupu is especially concerned with the problem of *burden*, which is a critical category in free exercise claims — i.e., a litigant must establish that a proposed or actual governmental action constitutes or will constitute a burden on his or her "exercise of religion." The burden issue was especially problematic in *Lyng*, one of the cases that is the focal point of Lupu's essay — i.e., the Court was not persuaded that the government's proposal to complete the Forest Service road would, if carried out, genuinely burden the religion of the Indian claimants in that case.

In fleshing out his argument for consideration of the common law tradition in free exercise cases, Lupu suggests the following possible "rule":

> Whenever religious activity is met by intentional government action analogous to that which, if committed by a private party, would be actionable under general principles of law, a legally cognizable burden on religion is present. (Lupu 1989, 966)

Lupu also cites as one historical basis for pursuing this route the statute of Virginia for Religious Freedom, which was a significant forerunner of the Free Exercise Clause. That statute provides in pertinent part "That no man shall . . . be enforced, restrained, molested or burthened, in his body or goods, nor shall otherwise suffer on account of his religious opinions or beliefs. . . ." (Lupu 1989, 968).

In applying common law principle specifically to *Lyng*, in which public land use was at stake, Lupu advances a number of accepted usages regarding property use and rights, including "the doctrine of easement by prescription" and "the ancient English common law formula of use continuing for so long that 'the memory of man runneth not to the contrary'" (Lupu 1989, 975–76). While these suggestions are quite technical and could require thorough grounding in the technicalities of the law for their successful application, the point worth underlining here is that Lupu is suggesting a legal approach that might break through the wall of court resistance to any Indian free exercise claim that involves public land. It might also help to rectify that imbalance of values that Justice Brennan alluded to in his dissent in *Lyng*.

In an analysis that parallels that of Lupu's in its stress on common law tradition, Ellen N. W. Sewell has suggested that one possible way to solve the conflict between Indian religious rights and the rights of the public as landowner would be "to categorize as a property right those Indian religious practices amenable to a property conception." Such a categorization would enable the courts to treat conflicting property claims "within a single scheme. Access to sites can be seen as a kind of easement. . . . Such 'religious easements' or 'religious usufructs' could even be thought of as a kind of 'reserved right'" similar, e.g., to water rights (Sewell 1983, 465).

Confronting Terminus

These strategies suggest various ways of putting Terminus in his proper place — i.e., as a marker and not as a bulwark or wall. A marker can more easily be moved than a fixed boundary designed to be impregnable. The metaphor may be useful in illuminating some inescapable realities in dealing with American Indian freedom of religion rights and claims.

The underlying reality is the marked differences between Indian cultures and the dominant European-shaped culture in the United States. These differences are evident in such obvious manifestations of culture as language, worldviews, religious rites and behavior, and aesthetic or artistic expressions and tastes. Specifically, e.g., Native American religions tend to be more site specific and land oriented than are the religious traditions of the majority of Americans. Indeed, specific locations may be essential to some Native American religions to a degree with few if any parallels in other American religious traditions. Add to these differences the prevailing property views and laws in America that are characterized by fixed boundaries, carefully drawn and zealously guarded rights of ownership, and the universal use of land as a commodity, and the gulf between traditional Indian approaches and those of the majority becomes a very deep one indeed. This gulf dominates American law, both in concept and practice.

Indian appeals to the Free Exercise Clause have not worked well, then, because the law has not shown the capacity to grasp and to accommodate the nature and significance of traditional Indian religions. This is due to a general inadequacy in free exercise doctrine as well as a certain myopia regarding those religions. That doctrine, as recently developed in the courts, has involved three steps: (1) Is a free exercise claim genuinely based on religion? Is it a legitimate religious claim? If the answer is in the affirmative, then the next question is (2) Does the proposed or actual governmental practice or legislation constitute a genuine burden on that religion? And if the conclusion is affirmative again, then (3) a balancing between governmental interests and the interests of the free exercise claimants must occur. Is there a state interest so compelling as to override the burden suffered by the free exercise claimant? Can the government achieve its objectives by alternative means? Etc.

Difficulties abound in pursuing these steps. First, the courts must get into the business of determining whether some view or practice is religious. In connection with this step courts have shown an inclination to refine matters by distinguishing between that which is *central* or even *indispensable* to the religion and that which is incidental to it. Court probings of centrality and indispensability have abounded in Indian sacred site cases, e.g., with devastating results for Indian claimants (Michaelsen 1985, Pepper 1982, and Justice Brennan's dissent in *Lyng*). Determining whether a genuine burden exists can also be a difficult matter, as suggested above. In this determination as well as in the balancing of competing interests courts have tended to give more weight to state interests than to those of religious claimants. A good summary of these difficulties is offered by Scott David Godshall, who finds "three shortcomings in present free exercise doctrine: it too narrowly defines the scope of protected beliefs, too broadly defines permissible burdens upon protected beliefs, and, finally, balances religious and state interests in a manner too often biased toward the interests of the state" (Godshall 1984, 1572).

Free exercise litigation is further complicated for Indian claimants by the fact that courts have not shown an inclination to confront and to cope with the significance of the unique status of Indians in this country. This is especially evident in cases dealing with public land. As Mark S. Cohen has noted, the fact that some courts have accorded Indians special protection in cases dealing with the alleged illegal use of substances such as peyote "creates a striking counterpoint to the sacred site cases, where most of the courts denied Indian religious claims without even considering the merit of the state interest involved" (Cohen 1987, 781).[4] Contrary to the typical free exercise claim, which seeks exemption from some governmental action on religious grounds — e.g., the military draft or compulsory education or uniform clothing regulations or compulsory insurance for employees — these sacred site cases seek to modify or to stop governmental actions involving the use and development of governmental land. Hence the relief sought in such cases is quite different from that sought in cases seeking individual exemption from a governmental act. Here public land is at stake; that presents a categorically different situation from the typical case in which free exercise doctrine has developed (see Gordon 1985, 1459, and Michaelsen 1985, 54).

The wariness and even air of suspicion with which courts approach such cases is quite evident in the Supreme Court's huffiness about Indian claims involving public land in the *Lyng* case. After using such language as "the religious servitude" that the Indian claimants seek "to impose" on the area involved and the "*de facto* beneficial ownership of some rather spacious tracts of public property," which those claimants would acquire if the Court acceded to their claims, the Court concludes magisterially that "whatever rights the Indians may have to the use of the area ... those rights do not divest the Government of its right to use what is, after all, *its* land" (*Lyng* 1988, 549). Justice Brennan rightly spots the majority's underlying concern in *Lyng* when he concludes his dissenting opinion with the assertion that "in the final analysis, the Court's refusal to recognize the constitutional dimension of [the Indian] respondents' injuries stems from its concern that acceptance of respondents' claim could potentially strip the Government of its ability to manage and use vast tracts of federal property.... These concededly legitimate concerns," he states further, "lie at the very heart of this case, which represents yet another stress point in the longstanding conflict between two disparate cultures — the dominant western culture, which views land in terms of ownership and use, and that of Native Americans, in which concepts of private property are not only alien, but contrary to a belief system that holds land sacred" (*Lyng* 1988, 562). Indeed, with its decision in *Lyng* the Supreme Court became, as Falk has pointed out, "the first appellate court in a sacred lands case to defer entirely to the federal government's property rights" (Falk 1989, 528). Terminus reigns in the highest court of the land.

Because of the unique status of Indians in America, case law dealing with them is, as Ellen Sewell points out, "Janus-faced: one face is that of Indian law, and the other, the face of relevant substantive law, which is applied ignoring the Indian or tribal status of a party" (Sewell 1983, 466). As noted above, some courts have acknowledged the unique status of Indian religious practices with a history antedating the advent of Europeans — such as the religious use of peyote — and have granted what might be regarded as special privilege to that status. However, the courts have not acknowledged the unique status of Indians in dealing with sacred site claims. Indeed, they have summarily dismissed any appeal to the notion of a governmental fiduciary responsibility toward American

Indian religious traditions. To deny such a responsibility, and to treat Indian free exercise claims in the same way as non-Indian claims may actually disadvantage the Indian claimants. Civil rights notions and lit-igation are generally based on universalistic and egalitarian principles that allow no place for group status, or, in the case of Indians, tribal status and the rights that Indian law has accorded that status. If Indian religious practices, and especially those having to do with land, are treated with the "respect" accorded religious practices generally in accordance with those principles, and if the First Amendment is, as Sewell puts it, "ap-plied relentlessly, without regard for the special status and traditional rights of tribes, the perverse result will be greater limitation of Indian exercise of religion than previously existed." But if the dual legal sta-tus of American Indians "is appreciated," she continues, if "application of universalistic principles is accompanied by acknowledgement of the corporate-like status of tribes, with its attendant particularistic rights or privileges, many of the constitutional problems vanish." For example, "Indian tribes' particularistic usages on federal lands can be recognized and legally sanctioned . . . without threatening the general principle of the ownership control of property because rights accorded to tribes do not necessarily create general precedents for religious rights in property" (Sewell 1983, 467, citations omitted).

Law as Medium

Putting Terminus in his proper place involves seeking different ways of viewing law, different metaphors from the dominant one of *bul-wark*. By this metaphor, Ball points out, "law is defensive, adamantine, preterhuman, static, pretentious. It is all limits and divisions and bring-ing to a halt" (Ball 1985, 17). Law as bulwark is part of a "family of metaphors . . . which tend to the individualistic and competitive: life as struggle, society as contract, politics as battlefield or marketplace, and nature as resource. Within this constellation humans are by nature individuals with conflicting self-interests" (Ball 1985, 120).

Are there not other metaphors, more humble, "decalcified, allowing movement and circulation, connecting rather than disconnecting?" Ball asks (1985, 27–28). And he proposes the metaphor of law as *medium*, as go-between, as facilitator of communication and relations between human beings. The "family cluster" to which this metaphor belongs tends "to the vital and pacific. . . . Nature is gift and occasion for a gift cycle, a sharing of the advantages of time and earth. Politics is the action of forming, exchanging, and distilling opinion — the action of a body politic. And law is then a medium of solidarity" (Ball 1985, 123).

Ball develops the metaphor of law as medium in the context of the law of the sea among nations. While that law has become increasingly concerned with boundaries and competing claims to resources, Ball finds in such ideas as free trade and free seas, and in the fact that the law of the sea has played such an important role in the development of international law, that that law does illustrate the metaphor of law as medium, albeit as a minor motif.

The metaphor of law as medium may also be fitting for reconceptualizing both free exercise doctrine and American Indian law. The religion clauses of the First Amendment were fashioned out of a concern to minimize governmental interference with religion and religious interference with the government. Thomas Jefferson, author of "A Bill for Establishing Religious Freedom," was primarily concerned with the latter. Roger Williams, a lesser known father or grandfather of the religion clauses, was primarily concerned with the former. The late eighteenth-century evangelical Protestants who were the ideological progeny of Williams joined with such Enlightenment rationalists as Jefferson and James Madison to bring about the enactment of Jefferson's "Bill" into law in Virginia in 1786 and the fashioning of the religion clauses of the First Amendment in 1791.

Both Jefferson and Williams spoke of a "wall of separation" between church and state (Jefferson 1801 and Williams 1644, 108; see Howe 1965). Both sought to build a civil society in which people would, at a minimum, not slit each other's throats, and, ideally, live in relative peace and harmony. Jefferson thought this would best be accomplished if religion had nothing to do with the state, if it, indeed, became an entirely personal, private matter. He was convinced that religion had had an adverse and corrupting influence on public life in the past, and he was concerned to eliminate that prospect in the new republic. Williams was equally convinced that the state had a corrupting influence on religion, and in the interest of enhancing what he called "pure religion" he sought to separate the state from it. With the passage of time and the enormous increase in governmental power in this country, Williams's concern seems more pressing than Jefferson's. While religion, in some forms, may still seek today to dominate civil affairs, the use and even domination of religion by government, with all of its impressive power, is a more real threat. This is clearly the case with regard to American Indian religions, at any rate.

More than a century ago Judge Alonzo Taft, in a dissent on the status of religion in Ohio, described what has become or should be the ideal relationship between the government and religion: "The government is neutral, and, while protecting all, it prefers none, and it *disparages* none" (*Minor* 1870, 415, Taft's emphasis). Taft's views, which were stated in dissent in a case that dealt with a contested Cincinnati School Board decision to eliminate devotional Bible reading from the public schools of that city, were cited with approval by Justice Clark in *Schempp* (1963,

214). Nonpreferential protection may be another form of what in recent years has been called "benevolent neutrality" (Miller and Flowers 1987). In any case, it suggests a governmental approach to religion that seeks neither to use nor to abuse it. Implied here, of course, is a generally positive view of religion. And Taft's reference to *all* suggests both inclusiveness and an underlying appreciation of the value of diversity. Such a view, while clearly assuming boundaries, also implies openness.

Openness involves an effort to learn about the other. Such learning may not only enhance one's own knowledge and understanding of the other but may also, if appropriately gained and used, enhance the status of the other. Indeed its impact may extend well beyond its immediate object.

In developing the metaphor of law as medium Ball leans on Lewis Hyde's remarkable essay *The Gift: Imagination and the Erotic Life of Property* (1983). A gift moves, Hyde points out, while a boundary marks resistance to momentum. A gift leaves one's hands and develops a life of its own. It may move in a circular route and eventually return in an unexpected and surprising form. But even when the power of Terminus is vested in a form of property that is portable, such as a commodity, that form tends to remain self-contained, bounded. Furthermore, Hyde points out, "its exchange will often establish a boundary where none existed before" (Hyde 1983, 61).

Appropriately enough, Hyde begins his analysis with an exploration of the origin and significance of the designation "Indian giver." That term of opprobrium perfectly illustrates, in its origins, the sharp contrast between European and Native American views of property: on the one side, something to be possessed, bounded, and protected by the language and other instrumentalities of the law; on the other, something to be shared, even given away, with the expectation that it will develop a life of its own and will return in some different form. "Imagine a scene," Hyde begins:

> An Englishmen comes into an Indian lodge, and his hosts, wishing to make their guest feel welcome, ask him to share a pipe of tobacco. Carved from a soft red stone, the pipe itself is a peace offering that has traditionally circulated among local tribes, staying in each lodge for a time but always given away again sooner or later. And so the Indians, as is only polite among their people, give the pipe to their guest when he leaves. The Englishman is tickled pink. What a nice thing to send back to the British Museum! He takes it home and sets it on the mantelpiece. A time passes and the leaders of a neighboring tribe come to visit the colonist's home. To his surprise he finds his guests have some expectation in regard to his pipe, and his translator finally explains to him that if he wishes to show his goodwill he should offer them a smoke and give them the pipe. In

consternation the Englishman invents a phrase to describe these people
with such limited sense of private property.

The "opposite of 'Indian giver,'" Hyde suggests, "would be something like 'white man keeper'...a person whose instinct is to remove
property from circulation, to put it in a warehouse or museum" or to put
it aside for use in production. "The Indian giver," Hyde points out, "(or
the original one, at any rate) understood a cardinal property of the gift:
whatever we have been given is supposed to be given away again, not
kept. Or, if it is kept, something of similar value should move on in its
stead." The one essential is that *the gift must always move*" (Hyde 1983,
3–4; Hyde's emphasis).

How does this apply to American Indian free exercise of religion
claims? What I am suggesting is that the law be seen for what it can
do to enhance human life, to encourage the expression of the human
spirit, and to improve relations among people. This no doubt entails as
an ultimate objective a shift in values from a stress on self-seeking and
possessiveness to an encouragement of openness and sharing. I suggest
as an intermediate step the exploration of all facets of the law to discover
those aspects of it which can expand our and the courts' understanding
of the meaning and potential of the Free Exercise Clause and of the
unique relationship between the U.S. government and American Indians
in such a way as to advance movement toward that ultimate objective.
Thus law may advance liberty.

*Robert S. Michaelsen is Professor Emeritus of Religion at the University of
California, Santa Barbara, with many publications regarding the American
Indian Religious Freedom Act.*

Epilogue

VERNON MASAYESVA

The American Indian Religious Freedom Act — AIRFA — has been called the law with no teeth. Sadly, this is true.

AIRFA was passed by Congress to force federal agencies to protect Indian religious rights on federal lands. Federal agencies and federal courts have given AIRFA such a narrow reading that it is practically meaningless.

AIRFA was passed by Congress to force federal agencies to admit that those agencies frequently engaged in conduct on federal lands that affected Indian rights to practice their religion at religious shrines, sacred burial sites, and sacred plant and animal gathering areas. Federal projects may destroy or expose such areas so as to make their use by Indians practicing their religion impossible.

Indian religious rights are entitled to protection under the Free Exercise Clause of the First Amendment to the U.S. Constitution. Cultural bias by many federal bureaucrats resulted in federal agencies not protecting Indian rights secured by the Free Exercise Clause. AIRFA was intended to force federal bureaucrats to look beyond their own cultural biases and to protect Indian religious rights.

What AIRFA has in fact brought about is far less than what Congress intended or the First Amendment requires. Now federal bureaucrats will come out for an "on-site" visit with the Indians to ask their concerns about a project. A nice visit is had with tribal government officials and other people who were invited to (or found out about) the meeting. The federal officials then go back and include a few paragraphs in their decision document about the effect of the federal project on Indian religious rights. A decision is then made. And all procedural niceties have been observed.

And that is the problem. AIRFA has been largely construed to require *only* that procedural steps be taken. Federal agencies will generally say that AIRFA does not command any *result*, only *process*.

AIRFA is different, therefore, from laws that protect endangered fish and animal species, or laws that protect water quality. Those laws require actual protection of fish, birds, or water — results. AIRFA, as federal agencies apply it, only requires procedure.

Even when federal courts and agencies face up to the First Amendment Free Exercise Clause, they have used a test that is bizarre and almost impossible to satisfy. Under this test Indians must show three things:

1. that the religious practice is central to their religion. How do people define which practices or beliefs in their religion are central and which are not?

2. that the religious belief or practice is *indispensable* to their religion. How can any people tell which practices or beliefs are indispensable? Can Catholics do without the Vatican?

3. that the practice or belief cannot be done elsewhere. If we push you out of the way with a bulldozer, can you go someplace else?

This three-part test is culturally biased. Indian religions are different from Christian and Jewish religions. Christian and Jewish religions are oriented toward a universal being — God — in heaven; places here on earth are largely of symbolic importance. For Indians, however, places and things here on earth often are more than mere symbols. God may actually be present in places or things here on earth.

Most bureaucrats and judges come to these problems from a European perspective. In so doing, they seriously misunderstand that differences in culture affect the significance of places and things in the world about us. The legal test used by courts does not really comprehend the nature of this cultural difference, this difference in religious belief.

A new beginning is needed. I am not prepared to say what the proper legal test is in every detail. But I have some suggestions:

1. Courts and administrators must learn to examine these issues better. Differences of cultural perspective and religious belief must be overcome. If an Indian says a rock contains the spirit of God, courts and judges must not dismiss this as romantic description. Keep in mind, to a Catholic consecrated bread is no longer bread but the very physical body of Christ. No court would challenge the Catholic belief in that regard. And no court should challenge as romantic overstatement that places or things contain the spirit of God either.

2. Federal agencies should borrow *cumulative impacts* analysis from environmental law. Too often, agencies only look at the effects of an isolated, particular project. No consideration is given to the effect that this and other actions may have. A dollar bill is made with a hundred

pennies. One penny seems like so little. But if you take enough away, you take away the whole dollar.

Indian religions have been suppressed by official government actors or by government-authorized missionaries. Indian religious sites have been bulldozed or carried off to museums. Religious objects have been stolen or sold. At some point, the religious experience can be lost through small steps.

Federal agencies and courts should consider past, present, and future actions as affecting Indian religion before approving any particular project. Direct and indirect effects of both federal and private action should be considered.

3. The current test of central and indispensable/site specific beliefs should be set aside. A common sense appraisal should be used. Regardless of whether beliefs are central and indispensable, government should not be able to violate rights unless very important national interests are at stake.

The First Amendment limits all the other powers of government found in the Constitution. Government should bend first, before it asks people to bend their beliefs or practices to accommodate government.

Many of the Europeans who came to this land did so to escape religious, racial, and political persecution in Europe. They sought to make this a better land than what they left behind. They adopted the Free Exercise of Religion Clause in the First Amendment to ensure against persecution here again.

The time has come when protection of Indian religious rights must also become a reality under the First Amendment.

Thank you.

Vernon Masayesva is vice-chairman of the Hopi Indian Tribe.

Notes

Prologue, by Christopher Vecsey

1. We have reprinted here the entire resolution, since many of the authors of the following chapters make reference to it.

PUBLIC LAW 95-341 [S.J.Res. 102]; Aug. 11, 1978

AMERICAN INDIAN RELIGIOUS FREEDOM

Joint Resolution American Indian Religious Freedom

Whereas the freedom of religion for all people is an inherent right, fundamental to the democratic structure of the United States and is guaranteed by the First Amendment of the United States Constitution;

Whereas the United States has traditionally rejected the concept of a government denying individuals the right to practice their religion and, as a result, has benefited from a rich variety of religious heritages in this country;

Whereas the religious practices of the American Indian (as well as Native Alaskan and Hawaiian) are an integral part of their culture, tradition and heritage, such practices forming the basis of Indian identity and value systems;

Whereas the traditional American Indian religions, as an integral part of Indian life, are indispensable and irreplaceable;

Whereas the lack of a clear, comprehensive, and consistent Federal policy has often resulted in the abridgement of religious freedom for traditional American Indians;

Whereas such religious infringements result from the lack of knowledge or the insensitive and inflexible enforcement of Federal policies and regulations premised on a variety of laws;

Whereas such laws were designed for such worthwhile purposes as conservation and preservation of natural species and resources but were never intended to relate to Indian religious practices and, therefore, were passed without consideration of their effect on traditional American Indian religions;

Whereas such laws and policies often deny American Indians access to sacred sites required in their religions, including cemeteries;

Whereas such laws at times prohibit the use and possession of sacred objects necessary to the exercise of religious rites and ceremonies;

Whereas traditional American Indian ceremonies have been intruded upon, interfered with, and in a few instances banned: Now, therefore, be it

American
Indian
Religious
Freedom.
42 USC 1996.

Resolved by the Senate and House of Representatives of the United States of America in Congress assembled, That henceforth it shall be the policy of the United States to protect and preserve for American Indians their inherent right of freedom to believe, express, and exercise the traditional religions of the American Indian, Eskimo, Aleut, and Native Hawaiians, including but not limited to access to sites, use and possession of sacred objects, and the freedom to worship through ceremonials and traditional rites.

42 USC 1996 note.

SEC. 2. The President shall direct the various Federal departments, agencies, and other instrumentalities responsible for administering relevant laws to evaluate their policies and procedures in consultation with native traditional religious leaders in order to determine appropriate changes necessary to protect and preserve Native American religious cultural rights and practices. Twelve months after approval of this resolution, the President shall report back to the Congresss the results of his evaluation, including any changes which were made in administrative policies and procedures, and any recommendations he may have for legislative action.

Presidential
report to
Congress.

Approved August 11, 1978.

2. The Supreme Court ruling in *Employment Division v. Smith* occurred after the chapters of this volume were already in press.

1 / A Legal Analysis of the American Indian Religious Freedom Act, by Sharon O'Brien

1. According to the decision, "... The Act does no more than direct federal officials to familiarize themselves with Native American religious values in order to avoid unwarranted and unintended interference with traditional native religious practices" (1530).

2. The bill introduced into the Senate is S. 1124.

3 / Repatriation, Reburial, and Religious Rights, by Walter R. Echo-Hawk and Roger C. Echo-Hawk

1. This is true, for example, of the important Cheyenne Dog Soldier pipe that is presently in the possession of the Smithsonian Institution. This pipe was taken by U.S. military forces in an attack on a Cheyenne village in the Battle of Summit Springs after its possessor, Chief Tall Bull, was killed in action. The Cheyennes have been patiently negotiating for years with the Smithsonian for the return of this important religious property for worship purposes by the Cheyenne Dog Soldier Society. See Testimony of William Parker (S. 187) before the Senate Select Committee on Indian Affairs (July 29, 1988), 72–85, 158–69.

2. Cole 1985, 181, 248–54. Sometimes the government proselytizing was accompanied by prosecutions of Natives for practicing traditional ceremonies, and museums were enriched by Native goods that were confiscated in these proceedings.

3. The Zuni war god that was stolen from its shrine on the Zuni Reservation and ultimately found its way to the Denver Art Museum is an example (Davis 1980).

4. Sledzik and Murphy (1987) cite this as Circular Letter #2, Surgeon General's Office, April 4, 1867, on file at the National Archives. "Memorandum for the Information of Medical Officers" was circulated in September 1868; it reported on contributions of Indian heads by that date and encouraged further submissions by army medical officers. A copy of this memorandum is on file at the Native American Rights Fund, dated September 1, 1868, and signed by Assistant Surgeon General C. H. Crane by order of the surgeon general. Sledzik and Murphy cite a letter from George Otis, dated September 1, 1868, sent to army medical officers, and on file at the Otis Historical Archives, National Museum of Health and Medicine.

5. See *Charrier v. Bell*, 496 So.2d 601 (La. App. 1 Cir. 1986), *cert. denied*, 498 So.2d 753 (La. 1986). In *Charrier*, the Court held the funerary offerings, when and if ever dug up, rightfully belong to the person (or descendants) who originally furnished the graves — which in that case was the Tunica-Beloxi Tribe.

6. See Antiquities Act of 1906, 16 U.S.C. 432; and Archaeological Resources Protection Act of 1979, 16 U.S.C. 470 aa-11. These statutes have actually been interpreted by federal agencies to convert dead persons into "federal property." If true, then this is a drastic and barbaric retreat from English and American common law, which do not recognize a property interest of any kind in dead human bodies. See, e.g., 25 A C.J.S. at 450; also, *Travelers Insurance Company v. Welsch*, 82 f.2d 799 (5th Cir. 1936); *Aetna Life Insurance Company v. Burton*, 12 N.E.2d 360 (Ind. 1938); *Alderman v. Ford*, 72 P.2d 981 (Kan. 1937); *Kingsley v. Forsythe*, 257 N.W. 95 (Minn. 1934); *Larson v. Chase*, 50 N.W. 238 (Minn. 1898).

7. This summary of Pawnee burial practices is from R. Echo-Hawk, "Pawnee Mortuary Traditions," foreword by Dr. Deward E. Walker, Jr., September 1988. Report prepared for the Native American Rights Fund.

8. Smithsonian Institution, National Museum of Natural History, National Anthropological Archives, Army Medical Museum Files, Box 2, File 509–31, Fryer to Otis, March 11, 1869 correspondence; see also Fryer to Otis February 12, 1869.

9. *Annotation: Corpse Removal and Reinterment of Remains*, 21 A.L.R. 2d 472, 475–76.

10. The traditional First Amendment test is stated and applied in cases such as *Thomas v. Review Board*, 450 U.S. 707, 718–19 (1981) and *Wisconsin v. Yoder*, 406 U.S. 205, 214–15 (1972). This balancing test applies with equal force in cases involving Indian religious freedom. See *Employment Division v. Smith, et al.*, 108 S.Ct. 1444 (1988).

11. Legal opinion letter of December 14, 1988, from Attorney General Spire to Executive Director of the Nebraska Indian Commission, on file at the Native American Rights Fund. Scientific interest has been held insufficient to justify

body snatching in the common law cases, *Annotation: Corpse Removal and Reinterment,* 479, and to alter Indian property rights in funerary items placed in the grave for the use of the decedent in the spiritual hereafter, *Charrier v. Bell,* 496 So.2d 601 (La. App. 1 Cir. 1986), *cert denied,* 498 So.2d 753 (La. 1986).

12. See, e.g., Bowman, "The Reburial of Native American Skeletal Remains: Approaches to the Resolution of a Conflict," *Harvard Environmental Law Review,* 13, no. 147 (1989); Echo-Hawk 1988; Rosen, "The Excavation of American Indian Burial Sites: A Problem in Law and Professional Responsibility," *American Anthropologist* 82 (1980): 5–27.

13. Quoted in Morris, "The Spirit and the Law: Indian Policy and Indian Religious Freedom," in G. P. Horse Capture, ed., *The Concept of Sacred Materials and Their Place in the World* (Cody, Wyo.: Buffalo Bill Historical Center, 1989), 4.

4 / Sacred Sites and Public Lands, by Steven C. Moore

1. Senators Cranston, Inouye, and DeConcini introduced S. 2250 in the 100th Congress, which was referred to the Select Committee on Indian Affairs. The committee held a hearing on the bill, but never took action to send the bill to the floor of the Senate. No companion bill was introduced on the House side.

Three bills amending AIRFA were introduced in the 101st Congress during 1989. On March 21, Congressman Morris Udall (Arizona) introduced H.R. 1546; on June 6 Senator John McCain (Arizona) introduced S. 1124; and on November 21, 1989, Senator Daniel Inouye (Hawaii) introduced S. 1979. H.R. 1546 and S. 1124 are very similar in text and substance to S. 2250. S. 1979 was far more expansive than the three other bills.

2. See July 18, 1989 testimony of Jeff Sirmon, Deputy Chief, U.S. Forest Services, before the U.S. House of Representatives Committee on Interior and Insular Affairs, opposing H.R. 1546. See also September 28, 1989, testimony of Alan J. West, Deputy Chief, Forest Service, before the U.S. Senate Select Committee on Indian Affairs, opposing S. 1124.

3. Arguably, the task is an easier one for the National Park Service, given its mission as a land preservation agency, as opposed to a land development agency. For instance, the Park Service recognizes that it has been previously "charged with the mission to preserve and interpret the cultural heritage of Native American tribes or groups," and that many parks contain "natural resources as well as features . . . that are associated with traditional sacred, subsistence or other cultural practices of contemporary Native American peoples, and necessary for their cultural continuity" (National Park Service, 35675).

4. Also, in several passages, the Park Service unduly restricts the scope of accommodation to Native Americans with "traditionally established interests in parks. . . ." (see 52 Fed. Reg., 35674). In other words, there must be some historical connection between traditional religious ceremonies and park lands before the service will allow an exemption from its permitting requirements (ibid, 35676). The key here is the Park Service's definition of "traditional": "beliefs and behaviors that have been transmitted across generations, and . . . identified by their Native American practitioners to be necessary for the perpetuation of

their cultures" (ibid.). First, such a threshold requirement imposes a stereotypical template on Indian cultures, "freezing" them in time and denying the reality that all religions are by nature dynamic and continually evolving. Second, the requirement that practitioners demonstrate that a belief or behavior is necessary for the perpetuation of an Indian culture casts the analysis in terms of extinction vs. survivability. In other words, Indian culture must be on the verge of extinction before being entitled to some measure of accommodation by Park Service bureaucrats.

5. This loophole smacks of the Forest Service's treatment of the religion claims in both the *Lyng* and *Means* decisions.

6. See May 18, 1988, testimony of Roland Robinson, Deputy Director, BLM, before the Senate Select Committee on Indian Affairs, opposing S. 2250; see also July 18, 1989, testimony of Dean Stepanek, Acting Deputy Director, BLM, before the House Interior Committee, opposing H.R. 61546.

7. See, e.g., the discussion of *Lyng* and *Means* in this chapter. Justice O'Connor's pronouncement in *Lyng*, that it is the United States government, after all, which *owns* the land, endorses and strengthens such bureaucratic arrogance. Is not the United States Government a government "of the people" — including Native Americans — and is there not a solemn trust relationship between the government (as trustee) and the Native (as beneficiary)?

8. The Advisory Council on Historic Preservation, responsible for enforcement of Section 106 of the National Historic Preservation Act, 16 U.S.C. §§170w *et seq*,. vehemently opposed the project on essentially the same grounds as those identified by Theodoratus.

9. Five years ago Sioux Indians from South Dakota experienced similar treatment from James Mathers, Forest Supervisor of the Black Hills National Forest. Mathers denied their application for a special use permit to construct a spiritual encampment in the forest, despite the existence of several Christian church camps and the Rapid City Country Club in the same forest. Federal District Court Judge O'Brien admonished Mathers for his "clear error of judgment": "In summary, the Court specifically finds the denial of the special use permit was arbitrary and capricious. The Court further finds that Forest Service policies as implemented by Mr. Mathers — including his decision to deny the special use application — have the effect of discriminating against Indians who are trying to practice their religion. The Court further finds that Mr. Mathers is subconsciously biased against Indian applicants. He acknowledges that Indian people should be treated equally — but just cannot bring himself to see that that happens" (*Means*).

10. See, e.g., *Thomas*, 715 ("Intrafaith differences...are not uncommon among followers of a particular creed, and the judicial process is singularly ill equipped to resolve such differences...").

5 / Protection of American Indian Sacred Geography, by Deward E. Walker, Jr.

1. A preliminary version of this paper was given as the invited keynote address to the Harvard Workshop on Sacred Geography, held on May 5–6, 1987,

Cambridge, Massachusetts, sponsored by the Harvard University Committee on the Study of Religion and the Center for the Study of World Religions.

I wish to express my appreciation to Dr. Raoul Birnbaum for his many valuable suggestions in developing this paper. I also wish to express my appreciation to the many American Indian religious leaders who have patiently endured my persistence in exploring subjects they believe most human beings should already understand.

6 / Law and the Limits of Liberty, by Robert S. Michaelsen

1. The 95th Congress enacted two major laws designed to protect the cultural integrity of Indian people: the joint resolution on American Indian Religious Freedom (S.J.R. Res. 102, 95th Cong., 2d Sess., Pub. L. No. 95-341, 92 Stat. 469 [codified in part at 42 U.S.C.A. §1996 & note]), and the Indian Child Welfare Act (Act of Nov. 8, 1978, Pub. L. No. 95-608, 92 Stat. 3069 [codified at 25 U.LS. C.A. §§1901–63]). AIRFA has two sections. The first culminates in the Congressional resolution "that henceforth it shall be the policy of the United States to protect and preserve for American Indians their inherent right of freedom to believe, express, and exercise the traditional religions of the American Indian, Eskimo, Aleut, and Native Hawaiians, including but not limited to access to sites, use and possession of sacred objects, and the freedom to worship through ceremonies and traditional rites." The second calls upon the President to implement this resolution through the administrative bodies that deal with Native Americans and to report back to the Congress with recommendations for legislative action within twelve months of the enactment of the resolution into law.

2. For example, in addition to AIRFA, Congress took action to return Blue Lake and its environs to the sole control of the Taos Pueblo and passed the Indian Education of Act of 1972, the Indian Self-Determination and Education Assistance Act of 1975, and the Indian Child Welfare Act of 1978. All of these acts extended the degree of tribal control of tribal affairs, and the last three made possible much more latitude than had existed previously for formal tribal control of education, including religious education. Selected specific American Indian religious practices were also recognized in federal actions in the 1970s. The use of peyote in the religious rites of the Native American Church was granted exemption from the provisions of the Comprehensive Drug Abuse Prevention and Control Act of 1970 in one of the federal regulations designed to implement that Act (21 CFR §1307.31). In 1978 the Bald Eagle Protection Act was amended to authorize the secretary of interior to permit the taking of bald and golden eagles "for religious purposes of Indian tribes" if compatible with the statute's conservation purposes (16 USCA §688a). And examination of state acts would turn up other instances of acknowledgement of the distinctive nature and needs of Indian religious practices.

3. The most recent efforts to give AIRFA more muscle centered in a measure introduced by Senators Cranston, Inouye, and DeConcini during the second session of the 100th Congress which specified that AIRFA be amended to include the following provisions:

Sec. 3. (a) Except in cases involving compelling governmental interests of the highest order, Federal lands that have been historically indispensable to a traditional America [sic] Indian religion shall not be managed in a manner that would seriously impair or interfere with the exercise or practice of such traditional American Indian religion.

(b) United States district courts shall have the authority to issue such orders as may be necessary to enforce the provisions of section S. 2250 (*Congressional Record–Senate* S. 3634, March 31, 1988). It is not clear what impact the Supreme Court's decision in *Lyng* might have on this proposed legislation. However, that case, which was decided on April 19, 1988, hung like a cloud over the hearing on the Cranston amendment, which was held less than a month later ("Improvement of the American Indian Religious Freedom Act," Hearing on S. 2250 before the Select Comm. on Indian Affairs, U.S. Senate, 100th Cong., 2d Sess. [May 18, 1988]). According to Senator Inouye an AIRFA amendment may be introduced again (135 *Cong. Rec.* S779, daily ed. Jan. 25, 1989).

4. Among the illegal substance cases mentioned by Cohen are *Woody, Whittingham,* and *Frank*. His note was written before the U.S. Supreme Court's decision in the sacred land case of *Lyng,* a decision that adds force to Cohen's observation concerning court stringency in sacred site cases. At the same time, the forthcoming decision of the Supreme Court in *Smith* could blunt the effect of the contrast Cohen highlights.

References

1 / A Legal Analysis of the American Indian Religious Freedom Act, by Sharon O'Brien

Court Cases

Badoni, 1977. Badoni v. Higginson, 455 F. Supp. 641 (D. Utah 1977).

Badoni, 1980. Badoni v. Higginson, 638 F.2d 172 (10th Cir. 1980).

Bear Ribs, 1979. Bear Ribs v. Taylor, Civ. No. 77-3985RJK(G) (C.D. Calif. April 1, 1979).

Bowen, 1986. Bowen v. Roy, 106 S.Ct. 2147 (1986).

Buerk, 1979. The United States of America v. Buerk, No. A. 77–121 (N.D.W.D. Ohio, Opinion and Order, Jan. 16, 1979).

Crow, 1982. Fools Crow v. Gullet, 541 F. Supp. 785 (D.S.D. 1982).

Dion, 1985. United States v. Dion, 762 F.2d 674 (8th Cir. 1985).

Frank, 1979. Frank. v. Alaska, Alaska, 604 P.2d 1068 (1979).

Indian Inmates, 1986. Indian Inmates of Nebraska Penitentiary v. Grammer, 649 F. Supp. 1374 (D. Neb. 1986).

Lyng, 1988. Lyng v. Northwest Indian Cemetery Protective Association, 108 S.Ct. 1319 (1988).

Marshno, 1980. Marshno v. McMannus, Case No. 79-3146 (D. Kan., Nov. 14, 1980).

Means, 1985. U.S. v. Means, 627 F. Supp. 247 (D.S.D. 1985).

Means, 1987. U.S. v. Means, Nos. 81-5131 and 81-5135 (D.S.D. Jan. 12, 1987).

Means, 1988. U.S. v. Means, 858 F.2d 404 (8th Cir. 1988).

New Mexico Navajo Ranchers, 1983. New Mexico Navajo Ranchers' Association v. I.C.C., 702 F.2d 227, 233 (D.C. Cir. 1983).

Northwest, 1985–86. Northwest Indian Cemetery Protective Association v. Peterson, 764 F.2d 581 (9th Cir. 1985) and 795 F.2d 688 (9th Cir. 1986).

Oneida Indian Nation, 1984. Oneida Indian Nation of New York v. Clark, 593 F. Supp. 257 (N.D.N.Y. 1984).

Peyote Way, 1983. Peyote Way Church of God. v. Smith, 556 F. Supp. 632 (N.D. Tex. 1983).

Reinert, 1984. Reinert v. Haas, 585 F. Supp. 477 (S.D. Iowa 1984).

Rush, 1984. United States v. Rush, 738 F.2d 497 (1st Cir. 1984).

S. of Fla., 1985. S. of Fla. D. of Bus. Reg. v. U.S. D. of Interior, 768 F.2d 1248 (11th Cir. 1985).

Sequoyah, 1979. Sequoyah v. Tennessee Valley Authority, 480 F. Supp. 608 (E.D. Tenn. 1979).

Sequoyah, 1980. Sequoyah v. Tennessee Valley Authority, 620 F.2d 1159 (Sixth Cir. 1980).

Shabazz, 1985. Shabazz v. Barnauskas, 600 F. Supp. 712 (M.D.F. 1985).

Standing Deer, 1987. Standing Deer v. Carlson, 831 F.2d 1525 (9th Cir. 1987).

Thirty-Eight Golden Eagles, 1986. United States v. Thirty-Eight (38) Golden Eagles, 649 F. Supp. 269 (D. Nev. 1986).

Ute Indian Tribe, 1981. Ute Indian Tribe v. State of Utah, 521 F. Supp. 1072 (D. Utah 1981).

Warner, 1984. United States v. Warner, 595 F. Supp. 595 (D.N.D. 1984).

Wilson, 1983. Wilson v. Block, 708 F.2d 735 (D.C. Cir. 1983).

Government Documents

Abourezk, James
1978   "Native Americans' Right to Believe and Exercise Their Traditional Native Religions Free of Federal Government Interference," March 21, 1979, to accompany S.J. Res. 102, U.S. Cong., Senate, 95th Congress, 2d Sess., Report No. 95–709, 11.

AIRFA Report
1979   *American Indian Religious Freedom Act Report.* P.L. 95–341. Washington, D.C., August.

Carter, Jimmy
1979   *Public Papers of the Presidents of the United States, Jimmy Carter, 1978* (Washington, D.C.: U.S. Government Printing Office), 2:1417–18.

House of Representatives
1989   H.R. 1546, 101st Cong., 1st Sess., 135 *Congressional Record* E898, March 21.

Udall, Morris
1978   "American Indian Religious Freedom." July 18, 1978. House of Representatives, *Congressional Record* 124, 21445.

2 / Peyote and the Law
by Omer C. Stewart

Aberle, D. F.
1965   *The Peyote Religion among the Navaho.* Chicago: Viking Fund Publications in Anthropology.

Aberle, D. F., and O. C. Stewart
    1957   *Navajo and Ute Peyotism: A Chronological and Distributional Study.* University of Colorado Studies, Series in Anthropology.

Aguirre Beltran, G.
    1963   *Medicina y Magia.* Mexico City: Instituto Nacional Indigenista.

Austin Statesman
    1954   "Jurors OK Peyote Sale to Indians in Laredo, Texas." March 15.

Baker, F.
    1964   "Father Peyote's 'Disciples,' " *Empire Magazine, Sunday Denver Post,* July 26, 4–5.

Bergmans, J. J.
    1921   Letter to Chas. H. Burke, Commissioner of Indian Affairs. August 2. Regarding Taos Peyotism. National Archives.

Bergquist, L.
    1957   "Peyote: The Strange Church of Cactus Eaters [Lodge Grass, Montana]." *Look* 21, no. 25 (December 10): 36–41.

Bolander, Walter L.
    1922   Letter to A. W. Leech, Supt. Northern Pueblos, Espanola, New Mexico. Report of arrest of Peyotists and seizure of Peyote drum, blankets, etc. National Archives.

California, State Senate
    1970   Senate Bill 946, Sec. 11. Amends Section 11540 of the Health and Safety Code. [Peyote illegal; original prohibition 1959 (see Mosk 1962, 273)].

Conley, William
    1967   Finding: State of Colorado v. Mana Pardeahtan. Criminal Action No. 9454. County Court for the City and County of Denver. June 27.

Dickens, Walter F.
    1917   Letter to Supt. O. J. Green, Shawnee Indian School, Shawnee, Oklahoma. From Red Lake Indian Agency, Red Lake, Minnesota. January 24. Indian Archives Division, Oklahoma Historical Society.

Gorman, Howard
    1940   *The Growing Peyote Cult and the Use of Peyote on the Navajo Indian Reservation.* By Vice-chairman, Navajo Tribal Council. May 18. 17 pages. See also Proceedings of the Meeting of the Navajo Tribal Council, June 3, 1940, 11–42. Window Rock, Arizona.

Hertzberg, Hazel W.
    1971   *The Search for an American Indian Identity: Modern Pan Indian Movements.* Syracuse, N.Y.: Syracuse University Press.

Humphreys, R. M.
 1916 "Peyote Replaces Whiskey on Reservation, Indians Get 'Jags' with the Mescal Bean." *Denver Times*, December 2.

Johnson, W. E.
 1909a Circular Letter, June 10, 1909, and replies. (Second peyote questionnaire). U.S. Bureau of Indian Affairs, Peyote Correspondence, Chief Special Officer, pt. lc.
 1909b [Documents Relating to a Campaign for the Suppression of Peyote.] MSS. U.S. Bureau of Indian Affairs, Peyote Correspondence, Chief Special Officer, pt. lc. Oklahoma City, Oklahoma Historical Society. Cheyenne and Arapaho-Vices.
 1909c Annual Report, 17–19. MS, Washington, D.C., National Archives. Records of the Bureau of Indian Affairs, Special Agent File, No. 54461-09-031.
 1909d Letter to the Commissioner of Indian Affairs, May 4, 1909. In U.S. Bureau of Indian Affairs, Peyote Correspondence, Chief Special Officer, pt. lc. Abstract printed in Johnson 1912, 239–42.
 1911a Letter to W. B. Freer, February 8, 1911. MS. Oklahoma City, Oklahoma Historical Society. Cheyenne and Arapaho-Vices.
 1911b Letter to R. G. Valentine, August 29, 1911. Abstract in Johnson 1912, 289–93.
 1912 "History, Use and Effects of Peyote." *Indian School Journal* 12, no. 7 (May): 239–42; no. 8 (June): 289–93.
 1918 Letter to W. B. Wheeler, April 10. U.S. Congress, Congressional Record, 61 (1921), pt. 5, 4681–82. See also U.S. Senate, Committee on Indian Affairs, Survey of Conditions, 1937, pt. 34, 18281–82.

Kazen, E. J.
 1968 Judge's Decision, Texas v. David S. Clark, March, no. 12, 879.

La Barre, W.
 1938 *The Peyote Cult*. University Publications in Anthropology. New Haven: Yale University Press.
 1960 "Twenty Years of Peyote Studies." *Current Anthropology* 1, no. 1 (January 1960): 45–60.

Larson, H. L.
 1919 Letter to H. J. Holgate, Deputy Special Officer from Chief Special Officer, Denver, May 21. Peyote File, National Archives, Washington, D.C.

Leonard, I. A.
 1942 "Peyote and the Mexican Inquisition, 1620." *American Anthropologist* 44:324–26.

McCormick, T. F.
 1928 Letter to Charles H. Burke, Commissioner of Indian Affairs. February 18. Revealed stand against Peyote, recommended Taos ordinance. National Archives.

1929   Letter to State Senator Ed Safford requesting a New Mexico state law against Peyote. National Archives.

McFate, Y.
1960   Decision of the Honorable Yale McFate in the Case of the State of Arizona v. Mary Attakai, no. 4089, Superior Court, Coconino County, Flagstaff, Arizona, July 26, 3:00 P.M. *American Anthropologist* 63 (1961): 1335–37.

Mooney, J.
1918   Statement. U.S. Congress. Committee on Indian Affairs, 59–68, 88–113, 145–48, 171–72.

Mosk, Stanley
1962   Subject: Religion—Use of Peyote. Opinion No. 62–93. Attorney General's Opinions, 39:276–79.

Nevada State Journal
1965   "Nevada Indians Assured Continued Use of Peyote." March 13. Reno.

Navajo Times
1967   "Resolution Allowing Peyote in NAC Rites Passed by Tribal Council Balloting." 8, no. 42 (October 19), 4. Window Rock, Arizona.

Newberne, R. E. L., and C. H. Burke
1925   Peyote: An Abridged Compilation from the Files of the Bureau of Indian Affairs, 3d ed.

Noland, James M.
1961   Interview of Judge Noland by Omer C. Stewart, Durango, Colorado. Field notes.

Oklahoma, Constitutional Convention
1907   Hearings before Medical Committee. Photograph and Catalog notes, Museum, Fort Sill, Oklahoma.

Oklahoma, District Court, Kingfisher County
1907   Territory of Oklahoma v. Taylor, et al. MS, Kingfisher, District Court, no. 1021.

Oklahoma Legislature
1899   Session Laws, Section 2652, 122–23. "Mescal bean" [peyote] prohibited.
1909   House, *Journal*, 118, 126, 180–81, 211, 353. [Failure to pass anti-peyote law.]
1927   Senate *Journal* 11:573, 594, 907. [Failure to pass anti-peyote law.]

Oklahoma, Legislature, House, Senate
1908   (Hearings on Mescal Bean Bill.) MS, Oklahoma Historical Society, Cheyenne Arapaho-Vices.

Platz, Lois
      1974   Letter to Omer C. Stewart from Office of the Clerk, Big
                      Horn County, Hardin, Montana, March 25. [Big Sheep Case
                      dismissed March 20, 1926.]

Randall, William
      1937   Remarks of Committee of Indians with Reference to the Use
                      of Peyote. Henry Standing Bear, Interpreter. 13 pages. RG 75,
                      National Archives.

Romero, Antonio
      1916   Letter to Mr. P. T. Lonergan, Albuquerque, First report of
                      Peyote use at Taos, for H. A. Larson, Chief Special Officer.
                      November 14. National Archives.

Safford, W. E.
      1915   "An Aztec Narcotic." *Journal of Heredity* 6, no. 7: 291–311.

Shreve, John B.
      1937   Letter to L. C. Mueller, Chief Special Officer, B.I.A. Washing-
                      ton, D.C. February 20. National Archives.

Stewart, O. C.
      1956   "Peyote and Colorado's Inquisition Law." *The Colorado Quar-
                      terly* 5, no. 1 (Summer): 79–90.
      1961a   "Peyote and the Arizona Court Decision." *American An-
                      thropologist* 63, no. 6: 1334.
      1961b   "The Native American Church (Peyote Cult) and the Law."
                      Denver Westerners Monthly Roundup 18, no. 1 (January): 5–18.
      1961c   "The Native American Church and the Law, with Description
                      of Peyote Religious Services." *Westerners Brand Book* 17:4–47.
      1963   Constitutional Rights of the American Indians. Hearings
                      before the Subcommittee on Constitutional Rights of the
                      Committee on the Judiciary United States Senate. 87th Con-
                      gress, 2d Sess. Part 3: 524–70.
      1970   "Anthropologists as Expert Witnesses for Indians: Claims and
                      Peyote Cases." Paper presented to AAA Annual Meeting,
                      November 20, 1970, San Diego.
      1972   Field notes based on interviews at Taos, New Mexico, with
                      Teles R. Romero. April 11 and 12.

Tobriner, J.
      1964   Opinion of the Supreme Court of the State of California in
                      Criminal Case no. 7788: The People v. Jack Woody et al. Con-
                      firming the Right to Use Peyote in Religious Services of the
                      Native American Church. August 24.

U.S. Congress, House, Committee on Indian Affairs
      1918   Peyote [Hearings on H.R. 2614, 65th Congress, 2d Sess.]
                      Washington, D.C.: U.S. Government Printing Office.

U.S. Department of Justice, Bureau of Narcotics
    1971   Regulations Implementing the Comprehensive Drug Abuse
                Prevention and Control Act of 1971. Special Exempt Persons
                307.31 Native American Church. Federal Register 36, no. 80
                (April 24).

U.S. District Court, Wisconsin, Eastern District
    1914   U.S.A. v. Mitchell Neck, alias Nah-qua-tah-tuck. MS, Mil-
                waukee, U.S. District Court. Crim. F, no. 280. Transcript of
                testimony not located; a summary is given in Safford 1915,
                306–7.

U.S. District Court, South Dakota, Western Division
    1916   U.S.A. v. Harry Black Bear. U.S. Congress, House, Commit-
                tee on Appropriations 1928: 124–25. Summary of testimony:
                Deadwood, South Dakota, *Daily Pioneer-Times*, September 7,
                1916, 1, cols. 4–5; September 8, 1916, 1, cols. 1–2.

Washington Daily News
    1942   "Pale Face Judge Frees Indian Whoopee Chief." March 19.

White, E. E.
    1888a   Order (Prohibiting Peyote at the Kiowa, Comanche, and Wi-
                chita Agency), June 6. MSS. Draft: Oklahoma City, Oklahoma
                Historical Society. Kiowa and Comanche-Vices. Final Copy:
                Washington, D.C., National Archives. Records of the Bureau
                of Indian Affairs, Letters Received, 1888, no. 15508 Inclos.

    1888b   Letter to the Commissioner of Indian Affairs, June 9, 1888.
                MS, Washington, D.C., National Archives. Records of the Bu-
                reau of Indian Affairs, Letters Received, 1888, no. 15508.

    1888c   Letter to the Commissioner of Indian Affairs, July 6, 1888. MS,
                Washington, D.C., National Archives. Records of the Bureau
                of Indian Affairs, Letters Received, 1888, no. 17455.

    1888d   Report of the Kiowa, Comanche, and Wichita Agency, 98–99.
                U.S. Bureau of Indian Affairs, Annual Report 1888: 95–101.

Woodson, A. E.
    1899   Report of Agent for Cheyenne and Arapaho Agency, 284. U.S.
                Bureau of Indian Affairs, Annual Report 1899: 282–86.

Young, Robert W.
    1961   *The Navajo Yearbook*. Window Rock, Arizona: Navajo Agency.

3 / Repatriation, Reburial, and Religious Rights, by Walter R. Echo-Hawk and Roger C. Echo-Hawk

Bieder, R. E.
    1986   *Science Encounters the Indian, 1820–1880: The Early Years of
                American Ethnology*. Norman: University of Oklahoma Press.

Blair, B.
    1979   "American Indians v. American Museums, A Matter of Religious Freedom." *American Indian Journal* 5:13–21.

Blakey, M. L.
    1987   "Skull Doctors: Intrinsic Social and Political Bias in the History of American Physical Anthropology." *Critique of Anthropology* 7, no. 2.

Cole, D.
    1985   *Captured Heritage: The Scramble for Northwest Coast Artifacts.* University of Washington Press.

Davis, B.
    1980   "Indian Religious Artifacts: The Curator's Moral Dilemma." *Indian Law Support Center Report* 2, 1.

Department of Interior
    1979   *Federal Agencies Task Force Report, American Indian Religious Freedom Act Report.*

De Smet, P. J.
    1863   "Letter of Father De Smet, November 1, 1859." *New Indian Sketches.* New York: D & J Sadler & Co.

Dorsey, G. A., and J. R. Murie
    1940   *Notes on Skidi Pawnee Society.* Alexander Spoehr, ed. Anthropological Series, Field Museum of Natural History, 27, no. 2.

Echo-Hawk, W. R.
    1986   "Museum Rights vs. Indian Rights: Guidelines for Assessing Competing Legal Interests in Native Cultural Resources." *Review of Law & Social Change* 14, no. 2. New York University.
    1988   "Tribal Efforts to Protect Against Mistreatment of Indian Dead: The Quest for Equal Protection of the Laws," *NARF Legal Review* 14, no. 1.

Gilmore, M. R.
    1912   "Uses of Plants by the Indians of the Missouri River Region." *Thirty-third Annual Report of the Bureau of American Ethnology.* Washington, D.C.: U.S. Government Printing Office.

Gould, S. J.
    1981   *The Mismeasure of Man.* New York: W. W. Norton & Co.

Harper, K.
    1986   *Give Me My Father's Body.* Iqaluit, N.W.T.: Blacklead Books.

Horse Capture, G. P., ed.
    1989   *The Concept of Sacred Materials and Their Place in the World.* Cody, Wyo.: Buffalo Bill Historical Center.

Lurie, N. O.
    1976   "American Indians and Museums: A Love-Hate Relationship." *The Old Northwest* 2:235.

McPhilimy, G.
> 1989 "Time to Close the Burial Pit." *Boulder Daily Camera*. May 25. Editorial, 12a.

Oehler, G. F., and D. Z. Smith.
> 1974 ed. *Description of a Journey and a Visit to the Pawnee Indians*. Fairfield, Washington: Ye Galleon Press.

Platt, E. G.
> 1918 "Some Experiences as a Teacher among the Pawnees." *Collection of the Kansas State Historical Society: 1915–1918* 14. Topeka: Kansas State Printing Plant.

Riding In, J. T.
> 1985 "Pawnee Removal: A Study of Pawnee-White Relations in Nebraska." Unpublished M.A. thesis. Los Angeles: University of California.

> 1989 "Murder, Justifiable Homicide, or Head Hunting? The Killing and Decapitation of Former Pawnee Scouts by U.S. Soldiers and Citizens." Manuscript on file at the Native American Rights Fund.

Ryan, L. J.
> 1925 "Doesn't Play Golf So Digs Up History." *Omaha World Herald*. September 13. Social Events section, 10.

Sledzik, P. S., and S. P. Murphy
> 1987 "Research Opportunities in Osteopathology at the Armed Forces Medical Museum." Unpublished paper presented at the Northeastern Anthropological Association Meetings, March 18–21. University of Massachusetts, Amherst.

Svingen, O. J.
> 1989 "History of the Expropriation of Pawnee Indian Graves in the Control of the Nebraska State Historical Society." Report prepared for the Native American Rights Fund, January.

White, R.
> 1983 *The Roots of Dependency: Subsistence, Environment, and Social Change among the Choctaws, Pawnees, and Navajos*. Lincoln: University of Nebraska Press.

Whiteford, G. L.
> 1937 "Prehistoric Indian Excavations in Saline County, Kansas." Salina: Consolidated.

Wilson, R. E.
> 1984 *Frank J. North: Pawnee Scout Commander and Pioneer*. Athens, Ohio: Swallow Press. (See Coons to North September 28, 1898, correspondence, 325–27.)

Witty, T. [Archeology Department of the Kansas State Historical Society
and the Division of Architectural Services]
    1984   "The Whiteford (Price) 'Indian Burial Pit,' Archaeological Site,
              Saline County, Kansas." Unpublished report submitted to the
              Historic Sites Board of Review, October.

Witty, T.
    1989   "New Law to Protect Unmarked Burial Sites in Kansas."
              Kansas Preservation 11, no. 6.

4 / Sacred Sites and Public Lands,
by Steven C. Moore

Court Cases

Badoni, 1980. Badoni v. Higginson, 638 F.2d 172 (10th Cir. 1980).

Bowen, 1986. Bowen v. Roy, 106 S.Ct. 2147 (1986).

Callahan, 1981. Callahan v. Woods, 658 F.2d 679, 687 (9th Cir. 1981).

Hobbie, 1987. Hobbie v. Unemployment Appeals Commission, 480 U.S. 136, 94
    L.Ed.2d 190, 197 (1987).

Lyng, 1988. Lyng v. Northwest Indian Cemetery Protective Association, 108 S.Ct.
    1319 (1988).

Means, 1985. United States v. Means, 627 F. Supp. 247, 269 (D.S.D. 1985);
    reversed, 858 F.2d 404 (8th Cir. 1988), *cert. denied*, 57 U.S.L.W. 3842 (1989).

Morton, 1977. Morton v. Mancari, 417 U.S. 535 (1977).

Northwest, 1986. Northwest Indian Cemetery Protective Association v. Peterson,
    795 F.2d 688 (9th Cir. 1986).

Sherbert, 1963. Sherbert v. Verner, 374 U.S. 398, 404 (1963).

Thomas, 1981. Thomas v. Review Board, 450 U.S. 707, 717 (1981).

Waltz, 1970. Waltz v. Tax Commission, 397 U.S. 664 (1970).

Wilson, 1983. Wilson v. Block, 708 F.2d 735 (D.C. Cir. 1983).

Yoder, 1972. Wisconsin v. Yoder, 406 U.S. 205, 220 (1972).

Government Documents

AIRFA Report, 1979. American Indian Religious Freedom Act Report. P.L. 95-341.
    Washington, D.C., August.

Archaeological Resources Protection Act, 1979.

Federal Land Policy and Management Act, 1976.

National Historic Preservation Act, 1966.

National Park Service, 1987. "Native American Relationships Policy," 52 Federal
    Register, September 22, 35674.

5 / Protection of American Indian Sacred Geography, by Deward E. Walker, Jr.

Andersen, Raoul R.
 1970 "Alberta Stoney (Assiniboine) Origins and Adaptations: A Case for Reappraisal." *Ethnohistory* 17:49–61.

Anderson, Gary C.
 1980 "Early Dakota Migration and Intertribal War: A Revision." *Western Historical Quarterly* 11, no. 11: 17–36.

Aquila, Richard
 1974 "Plains Indian War Medicine." *Journal of the West* 13, no. 2: 19–43.

Art, Karen Majcher
 1981 "Natural and Supernatural Resources: Mining on Navajo Land and the American Indian Religious Freedom Act." *Chicago Anthropology Exchange* 14, nos. 1–2: 4–26.

Bad Heart Bull, Amos and H. Blish
 1967 *A Pictographic History of the Oglala Sioux.* Lincoln: University of Nebraska Press.

Badhorse, Beverly
 1979 "Petroglyphs—Possible Religious Significance of Some." *Wyoming Archaeologist* 23, no. 2: 18–30.

Baker, Paul E.
 1955 *The Forgotten Kutenai.* Boise, Idaho: Mountain States Press.

Benedict, Ruth Fulton
 1922 "The Vision in Plains Culture." *American Anthropologist* 24: 1–23.
 1923 *The Concept of the Guardian Spirit in North America.* Menasha, Wis.: Memoirs of the American Anthropological Association, no. 29.

Boas, Franz, and J. R. Swanson
 1911 "Siouan." United States Bureau of American Ethnology, *Bulletin* 40, no. 1: 875–967.
 1918 "Kutenai Tales." Bureau of American Ethnology, *Bulletin* 49: 1–387.

Bowers, Alfred W.
 1950 *Mandan Social and Ceremonial Organization.* Chicago: Chicago University Press.
 1965 *Hidatsa Social and Ceremonial Organization.* Smithsonian Institution, Bureau of American Ethnology, *Bulletin*, 194.

Braroe, N. W., and E. E.
 1977 "Who's in a Name: Identity Misapprehension on the Northern Plains." *Diogenes* 98:71–92.

Brody, J. J.
1971   *Indian Painters and White Patrons*. Albuquerque: University of
New Mexico Press.

Brown, Joseph E.
1969   "The Persistence of Essential Values among North American
Plains Indians." *Studies in Comparative Religion* 3, no. 4 (Autumn): 216–25.
1982   *The Spiritual Legacy of the American Indian*. New York: Crossroad.
1983   "The Unlikely Associates: A Study in Oglala Sioux Magic and
Metaphysic." *Studies in Comparative Religion* 15, nos. 1–2:
92–100.

Brown, Mark H.
1969   *The Plainsmen of the Yellowstone*. Lincoln: University of Nebraska Press.

Brunton, Bill B.
1968   "Ceremonial Integration in the Plateau of Northwestern
North America." *Northwest Anthropological Research Notes* 2:
1–28.

Bullchild, Percy
1985   *The Sun Came Down: The History of the World as My Blackfeet
Elders Told It*. New York: Harper & Row.

Cahill, P. Joseph
1976   "Aspects of Modern Cree Religious Tradition in Alberta."
Studies in Comparative Religion 10, no. 4: 208–12.

Carrasco, David
n.d.   *Sacred Space and Religious Visions in World Religions*. Manuscript in author's possession, Department of Religious Studies,
University of Colorado, Boulder.
1982   Sacred Space and Religious Vision in World Religions: A
Context to Understand the Religious Claims of the Kootenai
Indians. Exhibit A in Walter A. Echo-Hawk Statement before
the Subcommittee on Civil and Constitutional Rights of the
House Committee on the Judiciary, June 10.

Carter, John G.
1938   "The Northern Arapaho Flat Pipe and the Ceremony of Covering the Pipe." Smithsonian Institution, Bureau of American
Ethnology, *Bulletin* 119:73–102.

Carter, Susanne
1981   *Land Management and the American Indian Religious Freedom Act*. Paper presented at the 34th Annual Northwest
Anthropological Conference, Portland, Oregon.

Chamberlain, A. F.
1893   "The Coyote and the Owl." *Memoirs of the International Congress of Anthropology*, Chicago, 282–84.

1894   "A Kootenay Legend." *Journal of American Folklore* 7:195–96.
1902   "Geographic Terms of Kootenay Origin." *American Anthropologist* 4:348–50.

Childears, Lucille
1950   "Montana Place Names from Indian Myth and Legend." *Western Folklore* 3:263–64.

Conner, Stuart
1970   *Religious Practices among the Crow Indians: Survival and Innovation in Indian Religion*. Paper presented at the 18th Annual Meeting of the American Society for Ethnohistory, Missoula, Montana.
1982   "The Vision Quest Experience." *Archaeology in Montana* 23, no. 33: 85–125.

Conolly, James B.
1958   "Four Bears." *North Dakota History* 25, no. 4: 93–106.

Cooper, John M.
1957   *The Gros Ventres of Montana: Part II, Religion and Ritual*. Washington, D.C.: Catholic University of America Press.

Dangberg, G. M.
1957   "Letters to Jack Wilson, the Paiute Prophet." United States Bureau of American Ethnology, *Bulletin* 164:279–96.

Daniels, Robert E.
1970   "Cultural Identities among the Oglala Sioux." In *The Modern Sioux*. Ed. E. Nurge. Lincoln: University of Nebraska Press, 198–245.

Danziger, Edmund J., Jr.
1970   "The Crow Creek Experiment: An Aftermath of the Sioux War of 1862." *North Dakota History* 37, no. 2: 104–24.

Deaver, Sherri
1986   *American Indian Religious Freedom Act (AIRFA) Background Data*. Ethnoscience, Billings, Montana, for Bureau of Land Management, May 15.

DeMallie, Raymond J.
1984   *The Sixth Grandfather: Black Elk's Teachings Given to John G. Neihardt*. Lincoln: University of Nebraska Press.

Dempsey, Hugh A.
1956   "Stone 'Medicine Wheels'—Memorials to Blackfoot War Chiefs." *Journal of the Washington Academy of Sciences* 46, no. 6: 177–82.
1984   *Big Bear: The End of Freedom*. Lincoln: University of Nebraska Press.

Denig, Edwin T.
1961   *Five Indian Tribes of the Upper Missouri*. Norman: University of Oklahoma Press.

Dorsey, George A.
1894   "A Study of Siouan Cults." Eleventh Annual Report of the
          Bureau of Ethnology, 11:361–544.
1897   "Siouan Sociology." *Fifteenth Annual Report of the Bureau of
          Ethnology* 15:205–44.
1903   "The Arapaho Sun Dance: The Ceremony of the Offerings
          Lodge." Chicago Natural History Museum, *Fieldiana: An-
          thropology* 4:1–228.
1905a   "The Cheyenne: I. Ceremonial Organization." *Field Colum-
          bian Museum Publication* 99, Anthropological Series 4, no. 1:
          1–55.
1905b   "The Cheyenne: II. The Sun Dance." *Field Columbian Museum
          Publication* 103, Anthropological Series 4, no. 2: 57–186.

Dorsey, George A., and A. L. Kroeber
1903   "Traditions of the Arapaho." *Field Columbian Museum Publi-
          cation* 81, Anthropological Series 5.

Doyle, David E.
1982   "Medicine Men, Ethnic Significance, and Cultural Resource
          Management." *American Antiquity* 47, no. 3: 634–42.

Dozier, Jack
1961   "History of the Coeur d'Alene Indians to 1900." Unpublished
          M.A. thesis. Moscow: University of Idaho.

Driver, Harold E.
1961   *Indians of North America*. Chicago: University of Chicago
          Press.

Dunn, Adrian R.
1963   "A History of Old Fort Berthold." *North Dakota History* 30,
          no. 4: 157–240.

Durkheim, Emile
1915   *Elementary Forms of the Religious Life*. Paris.

Dusenberry, Verne
1960   "Notes of the Material Culture of the Assiniboine Indians."
          Ethnos 25:44–62.
1962   *The Montana Cree: A Study in Religious Persistence*. Acta
          Universitatis Stockholmiensis, Stockholm Studies in Compar-
          ative Religion 3. Almqvist and Wiksell, Stockholm.

Dyck, Paul
1971   *Brule: The Sioux People of the Rosebud*. Flagstaff, Ariz.: North-
          land Press.

Eggan, Fred, ed.
1955   *Social Anthropology of North American Tribes*. 2d edition.
          Chicago: University of Chicago Press.

Eliade, Mircea
1949a   *The Myth of the Eternal Return*. Trans. Willard R. Trask. New
          York: Pantheon Books, 1954.

1949b	*Patterns in Comparative Religion.* Trans. Rosemary Sheed. New York: Sheed and Ward. 1958.
1950	"Shamanism." In *Ancient Religions.* Ed. Vergilius Ferm. New York: Philosophical Library.
1958	*Birth and Rebirth: The Religious Meanings of Initiations in Human Culture.* Trans. Willard R. Trask. New York: Harper & Row.
1987	*The Encyclopedia of Religion.* Ed. Mircea Eliade. Vols. 1–15. New York: Macmillan Publishing Company.

Ellis, F. H.
1974	"An Anthropological Study of the Navajo Indians." In *American Indian Ethnohistory: Indians of the Southwest.* Ed. D. A. Horr. New York: Garland Press.

Ewers, J. C.
1955a	"The Bear Cult among the Assiniboine and Their Neighbors of the Northern Plains." *Southwestern Journal of Anthropology* 11:1–14.
1955b	*The Horse in Blackfoot Culture.* Bureau of American Ethnology, *Bulletin,* 159.
1956	"The Assiniboine Horse Medicine Cult." *Primitive Man* 29: 57–68.
1958	*The Blackfeet: Raiders on the Northwestern Plains.* Norman: University of Oklahoma Press.
1968	*Indian Life on the Missouri.* Norman: University of Oklahoma Press.
1974	"Ethnological Report on the Chippewa Cree Tribe of the Rocky Boy Reservation and the Little Shell Band of Indians." In *Chippewa Indians. VI.* Compiled by D. A. Horr. New York: Garland Publishing, 9–182.
1980	*The Horse in Blackfoot Indian Culture.* Washington, D.C.: Smithsonian Institution Press.

Fahey, John
1974	*The Flathead Indians.* Norman: University of Oklahoma Press.

Feraca, Stephen E.
1963	*Wakinvan: Contemporary Teton Dakota Religion.* Studies in Plains Anthropology and History 1. Browning, Mont.

Flannery, Regina, ed.
1953	*The Gros Ventres of Montana: Part I, Social Life.* Washington, D.C.: Catholic University of America Press.

Fogelson, Raymond D.
1981	"Commentary." *Chicago Anthropology Exchange* 14, nos. 1–2: 130–45.

Fowler, Loretta
1982	*Arapahoe Politics, 1851–1978.* Lincoln: University of Nebraska Press.

Geertz, Clifford
1965   "Religion as a Cultural System." Ed. M. Banton. *Association of Social Anthropologists, Monographs* 3:1–46.

Gill, Sam D.
1983   *Native American Traditions: Sources and Interpretations.* Belmont, Calif.: Wadsworth Publishing Company.

Goode, William J.
1951   *Religion in Primitive Society.* New York: Free Press.

Grinnell, George B.
1922   "The Big Horn Medicine Wheel." *American Anthropologist* 24: 299–310.
1962   *Blackfoot Lodge Tales.* Norman: University of Oklahoma Press.
1972   *The Cheyenne Indians.* Vols. 1 and 2. Lincoln: University of Nebraska Press.
1985   *The Fighting Cheyennes.* Norman: University of Oklahoma Press.

Griswold, Gillett
1970   "Aboriginal Patterns of Trade Between the Columbia Basin and the Northern Plains." *Archaeology in Montana* 2, nos. 2–3: 1–96.

Haile, B.
1947   *Navajo Sacrificial Figurines.* Chicago: University of Chicago Press.

Hall, Robert L.
1985   "Medicine Wheels, Sun Circles, and the Magic of the World Center Shrines." *Plains Anthropologist* 30 (109): 181–93.

Hallowell, A. I.
1926   "Bear Ceremonialism in the Northern Hemisphere." *American Anthropologist* 28:1–175.

Hassrick, Royal B.
1965   *The Sioux.* Norman: University of Oklahoma Press.

Heidenreich, C. Adrian
1970   *The Survival of Traditional Religious Practices among the Crow Indians.* Paper presented at the 18th Annual Meeting of the American Society for Ethnohistory, Missoula, Montana.
1985   "The Native Americans' Yellowstone." *Montana: The Magazine of Western History* 35, no. 4: 2017.

Hewes, Gordon
1961   "Early Tribal Migrations in the Northern Great Plains." *Plains Archaeological Conference News Letter* 1:49–61.

Hilger, Sister M. Inez
1959   "Some Customs of the Chippewa." *North Dakota History* 26, no. 3: 123–26.

Hoebel, E. Adamson
    1960   *The Cheyennes*. New York: Holt, Rinehart, and Winston.

Holt, Barry H.
    1982   "Navajo Sacred Areas: A Guide for Management." *Contract Abstracts* 2, no. 2: 42–45.

Horse Capture, George, ed.
    1980   *The Seven Visions of Bull Lodge*. Ann Arbor, Michigan: Bear Claw Press.

Howard, James H.
    1952a   "A Yanktonai Dakota Mide Bundle." *North Dakota History* 19, no. 2: 133–39.
    1952b   "The Sun Dance of the Turtle Mountain Ojibwa." *North Dakota History* 19, no. 4: 249–64.
    1953   "Notes on Two Dakota 'Holy Dance' Medicines and Their Uses." *American Anthropologist* 55:608–9.
    1960   "Two Teton Dakota Winter Count Texts." *North Dakota History* 27, no. 2: 67–81.
    1966   *The Dakota or Sioux Indians: A Study in Human Ecology*. University of South Dakota, Dakota Museum, Vermillion.
    1972   "Notes on the Ethnogeography of the Yankton Dakota." *Plains Anthropologist* 17:281–307.
    1976   "Yanktonai Ethnohistory and the John K. Bear Winter Count." *Plains Anthropologist, Memoir* 11.
    1977   *The Plains-Ojibwa or Bungi, Hunters and Warriors of the Northern Prairies with Special Reference to the Turtle Mountain Band*. Reprints in *Anthropology* 7. J & L Reprint Company, Lincoln, Nebraska.
    1984   *The Canadian Sioux*. Lincoln: University of Nebraska Press.

Hultkrantz, Åke
    1953   *Conceptions of the Soul among North American Indians*. Stockholm, Sweden.
    1954a   "The Indians in Yellowstone Park." *Annals of Wyoming* 29, no. 2: 125–29.
    1954b   "The Indians and the Wonders of Yellowstone: A Study of the Interrelations of Religion, Nature, and Culture." *Ethnos* 19:34–68.
    1957   *The North American Indian Orpheus Tradition*. Stockholm, Sweden.
    1961   "The Shoshones in the Rocky Mountain Area." *Annals of Wyoming* 33, no. 1: 19–41.
    1970   "Anthropological Approaches to the Study of Religion." *History of Religions* 9, no. 4: 337–52.
    1981   *Belief and Worship in Native North America*. Ed. Christopher Vecsey. Syracuse, N.Y.: Syracuse University Press.
    1983   *The Study of American Indian Religions*. Ed. Christopher Vecsey. New York: Crossroad.

Hurt, Wesley R.
  1960a   "Factors in the Persistence of Peyote in the Northern Plains."
          Plains Anthropologist 5:16–27.
  1960b   "The Yankton Dakota Church: A Nationalistic Movement of
          Northern Plains Indians." In *Essays in the Science of Culture.*
          Ed. G. Dole and R. Carneiro, 267–87.

Hyde, George E.
  1937   *Red Cloud's Folk: A History of the Oglala Indians.* Norman: Uni-
          versity of Oklahoma Press.
  1952   "The Mystery of the Arikaras." *North Dakota History* 19, no. 2:
          25–58.
  1959   *Indians of the High Plains: From the Prehistoric Period to the
          Coming of Europeans.* Norman: University of Oklahoma Press.

Jenness, Diamond
  1932   *The Indians of Canada.* National Museum of Canada, *Bulletin,*
          65.

Jorgensen, Joseph G.
  1972   *The Sun Dance Religion.* Chicago: University of Chicago Press.
  1984   "Land Is Cultural, So Is a Commodity: The Locus of
          Differences among Indians, Cowboys, Sod-Busters, and En-
          vironmentalists." *Journal of Ethnic Studies* 12, no. 3: 1–21.

Kehoe, Alice B.
  1968   "The Ghost Dance Religion in Saskatchewan Canada." *Plains
          Anthropologist* 13:296–304.
  1970   "The Dakotas in Saskatchewan." In *The Modern Sioux.* Ed. E.
          Nurge. Lincoln: University of Nebraska Press, 148–72.
  1981   *North American Indians: A Comprehensive Account.* Englewood
          Cliffs, N.J.: Prentice-Hall.

Kehoe, Thomas F.
  1972   "Stone 'Medicine Wheel' Monuments in the Northern Plains
          of North America." *Atti del XL Congresso Internazionale delgi
          Americanistic* 2:183–99.
  1979   "Stones, Solstices and Sun Dance Structures." *Plains An-
          thropologist* 22:85–95.

Kehoe, Thomas F. and Alice B.
  1959   "Boulder Effigy Monuments in the Northwestern Plains."
          Journal of American Folklore 72:113–27.

Kelley, R. E.
  1972   *Navajo Ritual Human Figurines: Form and Function.* Museum
          of Navajo Ceremonial Art, Santa Fe, N.M.

Kluckhohn, C.
  1967   *Navajo Witchcraft.* Boston: Beacon Press.

Kluckhohn, C., W. W. Hill, and L. W. Kluckhohn
  1971   *Navajo Material Culture.* Cambridge: Belknap Press.

Kluckhohn, C., and D. Leighton
    1948   *The Navajo*. Cambridge: Harvard University Press.

Kroeber, Alfred A.
    1908   "Ethnology of the Gros Ventres." *Anthropological Papers of the American Museum of Natural History* 1, no. 4: 145–287.
    1983   *The Arapaho*. Lincoln: University of Nebraska Press.

Lancaster, Richard
    1966   *Piegan*. New York: Doubleday.

Landes, Ruth
    1968   *Ojibwa Religion and the Midewiwin*. Madison: University of Wisconsin Press.

Lantis, Margaret
    1950   "The Religion of the Eskimos." In *Ancient Religions*. Ed. Vergilius Ferm. New York: Philosophical Library.

Lame Deer, John (Fire), and Richard Erdoes
    1972   *Lame Deer Seeker of Visions*. New York: Washington Square Press.

Leforge, Thomas H.
    1974   *Memoirs of a White Crow Indian*. Lincoln: University of Nebraska Press.

Leslie, Charles, ed.
    1960   *Anthropology of Folk Religion*. New York: Vintage Books.

Lewis, Thomas H.
    1980   "The Changing Practice of the Oglala Medicine Man." *Plains Anthropologist* 25, no. 89: 264–67.

Liberty, Margot
    1980   "The Sun Dance." In *Anthropology on the Great Plains*. Ed. W. R. Wood and M. Liberty. Lincoln: University of Nebraska Press, 165–78.

Linderman, Frank B.
    1932   *Pretty-Shield: Medicine Woman of the Crows*. Lincoln: University of Nebraska Press.

Linton, Ralph
    1943   "Nativistic Movements." *American Anthropologist* 45:230–40.

Long, James L. (First Boy)
    1942   *Land of Nakoda: The Story of the Assiniboine Indians*. Helena, Mont.: State Publishing Company.

Lowie, Robert H.
    1909   "The Northern Shoshone." *Anthropological Papers of the American Museum of Natural History* 2 no. 2: 169–306.
    1910   "The Assiniboine." *Anthropological Papers of the American Museum of Natural History* 4, no. 1: 1–269.

1913a	"Dance Associations of the Eastern Dakota." *Anthropological Papers of the American Museum of Natural History* 11, no. 2: 101–42.
1913b	"Societies of the Crow, Hidatsa, and Mandan Indians." *Anthropological Papers of the American Museum of Natural History* 11, no. 3: 145–358.
1915a	"Dances and Societies of the Plains Shoshone." *Anthropological Papers of the American Museum of Natural History* 11, no. 10: 803–35.
1915b	"Societies of the Arikara Indians." *Anthropological Papers of the American Museum of Natural History* 11, no. 8: 645–78.
1917	"Notes on the Social Organization and Customs of the Mandan, Hidatsa, and Crow Indians. *Anthropological Papers of the American Museum of Natural History* 21, no. 1: 1–100.
1918	"Myths and Traditions of the Crow Indians." *Anthropological Papers of the American Museum of Natural History* 25, no. 1: 1–308.
1919a	"The Sundance of the Wind River Shoshoni and Ute." *Anthropological Papers of the American Museum of Natural History* 156: 405–10.
1919b	"The Tobacco Society of the Crow Indians." *Anthropological Papers of the American Museum of Natural History* 21, no. 2: 101–200.
1922	"The Religion of the Crow Indians." *Anthropological Papers of the American Museum of Natural History* 25, no. 2: 309–444.
1924	*Primitive Religion.* New York: Liveright, 1948 new edition.
1935	*The Crow Indians.* Lincoln: University of Nebraska Press.
1954	*The Indians of the Plains.* New York: McGraw-Hill.

McCool, Daniel
1981	"Federal Indian Policy and the Sacred Mountains of the Papago Indians." *Journal of Ethnic Studies* 9, no. 3: 57–69.

Mails, Thomas E.
1973	*Dog Soldiers, Bear Men and Buffalo Women: A Study of the Societies and Cults of the Plains Indians.* Englewood Cliffs, N.J.: Prentice-Hall.
1978	*Sundancing at Rosebud and Pine Ridge.* Center for Western Studies, Augustana College, Sioux Falls, S.D.
1979	*Fools Crow.* New York: Doubleday.

Malinowski, Bronislaw
1925	*Magic, Science, and Religion.* Garden City, N.Y.: Doubleday, 1955 new edition.

Mandelbaum, David G.
1940	"The Plains Cree." *Anthropological Papers of the American Museum of Natural History* 37, no. 2: 167–316.

Merton, Robert
    1949   "Manifest and Latent Functions." In *Social Theory and Social Structure*. Glencoe, N.Y.: Free Press.

Michaelsen, Robert S.
    1983   " 'We Also Have a Religion'—The Free Exercise of Religion among Native Americans." *American Indian Quarterly* 7, no. 3: 111–42.
    1986   "American Indian Religious Freedom Litigation: Promise and Perils." *Journal of Law and Religion* 3:47–76.

Miller, David H.
    1959   *Ghost Dance*. Lincoln: University of Nebraska Press.

Mooney, James
    1965   *The Ghost Dance Religion and the Sioux Outbreak of 1890*. Chicago: University of Chicago Press.

Moore, John H.
    1973   Review: Seven Arrows. Hyemeyohsts Storm. *American Anthropologist* 75, no. 4: 1040–42.
    1984   "Cheyenne Names and Cosmology." *American Ethnologist* 11, no. 2: 291–312.

Myerhoff, Barbara G.
    1978   "Return to Wirikuta: Ritual Reversal and Symbolic Continuity on the Peyote Hunt of the Huichol Indians." In *The Reversible World: Symbolic Inversion in Art and Society*. Ed. Barbara A. Babcock. Ithaca, N.Y.: Cornell University Press, 236–39.

Nabokov, Peter
    1967   *Two Leggings, the Making of a Crow Warrior*. New York: Thomas Y. Crowell.

Neihardt, John G.
    1961   *Black Elk Speaks*. Lincoln: University of Nebraska Press.

Neuman, Robert W.
    1975   *The Sonota Complex and Associated Sites on the Northern Great Plains*. Nebraska State Historical Society Publications in Anthropology, 6.

Nichols, Roger L.
    1982   "The Arikara Indians and the Missouri River Trade: A Quest for Survival." *Great Plains Quarterly* 2:77–93.

Norbeck, Edward
    1961   *Religion in Primitive Society*. New York: Harper & Row.

Nurge, Ethel, ed.
    1970   *The Modern Sioux, Social Systems and Reservation Culture*. Lincoln: University of Nebraska Press.

Ortiz, Alfonso
    1975   "The Tewa World View." In *Teachings from the American Earth: Indian Religion and Philosophy*. Ed. Dennis and Barbara Tedlock. New York: Liveright, 179–89.

Parker, Arthur C.
    1912   "The Code of Handsome Lake, the Seneca Prophet." New York State Museum, *Bulletin* 163:20–26.

Parks, D. R., M. Liberty, and A. Ferenci
    1980   "Peoples of the Plains." In *Anthropology on the Great Plains*. Ed. W. R. Wood and M. Liberty. Lincoln: University of Nebraska Press.

Parks, D. R., and W. Wedel
    1985   "Pawnee Geography: Historical and Sacred." *Great Plains Quarterly* 5:143–76.

Peterson, Karen D.
    1971   *Plains Indian Art from Fort Marion*. Norman: University of Oklahoma Press.

Pepper, G. H., and G. L. Wilson
    1915   "An Hidatsa Shrine and the Beliefs Respecting It." *Memoirs of the American Anthropological Association* 2:279–328.

Phinney, Archie
    1934   *Nez Percé Texts*. New York: Columbia University Contributions to Anthropology, no. 25.

Point, Nicholas
    1967   *Wilderness Kingdom: Indian Life in the Rocky Mountains 1840–1847*. New York: Holt, Rinehart, and Winston.

Potts, W. J.
    1892   "Creation Myth of the Assiniboines." *Journal of American Folklore* 5:72–73.

Powell, Peter J.
    1969   *Sweet Medicine: The Continuing Role of the Sacred Arrows, the Sun Dance, and the Sacred Buffalo Hat in Northern Cheyenne History*. 2 vols. Norman: University of Oklahoma Press.

Powers, William K.
    1970   "Contemporary Oglala Music and Dance: Pan-Indianism vs. Pan-Tetonism." In *The Modern Sioux*. Ed. E. Nurge. Lincoln: University of Nebraska Press, 268–90.
    1975   *Oglala Religion*. Lincoln: University of Nebraska Press.
    1982   *Yuwipi: Vision and Experience in Oglala Ritual*. Lincoln: University of Nebraska Press.

Radin, Paul
    1927   *Primitive Man as Philosopher*. New York: Dover.
    1937   *Primitive Religion: Its Nature and Origin*. New York: Dover.

1956   *The Trickster: A Study in American Indian Mythology.* New York: Philosophical Library.

Ray, Verne F.
1939   *Cultural Relations in the Plateau of Northwestern America.* Publications of the Frederick Webb Hodge Anniversary Publications Fund 3. Los Angeles.
1942   "Culture Element Distribution: Plateau (22)." *Anthropological Records* 8, no. 2: 99–262.

Reichard, Gladys A.
1930   "The Style of Coeur d'Alene Mythology." *Proceedings of the International Congress of Americanists* 24:243–53.
1947   "An Analysis of Coeur d'Alene Indian Myths." *Memoirs of the American Folklore Society*, no. 41.
1950   *Navajo Religion: A Study of Symbolism.* Bollingen Series 18. New York: Pantheon Books.

Rodnick, David
1937   "Political Structure and Status among the Assiniboine Indians." *American Anthropologist* 39:408–16.
1938   "The Fort Belknap Assiniboine of Montana." Master's thesis, Department of Anthropology, University of Montana, Missoula.
1939   "An Assiniboine Horse Raiding Expedition." *American Anthropologist* 41:611–16.

Rogers, E. S.
1971   "The Assiniboine." *The Beaver* (Autumn): 40–43.

Schaafsma, P.
1963   *Rock Art of the Navajo Reservoir District.* Museum of New Mexico Papers in Anthropology 7.

Schaeffer, Claude E.
1934–69   *The Claude Everette Schaeffer Papers, 1934–1969.* Personal and Anthropological Papers, Re: Flathead, Kootenai, and Blackfoot Indian Culture. Manuscripts in the Glenbow-Alberta Institute, Archives Division, Calgary, Alberta, Access Number 2464.
1947   "The Bear Foster Parent Tale: A Kootenai Version." *Journal of American Folklore* 60:286–88.
1966   *Bear Ceremonialism of the Kutenai Indians.* Museum of the Plains Indian, Studies in Plains Anthropology and History 4.

Schultz, James W.
1962   *Blackfeet and Buffalo.* Norman: University of Oklahoma Press.

Shimkin, D. B.
1947   "Wind River Shoshone Ethnogeography." *University of California Publications in Anthropological Records* 5, no. 4: 245–80.

1953 *Wind River Shoshone Sun Dance.* Anthropological Paper 41. Washington, D.C.: Smithsonian Institution.

Skinner, Alanson P.
1913 "Menomini Social Life and Ceremonial Bundles." *Anthropological Papers of the American Museum of Natural History* 13: 147–49.
1914 "Political Organization, Cults, and Ceremonies of the Plains-Ojibway and Plains-Cree Indians." *Anthropological Papers of the American Museum of Natural History* 11, no. 6: 475–542.
1919 "A Sketch of Eastern Dakota Ethnology." *American Anthropologist* 21, no. 2: 1164–74.

Slotkin, J. S.
1956 *The Peyote Religion: A Study in Indian-White Relations.* Glencoe, N.Y.: Free Press.

Spencer, Rogert F. et al.
1965 *The Native Americans.* New York: Harper & Row.

Spier, Leslie
1921 "The Sun Dance of the Plains Indians: Its Development and Diffusion." *Anthropological Papers of the American Museum of Natural History* 16, no. 7: 451–528.

Spinden, Herbert Joseph
1908 *The Nez Percé Indians.* Menasha, Wis.: Memoirs of the American Anthropological Association, no. 2.

Standing Bear, Luther
1975 *My People, the Sioux.* Lincoln: University of Nebraska Press.
1978 *Land of the Spotted Eagle.* Lincoln: University of Nebraska Press.

Stands-in-Timber, John and M. Liberty
1967 *Cheyenne Memories.* New Haven: Yale University Press.

Steinmetz, Reverend Paul B., S.J.
1980 *Pipe and Peyote among the Oglala Lakota,* Stockholm Studies in Comparative Religion, Almqvist and Wiksell International.

Steward, Julian
1938 *Basin Plateau Aboriginal Sociopolitical Groups.* Smithsonian Institution, Bureau of American Ethnology, *Bulletin,* 120.

Stewart, Omer C.
1980a "The Ghost Dance." In *Anthropology on the Great Plains.* Ed. W. R. Wood and M. Liberty. Lincoln: University of Nebraska Press, 179–87.
1980b "The Native American Church." In *Anthropology on the Great Plains.* Ed. W. R. Wood and M. Liberty. Lincoln: University of Nebraska Press, 188–96.
1983 "Peyotism in Montana." *Montana: Magazine of Western History* 33, no. 2: 2–15.

Swanson, Guy E.
1960   *The Birth of the Gods: The Origin of Primitive Beliefs.* Ann Arbor: University of Michigan Press.

Teit, James A.
1917a   "Coeur d'Alene Tales." *Memoirs of the American Folklore Society* 1:119–28.
1917b   "Pend d'Oreille Tales." *Memoirs of the American Folklore Society* 11:114–18.
1930   "The Salishan Tribes of the Western Plateau." *Annual Report of the Bureau of American Ethnology* 45:295–396.

Thompson, Stith, ed.
1929   *Tales of the North American Indians.* Cambridge, Mass.

Titiev, Mischa
1960   "A Fresh Approach to the Problem of Magic and Religion." *Southwestern Journal of Anthropology* 16:292–98.

Trenholm, Virginia C. and M. Carley
1964   *The Shoshonis: Sentinels of the Rockies.* Norman: University of Oklahoma Press.

Turney-High, H. H.
1937   *The Flathead Indians of Montana.* Menasha, Wis.: Memoirs of the American Anthropological Association, no. 43.
1941   *Ethnography of the Kutenai.* Menasha, Wis.: Memoirs of the American Anthropological Association, no. 56.

Underhill, Ruth
1965   *Red Man's Religion: Belief and Practices of the Indians North of Mexico.* Chicago: University of Chicago Press.

Van Gennep, Arnold
1908   *The Rites of Passage.* With an Introduction by Solon T. Kimball. Chicago: University of Chicago Press, 1960 new edition.

Van Valkenburgh, R.
1974   "Navajo Sacred Places." In *American Indian Ethno-history: Indians of the Southwest.* Ed. D. A. Horr. New York: Garland Press.

Vecsey, Christopher
1980   "American Indian Environmental Religions." In *American Indian Environments: Ecological Issues in Native American History.* Ed. C. Vecsey and R. W. Venables. Syracuse, N.Y.: Syracuse University Press, 1–37.

Voget, Fred W.
1984   *The Shoshoni-Crow Sun Dance.* Norman: University of Oklahoma Press.

Walker, Deward E., Jr.
1964   *A Survey of Nez Percé Religion.* Board of National Missions, United Presbyterian Church in the U.S.A., New York.

1966   "The Nez Percé Sweat Bath Complex: An Acculturational Analysis." *Southwestern Journal of Anthropology* 22, no. 2: 133–71.

1967a   *Mutual Cross-Utilization of Economic Resources in the Plateau: An Example from Aboriginal Nez Percé Fishing Practices.* Washington State University, Laboratory of Anthropology, Report of Investigations, no. 41.

1967b   "Nez Percé Sorcery." *Ethnology* 6, no. 1: 66–96.

1968   *Conflict and Schism in Nez Percé Acculturation: A Study of Religion and Politics.* Washington State University Press, Pullman.

1969   "New Light on the Prophet Dance Controversy." *Ethnohistory* 16, no. 3: 245–55.

1970   "Ethnology and History." *Idaho Yesterdays* 14, no. 1: 24–29.

1978   *Indians of Idaho.* Moscow: University of Idaho Press.

1980   *Myths of Idaho Indians.* Moscow: University of Idaho Press.

Walker, Deward E., Jr., ed.

1970a   *Systems of North American Witchcraft and Sorcery.* Anthropological Monographs of the University of Idaho, no. 1. Moscow: University of Idaho Press.

1970b   *The Emergent Native Americans.* Boston: Little, Brown.

Walker, James R.

1917   "The Sun Dance and Other Ceremonies of the Oglala Division of the Dakota." *Anthropological Papers of the American Museum of Natural History* 16:51–221.

1980   *Lakota Belief and Ritual.* Lincoln: University of Nebraska Press.

1983   *Lakota Myth.* Lincoln: University of Nebraska Press.

Wallace, Anthony F. C.

1956a   "New Religions among the Delaware Indians, 1680–1900." *Southwestern Journal of Anthropology* 12, no. 1: 1–22.

1956b   "Revitalization Movements." *American Anthropologist* 58: 264–81.

Wedel, Mildred M.

1974   "LeSeur and the Dakota Sioux." In *Aspects of Upper Great Lakes Anthropology: Papers in Honor of Lloyd A. Wilford.* Ed. E. Johnson. Publication of the Minnesota Historical Society, Minnesota Prehistoric Archaeology Series 11: 157–71.

Whiting, Beatrice B.

1950   *Paiute Sorcery.* Viking Fund Publications in Anthropology 15. New York.

Wildschut, William

1960   *Crow Indian Medicine Bundles.* Ed. J. C. Ewers. New York: Museum of the American Indian.

Will, George F.

1928   "Magical and Sleight of Hand Performances by the Arikara." *North Dakota History* 3, no. 1: 50–65.

1930a	"Arikara Ceremonials." *North Dakota History* 4, no. 4: 247–74.
1930b	"The Mandan Lodge at Bismarck." *North Dakota History* 5, no. 1: 38–48.

Wilson, G. L.
1928	"Hidatsa Eagle Trapping." *Anthropological Papers of the American Museum of Natural History* 30, no. 4: 101–245.

Wissler, Clark
1912	"Societies and Ceremonial Associations of the Oglala Division of the Teton-Dakota." *Anthropological Papers of the American Museum of Natural History* 11, no. 1: 1–99.
1913	"Societies and Dance Associations of the Blackfoot Indians." *Anthropological Papers of the American Museum of Natural History* 11, no. 4: 359–460.
1916	"General Discussion of Shamanistic and Dancing Societies." *Anthropological Papers of the American Museum of Natural History* 11, no. 12: 853–76.

Woolworth, Alan R.
1956	"Grandmother's Lodge." *North Dakota History* 23, no. 2: 79–102.
1959	"Unusual Artifacts from the Central and Northern Plains." *North Dakota History* 26, no. 2: 93–100.

Wright, Gary A.
1978	"The Shoshonean Migration Problem." *Plains Anthropologist* 23: 113–37.

Young, M. Jane
1985	"Images of Power and the Power of Images: The Significance of Rock Art for Contemporary Zunis." *Journal of American Folklore* 98:3–48.

6 / Law and the Limits of Liberty, by Robert S. Michaelsen

Andreason, Cynthia Thorley
1984	"Indian Worship v. Government Development: A New Breed of Religion Cases." *Utah Law Review* 1984:313.

Ball, Milner
1985	*Lying Down Together: Law, Metaphor, and Theology.* Madison: University of Wisconsin Press.

Cohen, Mark S.
1987	"American Indian Sacred Religious Sites and Government Development: A Conventional Analysis in an Unconventional Setting." *Michigan Law Review* 85:771.

Cotton, John
    1634   "God's Promise to His Plantation." A Sermon Preached in Northampton, England, 1630. London.

Craven, Rex P.
    1983   "The American Indian Religious Freedom Act—An Answer to the Indians' Prayers?" *South Dakota Law Review* 29:131.

Ensworth, Laurie
    1983   "Native American Free Exercise Rights to the Use of Public Lands." *Boston University Law Review* 63:141.

Falk, Donald
    1989   "Lyng v. Northwest Indian Cemetery Protective Association: Bulldozing First Amendment Protection of Indian Sacred Lands." *Ecology Law Quarterly* 16:515.

Godshall, Scott David
    1984   "Land Use Regulation and the Free Exercise Clause." *Columbia Law Review* 84:1562.

Gordon, Sarah B.
    1985   "Indian Religious Freedom and Governmental Development of Public Lands." *The Yale Law Journal* 94:1447.

Gould, Diane Brazen
    1986   "The First Amendment and the American Indian Religious Freedom Act: An Approach to Protecting Native American Religion." *Iowa Law Review* 71:869.

Hanke, Lewis
    1965   *The Spanish Struggle for Justice in the Conquest of America.* Boston: Little, Brown.

Higginbotham, C. Dean
    1982   "Native Americans versus Archaeologists: The Legal Issues." *American Indian Law Review* 10:91.

Howe, Mark DeWolfe
    1965   *The Garden and the Wilderness: Religion and Government in American Constitutional History.* Chicago: University of Chicago Press.

Hyde, Lewis
    1983   *The Gift: Imagination and the Erotic Life of Property.* New York: Vintage Books.

Jefferson, Thomas
    1801–9   Indian Addresses. *The Works of Thomas Jefferson.* New York: Townsend MacCoun, 1884, 8:179–240.

    1801   To a Committee of the Danbury Baptist Association in the State of Connecticut, 1-1-1801. *Writings.* New York: Library of America, 1984, 510.

Keightly, Thomas, and L. Schmitz
    1976   *Classical Mythology: The Myths of Ancient Greece and Ancient Italy.* Chicago: Ares Publishers.

King, William
    1965   *Heathen Gods and Heroes.* Carbondale: Southern Illinois Press.

Lupu, Ira C.
    1989   "Where Rights Begin: The Problem of Burdens on the Free Exercise of Religion." *Harvard Law Review* 102:933.

Michaelsen, Robert S.
    1983a   "The Significance of the American Indian Religious Freedom Act of 1978." *Journal of the American Academy of Religion* 52: 93.
    1983b   "'We Also Have a Religion': The Free Exercise of Religion among Native Americans." *American Indian Quarterly* 7 (Summer) 111–42.
    1984   "Civil Rights, Indian Rights." *Society* 21 (May/June): 42.
    1985   "American Indian Religious Freedom Litigation: Promise and Perils." *Journal of Law and Religion* 3:47.
    1988   "Is the Miner's Canary Silent? Implications of the Supreme Court's Denial of American Indian Free Exercise of Religion Claims." *Journal of Law and Religion* 6:97.

Miller, Robert T., and Ronald B. Flowers, eds.
    1987   *Toward Benevolent Neutrality: Church, State, and the Supreme Court.* 3d ed. Waco, Tex.: Baylor University Press.

Pepper, Stephen L.
    1982   "The Conundrum of the Free Exercise Clause—Some Reflections on Recent Cases." *Northern Kentucky Law Review* 9: 265.

Sewell, Ellen M. W.
    1983   "The American Indian Religious Freedom Act." *Arizona Law Review* 25:429.

Smith, Mary H.
    1986   "Wilson v. Block." *Natural Resources Journal* 26:169.

Williams, Roger
    1644   Mr. Cottons Letter Lately Printed, Examined and Answered. London. In *The Complete Writings of Roger Williams*, 1963, 1: 314.

Court Cases

Bowen, 1985. Bowen v. Roy, 476 U.S. 693. Challenged ruling that statutes that require state agency to use Social Security number for certain programs do not violate the Free Exercise Clause and do not, standing alone, impair appellees' freedom to exercise their religion.

Black, 1986. Black v. Employment Div., 721 P.2d 451 (Or.) Denial of unemployment compensation for use of peyote in a bona fide service of the Native American Church is a violation of plaintiff's free exercise of religion rights. See also *Smith*.

Cherokee Nation, 1831. Cherokee Nation v. Georgia, 30 U.S. (5 Pet.) 1.

Crow, 1982. Crow v. Gullet, 541 F. Supp. 785 (D.S.D.). Development of state park in area sacred to Lakota and Cheyenne does not violate their free exercise of religious rights.

Frank, 1979. Frank v. Alaska, 604 P.2d 1068 (Alaska Supreme Ct.). Taking of moose out of season for bona fide potlatch is permissible under Free Exercise Clause.

Hopi, 1981. Hopi Indian Tribe v. Block, 8 *Indian Law Review* 3073 (D.D.C.). Expansion of ski facilities on mountain sacred to Hopi does not violate their free exercise rights.

Lyng, 1988. Lyng v. Northwest Indian Cemetery Protective Assoc. 485 U.S. 439, 99 L Ed. 2d 534. Development of Forest Service road through area sacred to Northwest California Indians does not violate their free exercise rights. See *Northwest*.

Manybeads, 1989. Jenny Manybeads v. U.S., U.S. Dist. Ct., Dist. of Arizona, CIV 88-410 PCT EHC, 10-20-90. Navajo appeal to First Amendment and AIRFA to put a stop to their removal from Hopi Partitioned Land under the Navajo-Hopi Land Settlement Act of 1974, denied.

Means, 1985. U.S. v. Means, 627 F.Supp 247 (D.S.D.). Forest Service agent failed to comply with AIRFA in denying plaintiffs' application for a permit to establish Yellow Thunder Camp in the Black Hills.

Minor, 1870. Minor v. Bd. of Ed. of Cincinnati. In *The Bible in the Public Schools*. New York: De Capo Press, 1967.

New Mexico Navajo Ranchers, 1983. New Mexico Navajo Ranchers' Assoc. v. Interstate Commerce Comm., 702 F.2d 227 (D.C. Cir.). In keeping with AIRFA the commission must reconsider plaintiffs' claim that land on which railroad proposed is sacred to Navajo.

Northwest, 1983. Northwest Indian Cemetery Protective Assoc. v. Peterson, 552 F. Supp. 951 (N.D. Calif.). Forest Service proposal to develop road through area sacred to Northwest California Indians is in violation of their free exercise of religion rights. Affirmed, 795 F.2d 688 (9th Cir. 1986), reversed in *Lyng*.

Peyote Way, 1983. Peyote Way Church of God v. Smith, 556 F. Supp. 632 (N.D. Tex.). Under AIRFA law protecting Indian use of peyote in bona fide service of the Native American Church does not violate plaintiffs' equal protection rights.

Roy, 1984. Roy v. Cohen 590 F. Supp. 600 (M.D.Pa.). State required use of Social Security number for receipt of benefits under some state programs is in violation of plaintiff's free exercise of religion rights. Reversed in *Bowen*.

Schempp, 1963. Abington School Dist. v. Schempp, 374 U.S. 203. School sponsored devotional Bible reading and prayer in the public schools violates the Establishment Clause of the First Amendment.

Smith, 1986. Smith v. Employment Div., 721 P.2d 445 (Or.). Denial of unemployment compensation for use of peyote in a bona fide service of the Native American Church violates plaintiff's free exercise of religion rights. Remanded by U.S. Supreme Court, 1988, for determination whether use of peyote unlawful in Oregon under any circumstances, 56 USLW 4357. (Incorporates *Black*).

Smith, 1988. Employment Div. v. Smith, 763 P.2d 146 (Or.). On remand, use of peyote does violate Oregon law, but that law violates plaintiffs' free exercise of religion rights.

Whittingham, 1973. State v. Whittingham, 504 P.2d 950 (Ariz. Ct. of Appeals). Use of peyote in bona fide service of the Native American Church accords with free exercise of religion rights.

Wilson, 1983. Wilson v. Block, 708 F.2d 735 (D.C. Cir.). Upholds *Hopi*.

Woody, 1964. People v. Woody, 394 P.2d 813 (Sup. Ct. Calif.). Use of peyote in bona fide service of the Native American Church accords with free exercise of religion rights.

Government Documents

AIRFA Hearings, 1978. American Indian Religious Freedom. *Hearings* before the Select Committee on Indian Affairs . . . on S.J. Res. 102, February 24 and 27, U.S. Senate, 95th Congress, 2d Sess.

AIRFA Report, 1979. *American Indian Religious Freedom Act Report*. P.L. 95-341. Washington, D.C., August.

Index